Empowerment Through Agency Enhancement

Mine Sato • Nobuo Sayanagi • Toru Yanagihara

Empowerment Through Agency Enhancement

An Interdisciplinary Exploration

Mine Sato
Yokohama National University
Yokohama, Kanagawa, Japan

Nobuo Sayanagi
Yamanashi Eiwa College
Kofu, Yamanashi, Japan

Toru Yanagihara
Takushoku University
Tokyo, Tokyo, Japan

ISBN 978-981-19-1226-9   ISBN 978-981-19-1227-6 (eBook)
https://doi.org/10.1007/978-981-19-1227-6

© The Editor(s) (if applicable) and The Author(s), under exclusive licence to Springer Nature Singapore Pte Ltd. 2022
This work is subject to copyright. All rights are solely and exclusively licensed by the Publisher, whether the whole or part of the material is concerned, specifically the rights of translation, reprinting, reuse of illustrations, recitation, broadcasting, reproduction on microfilms or in any other physical way, and transmission or information storage and retrieval, electronic adaptation, computer software, or by similar or dissimilar methodology now known or hereafter developed.
The use of general descriptive names, registered names, trademarks, service marks, etc. in this publication does not imply, even in the absence of a specific statement, that such names are exempt from the relevant protective laws and regulations and therefore free for general use.
The publisher, the authors and the editors are safe to assume that the advice and information in this book are believed to be true and accurate at the date of publication. Neither the publisher nor the authors or the editors give a warranty, expressed or implied, with respect to the material contained herein or for any errors or omissions that may have been made. The publisher remains neutral with regard to jurisdictional claims in published maps and institutional affiliations.

This Palgrave Macmillan imprint is published by the registered company Springer Nature Singapore Pte Ltd.
The registered company address is: 152 Beach Road, #21-01/04 Gateway East, Singapore 189721, Singapore

Acknowledgements

The authors are grateful to supports given by the staff of JICA Research Institute (currently JICA Sadako Ogata Research Institute for Peace and Development) especially to the former director Hiroshi Kato, who was instrumental in providing the platform for the research project, "An Interdisciplinary Study on Agency Enhancement Process and Factors". Special appreciation goes to Prof. Tomomi Kozaki (Senshu University) and Prof. Yusuke Nakamura (Tokyo University) for their contributions to the project. The authors also dedicate their gratitudes to the members of Life Improvement Circle in Matsukawa Town in Nagano Prefecture, who have kindly shared their precious experiences to improve their own life conditions through self-reliant manners, which efforts have lasted over half a century. Their beautiful laughter and wisdoms to live every single day through fully exercising their own agency deeply inspired the authors to elaborate this project.

Sato would like to thank the staff of *Alianza Comunitaria* in Nicaragua, especially Mr Itsuo Kuzasa and Mr. Tetsuo Nohara for their special supports to conduct research. Special gratitudes go to the members of Life Improvement Research Forum where she incubated this research project through sometimes tense but always meaningful discussions. She also wants to dedicate profound appreciation to Honorary Professor Jun Nishikawa (Waseda University), who has always given critical advice to her research ideas.

Finally, and mostly, she is extremely grateful to the co-authors of this book, Prof. Toru Yanagihara and Prof. Nobuo Sayanagi, who have always been so patient and consistent to complete this book project. She truly hopes to continue dialogues and research projects with them.

Nobuo Sayanagi is indebted to all of the parties that have allowed him, a complete outsider to the international development community, to become so immersed in the field. Dr. Jiro Aikawa, the mastermind of the SHEP approach who currently serves as the senior technical advisor for JICA overseeing the implementation of the project in over 30 countries, has provided him countless opportunities for research and collaboration. Sayanagi is also grateful to the many staff members who have supported the SHEP approach over the years, especially Mr. Hirotaka Nakamura, who he had the pleasure of working with again in his research of the PAPRIZ program in Madagascar. Gratitudes are also due to the staff members of the PAPRIZ team led by Mr. Ryuzo Habara, who meticulously coordinated the survey itineraries for Sayanagi's six (as of date) visits to Madagascar. His research in Madagascar was enabled by the SATREPS Madagascar research project, a.k.a. Fy Vary. Sayanagi is especially thankful to Mr. Shigeki Yokoyama of JIRCAS, who invited him to join the Fy Vary team, Dr. Yasuhiro Tsujimoto of JIRCAS, the PI of the Fy Vary research. Presenting at Fy Vary meetings as the only psychologist was a learning experience in itself and has inspired much of what is written in Chaps. 3 and 9. Sayanagi also thanks his Malagasy colleagues on the Fy Vary project. Sayanagi extends a special acknowledgement to Ms. Yuka Ebihara, who introduced him to Prof. Sato. She was a radio personality when he worked as a staff member at one of the leading FM radio stations in Tokyo. It had been a long time since they both left their radio jobs, and it is of great luck that their lives would cross again in such a way. If it weren't for her, Sayanagi probably would not have ever been able to conduct research in this field, which has become a very important part of his life. Finally, Sayanagi is forever grateful to his two co-authors, Prof. Yanagihara and Prof. Sato. Prof. Yanagihara has been his de facto mentor in poverty studies, also gave him the opportunity to collaborate in a project on unemployed youth in Japan. And Prof. Sato is the one person that has made this psychological research in development aid all possible. If she hadn't thought of adding a psychologist to the research team, or didn't ask Ms. Ebihara for suggestions, Sayanagi would not be where he is today. He hopes that the trio's adventures together will continue.

Contents

1 Introduction: What Moves Researchers to Take Initiatives to This
   Interdisciplinary Research Project 1

Part I Understanding Agency and Its Development 9

2 Beyond Aloof Cynicism: A Critical Overview of Anthropological
   Perspectives on Agency and Its Development..................... 11

3 A Psychological Perspective on Agency in the Context of Behavior
   Change 27

4 Agency as Base for "Bounded Rationality", Core of "Human
   Capital", and Key to "Human Capabilities" 37

**Part II Enhancing Agency: Its Plausible Mechanisms and Influential
   Factors** 63

5 What Is Done for Facilitating Agency Development in Practice?:
   Documenting and Crystallizing an Unsung Practical Knowledge
   of a Third-Country Expert..................................... 65

6 Breaking the Poverty Trap: A Psychological Framework for
   Sustainably Facilitating Agency and Behavior Change in
   Development Aid Beneficiaries 89

7 User-Centered Approaches to Service Transactions and Agency of
   Service Users 123

Part III Visualizing and Measuring Agency 151

8 Writing, Telling, Expressing Self in Association with Others:
   Revisiting and Examining Life Record Movement as an Origin of
   Story-Based Methods in Japan 153

vii

9	**The Psychological Measurement of Agency: Recent Developments and Challenges of Psychometrics in Poverty Contexts**	175
10	**Visualization of the Stages of Agency Development**	187
11	**Conclusion**	217
Index		231

List of Figures

Fig. 6.1   Relatedness support and competence support as moderating variables of autonomy support. (This hypothesis has been modified from its original form in Sayanagi (2017a) to include direct paths from relatedness- and competence-support to the dependent variable. Note: Arrows between factors indicate cause and effect. Arrows pointing at other arrows indicate a moderating effect.) 106

Fig. 9.1   Relationship between reliability and validity in psychometric scales (figure adapted from Toshima & Seiwa, 1993) 179

List of Tables

Table 4.1	Cross-cutting distinctions: (i) well-being and agency, and (ii) achievement and freedom	56
Table 5.1	Types of power	69
Table 5.2	Dimensions of empowerment	69
Table 5.3	A process model of agency development of community members	70
Table 5.4	Poverty Indicators of the three cities	75
Table 5.5	Structure of the MMO training: Categorizing the training chapters	77
Table 5.6	A process model of agency development of MMO participants	83
Table 7.1	Classification of natures of service	128
Table 7.2	Illustration of the four types of services	129
Table 7.3	Typology of user-provider relationship in service transactions	132
Table 7.4	Types of user-provider relations and degrees of transaction intensity and discretion	133
Table 7.5	Typology of services and User Agency (UA) … and implicit stages of Agency Development	134
Table 8.1	Types of power	171
Table 10.1	Fulfillment of the minimum quality-of-life conditions on Entry / Exit of the *Programa Puente* (PP)	199
Table 10.2	Minimum quality-of-life conditions met at the entry into and the exit from *Programa Puente* (PP)	201
Table 10.3	Evaluation of the CHS as a whole by participating families	206
Table 10.4	Evaluation of AFs by participating families	206
Table 10.5	Evaluation of works on intrafamily relations by participating families	206
Table 10.6	Area of most significant learning	208
Table 10.7	Subcategory of most significant learning under "Family"	208
Table 10.8	Area of most significant functioning attributed to *Program Puente* (at the time of exit)	209

Table 10.9	Area of most significant functioning attributed to *Program Puente* (three years after exit)	209
Table 10.10	Areas of attention expressed in 'family projects' (on exit from *Programa Puente*)	211
Table 11.1	Comparison of the three definitions	219

Chapter 1
Introduction: What Moves Researchers to Take Initiatives to This Interdisciplinary Research Project

This introductory section gives an overview of the book and tells the story behind the elaboration and development of the interdisciplinary project commenced in 2012 at JICA Research Institute in Japan, which three researchers from different disciplines: Economics, Psychology, and Anthropology continue. As I (Sato, a development anthropologist) am the person who took the initiative for this book project and invited the other members, I would like to explain the objectives of the book, how this book project was incubated and developed, why an interdisciplinary approach is appropriate, as well as a brief introduction of each part and chapter.

This project focuses on understanding the definitions, factors, and mechanisms involved in agency and its development in three related contexts: participatory development, social work, and service provisions. The project's main objectives are to (1) recognize the critical roles of agency, (2) examine its definitions and positioning, (3) understand multi-layered conditions and make working theories on how agency development can happen, and (4) share ideas for visualizing and measuring agency development.

The research has its starting point in the recognition of the critical role played by "agency" (commonly understood as will for and practice of self-determination and self-management, its academic definitions are to be discussed in Part I) on the part of the intended beneficiaries of services and projects for effective implementation and sustainability. It is designed to address this subject matter with its principal focus on human beings' inner capacities and orientations, posing questions as to how such capacities and orientations could be enhanced and activated *in practice* by external actors in the field of public policies for socioeconomic and international development. The project transcends traditional disciplinary boundaries by combining anthropological, psychological, and economic approaches and perspectives.

1 A Life-Long Inquiry: What Makes People Move

The concepts and purposes of this book project are somewhat formal and academic, but it has been a life-long inquiry for me. Although not knowing the term agency, "what moves people to take initiatives" has been a repeated inquiry since my childhood. I was born in the 1970s as a sibling of the post-war baby boomers in a newly developed suburban community. As many people quickly came to live in the area, public and private services and recreation opportunities were not sufficiently provided. Consequently, self-supported community activities were preconditions to living well. Many community activities were organized by the neighborhood association, such as local patrols, monthly community clean-ups, and "watermelon-cracking" events for kids during summer vacation. At school, I was often involved with student councils. Many activities such as Sumo wrestling championships and community mapping for identifying safety hazards were organized and run by the students with the help of teachers. However, there were always a certain number of teachers and students who were "reluctant" to organize or take part in such activities. I wondered why and assumed that they were either shy, the activities were boring, or they felt excluded for some reason, but I was never able to figure out why.

Family situations were similar in my community. As a child, my parents sometimes sent me to neighborhood families who never paid neighborhood dues or showed up to community activities to pass community circulars to them. Some looked economically challenged, some looked rich, and some looked elderly with limited mobility. Some never answered the door chimes. Through my experiences at home and school, I often wondered what makes the difference between people who take the initiative and those who do not. Are the factors physical, gender-related, environmental, economic, socio-cultural, personality-related, or all combined? I wanted to know the answers, but no adult could give me convincing explanations at all.

2 A Long Way to Design a Research Project to Bridge Practices and Theories

As a university student, I majored in International Relations and became interested in developing countries, notably female empowerment and participatory community development. After graduating from university in Japan, I studied abroad for higher degrees as well as working in the field of International Development and Cooperation, such as JOCV (Nicaragua, 1997–1999), JICA (Nicaragua, 2002–2004), and UNICEF (Pakistan, 2005–2007), always in the field of participatory/community development with empowerment components though the sectors were varied. I have often felt challenged to persuade the "beneficiary populations" to take initiatives for planning and taking specific actions that would "improve" their living conditions from an outsider's viewpoint. I have also noticed that those who looked most vulnerable would often not even come to meetings organized by the projects with local leaders for decision making and actual activities though being invited. I have raised many hypotheses on their non-participation; internal conflicts within a community, "cultural aspects" that do not allow them to take part in, a mismatch between project designs and the beneficiaries' needs, and so on. However, I could not definitively figure out the factors or any solutions. Through those working experiences, I have become eager to know whether there could be any theories or methods to empower people that would actually work in practice. I have also remembered my childhood experiences and the inquiries regarding community participation. Although the contexts were quite different, the inquiry was the same and still unanswered.

I went back to Japan in 2007 and worked for the Japan Bank for International Cooperation (JBIC) and the Japan International Cooperation Agency (JICA) as a "social development specialist" for promoting people's participation and social development aspects in development programs and projects. Through this job, I got interested in Japanese community development and female empowerment experiences. I participated in a research forum under the Japan Society for International Development (JASID) regarding post-war life improvement experiences, organized by Prof. Toru Yanagihara (Development Economics, Takushoku University). The research forums' primary theme was to examine the applicability of post-war life improvement programs introduced by the Allied Powers General Headquarters (GHQ) and adopted nationwide, which had self-sustaining and empowerment aspects for promoting the quality of life of rural women through supporting their self-help efforts. I later became a co-organizer of the forum, which lasted until 2010.

In 2011, I started working for JICA-Research Institute, currently JICA Sadako Ogata Research Institute for Peace and Development (JICA-RI). In 2012, I co-designed a research project with Prof. Yanagihara regarding enhancing the agency of marginalized populations in developing countries with reference to Japanese post-war life improvement experiences. It was launched as the research project, "An Interdisciplinary Study on Agency Enhancement Process and Factors," between 2013 and 2015.[1] We wanted a psychologist's involvement since the topic should be related to "motivation." However, I could not identify any Japanese psychologists dealing with International Development. I kept sending messages to psychologists to invite their participation in the project, but my offer was declined for a couple of months. Finally, one of my co-workers, Ms. Yuka Ebihara, introduced me to Prof. Nobuo Sayanagi (Educational Psychology, Yamanashi Eiwa College), who had lived in a developing country in his childhood. I talked with him about the project a couple of times, and he finally agreed to join the research team. We also invited Prof. Tomomi Kozaki (Senshu University, Latin American Studies) and Prof. Yusuke Nakamura (Cognitive Artifacts and Social Change, Tokyo University) to the research project.

---

[1] For details and publications, refer to https://www.jica.go.jp/jica-ri/research/strategies/strategies_20130101-20150331.html.

There are a couple of larger contexts behind designing the research project. Since the 1980s, theoretical contributions to public policy and practice discussions, including international cooperation, have seen attempts to adopt bottom-up models. The bottom-up approach emphasizes the importance of will and commitment amongst community members concerning their initiatives and actions to maintain or improve quality of life as an alternative to the dominant top-down development model in which outsiders diagnose the problems and prescribe solutions. Enhancing the agency of marginalized communities thus has become the key to empowering them through applying bottom-up development approaches.

In this context, agency, and its conditions in marginalized populations have been studied in the field of International Development Studies, primarily from economic, sociological, and anthropological perspectives. Many development practitioners, including myself, have also reported how they try to facilitate such processes. Although their findings are fruitful, we identify some "blind spots" in those studies and reports. First, the researchers tend to focus on explanations such as definitions and measurements, not on application: how external actors or interventions can facilitate agency development of such a population. Sociology is particularly known for having a long tradition of developing discussions on agency. However, such sociological research focuses on *what* (such as definitions and measurements), not on *how* (plausible ways for developing agency). Second, the reports by development practitioners tend to be somewhat anecdotal and are not systematically formulated to identify the factors and mechanisms involved. Third, although exercising agency is a phenomenon that cannot be explained through a single academic discipline, few interdisciplinary studies are attempted. Fourth, although agency and its conditions are tightly related to Psychology, very few psychological studies have been conducted in the field of International Development and poverty alleviation of developing countries. In sum, there is a lack of research on *how* external actors can facilitate agency enhancement through interdisciplinary approaches.

To challenge the above-explained theme, the project was launched by the five researchers, and we published five papers in English and one paper in Spanish. After the termination of the research project, three out of the five members, who were the authors of this book project, took the initiative to examine the project theme further. They hosted two international conference sessions at HDCA (Human Development and Capability Association), three national conference sessions at JASID (Japan Society for International Development) as well as publishing a special issue for the Journal for International Development Studies (JASID).

The interdisciplinary team is comprised of Economics and Public Policies (Yanagihara), Psychology (Sayanagi), and Anthropology (Sato). Yanagihara has recently centered his research interest in applying institutional and behavioral economics analysis to modeling service transactions, case studies of social work, and empowerment. In addition, he organized research forums regarding Japanese experiences of post-war life improvement programs and their application to development programs between 2006 and 2010. Sayanagi, who specializes in Self-Determination Theory, joined us in 2013 and has worked at monitoring JICA projects and contributed to the publication of a guidebook regarding motivation and international cooperation.[2] Sato has worked as a development practitioner (community empowerment and participatory development) and built her academic career in Development Anthropology. As a scholar-practitioner, she has tried to extract working theories of agency development from practical knowledge of the field through applying anthropological methods.

As our academic and professional backgrounds are quite different, "transactional costs" were extremely high in the beginning to communicate and understand one another, as though we spoke in different languages. However, we could somehow endure and enjoy the process as we were sure that taking an interdisciplinary approach and combining Economic, Phycology, and Anthropology are appropriate and effective means for inquiring into agency development for the following reasons. First, the three disciplines, which have rich pools of preceding studies of the research subject, have vastly different theories and academic stances regarding "agency" and its development. Our review found that some prominent scholars have taken interdisciplinary approaches to study "agency and its development," combining the two disciplines out of the three. For instance, Margaret Mead, in *Coming of Age in Samoa* (1928), combines Anthropology and Psycology. She articulates cultural influences on psychosexual development in adolescent girls based on her fieldwork on the island of Ta'u in the Samoan Islands, comparing findings with those of American girls. The book is written as an anthropological text, but the contents are also psychosocial. Social Economist Naila Kabeer, known in the field of Gender and Development, mixed socioeconomic analyses and anthropological research methods for *The Power to Choose* (2002). She examines the lives of Bangladeshi garment workers in Bangladesh and Britain to argue how globalization affects women of both countries. The Nobel Prize-winning economist James Heckman is an expert in the economics of human development. He has recently collaborated with psychologists to develop personality measurement systems and published various books and articles such as *Handbook of the Economics of Education* (2011).

Second, the three disciplines have distinct roles in the project. Economics has its strength in formulating hypotheses building on the existing theoretical and empirical works and the statistical verification methodology of hypotheses. Psychology is a discipline that has garnered a body of empirical evidence on, among other things, operable factors that enhance and thwart motivation which can be critical to the success or failure of aid projects. Anthropology and its ethnographic approaches have advantages in understanding local contexts and realities in detail and verbalizing practical knowledge, allowing researchers to conduct up-close qualitative research with the researched communities. It is expected that these methodologies could be usefully employed to explore interdisciplinary collaborations in complementary manners.

In his famous Nicomachean Ethics, Aristotle divides knowledge generation into three approaches: *episteme*, *techné*, and *phronesis*. *Episteme* attributes are universal, invariable, and context-independent, which is based on general analytical

---

[2] https://libopac.jica.go.jp/images/report/12092193.pdf.

rationality. *Techne* is defined as the set of principles, or rational methods, aiming at making or doing, based on practical instrumental rationality governed by a conscious goal. *Phronesis* is based on practical value-rationality, which is pragmatic, variable, and context-dependent. It can be practically said that Yanagihara's approach is linked with *episteme*. He specializes in Economics and Public Policy and is always highly interested in definitions, logic, and theories. Sayanagi's approach is more related to *Techne*. His research methods are also quite rigorous, constantly adjusting questionnaires experimentally as though he were a craftsman. Anthropology is strongly associated with *phronesis*, respecting contextualized realities and knowledge. This approach is appropriate to investigate a case in-depth and extract working theories in a contextualized and open-ended manner.

Thus, we believe that conducting research on agency and its development from interdisciplinary approaches with a combination of the three academic disciplines can be an appropriate option for this book project.

3 Structure of the Book

This book consists of three parts, and each part includes three chapters written from each discipline. Part I, "Understanding Agency and Its Development," explores how each discipline defines and makes inquiries into agency and its development.

Chapter 2, "Beyond Aloof Cynicism: A Critical Overview of Anthropological Perspectives on Agency and its Development," provides a selective literature review related to the theme of agency and its development in Social and Cultural Anthropology. It first discusses how culture is defined and can be related to agency and its development. Second, the author explores how academic Anthropology defines and discusses agency development. Subsequently, how Development Anthropology defines and discusses "agency (development)" in its texts are to be explored. Finally, the author suggests an alternative form of anthropology that can serve to make working theories on agency development drawn from insiders' realities and tacit knowledge.

Chapter 3, "A Psychological Perspective on Agency in the Context of Behavior Change," starts with an introduction on the assumptions behind psychological concepts, or *constructs*, which do not necessarily have any entity or substance. The chapter then provides a tentative definition for the agency construct that is relevant to behavior change and taking initiatives, selectively reviews concepts that are related to the definition, especially self-efficacy and autonomous motivation. The refined definition of agency proposed in this chapter, informed by SDT, is *the ability and capacity to self-determinedly act towards the goal(s) of improving the environment and/or circumstances.* We further argue that autonomous motivation is the more appropriate concept to be used for behavior change, especially in the context of international development, as it is a predictor of behavior changes and associated with eudaimonic well-being.

3 Structure of the Book

Chapter 4, "Agency in Economics: Rationality, Human Capital, and Human Capability," first puts forth the author's definition of the term "agency" and then proceeds to provide a selective review of literature in economics related to the theme of agency and its development. The exposition will be presented in three distinct contexts: (1) micro-and behavioral economics, (2) human capital theory, and (3) capability approach. The key features of (1) and (2) represent recent scholastic innovations in economics motivated by the desire to make economic research more empirically relevant by incorporating viewpoints and findings from psychology and neuroscience. By contrast, (3) reflects attempts spearheaded by Amartya Sen to bridge economics and philosophy (ethics, in particular). Finally, interconnections among these three areas of research will be discussed to identify issues for possible cross-fertilization.

Part II, "Enhancing Agency: Its Plausible Mechanisms and Influential Factors," tries to propose plausible hypotheses and working theories on agency development as well as analyzing enhancing and thwarting factors.

Chapter 5, "What Is Done for Facilitating Agency Development in Practice?: Documenting and Crystallizing an Unsung Practical Knowledge of a Third-Country Expert," tries to understand what is being done to facilitate agency development (empowerment) in practice by connecting research (academic theories) and practice (development projects) with clarifying context-specific factors. Through analyzing and crystalizing a case study led by a Nikkei Brazilian expert in Nicaragua, the paper tries to frame a hypothesis on plausible dynamics for enhancing agency in practice.

Chapter 6, "A Psychological Framework for Breaking the Poverty Trap," proposes a hypothesis for promoting autonomous motivation, the central mechanism of agency, in marginalized populations. The hypothesis is a modification of Self-Determination Theory but also draws from behavior modification approaches. The modification to self-determination theory accommodates for the low levels of perceived competence common among populations that become the beneficiaries of aid programs. Finally, the proposed framework is used to examine some international development schemes that aim for the behavior change of their beneficiaries, and future applications of the framework in research and practice are discussed.

Chapter 7, "User-Centered Approaches to Service Transactions and the Empowerment of Service Users," is concerned with the issues surrounding the "User-Centered Approach (UCA)" to service provision, one context in which "agency" on the part of service users is notably featured. First conceptual and analytical approaches to service transaction and utilization are presented, followed by articulation and classification of the nature of services based on New Institutional Economics and conjectures on two types of failures. Second, in discussing the effectiveness of the UCA models (co-production and self-management), typologies of user-provider relations and user agency in service transactions and utilization will be presented. Third, the conceptual distinction between and empirical illustrations of the activation and augmentation of user agency is provided and related to different types of empowerment interventions.

Part III, "Visualizing and Measuring Agency," deals with how to make processes of agency development "visible" through verbalizing, patterning, and making frameworks for evaluations.

Chapter 8, "Writing, Telling, Expressing Self in Association with Others: Revisiting and Examining Life Record Movement as an Origin of Story-based Methods in Japan," traces historical elaborations of Life Record Movement (LRM) in the post-war context, in search of finding meaningful suggestions to current social and international projects that incorporate agency development (empowerment) components. The author focuses on its participants' realities reflected in primary and secondary sources and personal changes experienced by them.

Chapter 9, "The Psychological Measurement of Agency in Poverty Contexts: Recent Developments and Challenges of Psychometrics in Poverty Contexts," first outlines the underlying assumptions concerning the measurement of psychological constructs, or *psychometrics*. The main objective of the chapter is to review the psychological literature on the measurement of autonomous motivation. There is a special focus on the challenges of psychometrics in poverty contexts, and recent developments regarding the measurement of autonomous motivation in development aid studies are described in detail. Finally, future directions in conducting psychological research on agency in such contexts are proposed.

Chapter 10, "Visualization of the Stages of Agency Formation/Development: The Design and Performance of the Program for the Poorest in Chile," represents an in-depth study of the case of the Chile Solidario Program (CHS), designed and implemented by the government to assist the poorest segment of the population to move out of the poverty trap. CHS. The unique feature of CHS was its emphasis on agency development as a key condition for overcoming the difficulties of daily life and setting the goals for a better life at present and in the future. Following the description of the key features of CHS, its results in the realm of agency development are presented based on official documents and, to visualize the process of agency formation/development, a conceptual scheme of stage transition is formulated and illustrated by views and sentiments expressed by program participants. The critical role of social workers in providing psychosocial support through the process of stage transition is emphasized, and conditions for their effective performance are identified.

Finally, in the closing chapter (Chap. 11), all the above chapters are to be dissected to extract differences and similarities of definitions, mechanisms, and the visualization/measurement of agency and its development.

Part I
Understanding Agency and Its Development

Chapter 2
Beyond Aloof Cynicism: A Critical Overview of Anthropological Perspectives on Agency and Its Development

1 Introduction

This chapter provides a selective literature review of Sociocultural Anthropology (a portmanteau to refer to Social Anthropology and Cultural Anthropology, expressed as Anthropology in this chapter) exclusively related to the theme of agency and its development. The review seeks to uncover hidden connections between culture and agency as well as its development.

There are two main reasons for exploring this theme. First, the author has wondered for a long time why relations between culture and agency have not been seriously discussed, while they should be closely linked because the notion of agency includes value, which should be related to culture. Second, development anthropologists, including the author herself, have been committed to development practices, especially to social development projects aimed at the participation and empowerment of the targeted populations. However, they have seldom elaborated working theories of agency development, which remains a big question for the author, who has also been working as a development scholar/practitioner for a long time.

To explore the theme and answer the two inquiries above, in this chapter, the author first discusses how culture is defined and can be related to agency and its development. Second, the author explores how academic Anthropology has defined and discussed agency development, although it would not necessarily be explicitly expressed and explained in its texts. Subsequently, she further discusses how applied Anthropology, in this case, Development Anthropology (a school of Applied Anthropology), has defined and discussed "agency" and its development in their texts. Finally, the author suggests an alternative form of anthropology that can make working theories on agency development drawn from 'insiders' realities and tacit knowledge.

© The Author(s), under exclusive license to Springer Nature Singapore Pte Ltd. 2022
M. Sato et al., *Empowerment Through Agency Enhancement*,
https://doi.org/10.1007/978-981-19-1227-6_2

2 Definitions of Culture, Agency, and Its Development

2.1 Defining and Relating Culture and Agency

Anthropology was initially a compound of the Greek words for "human being" and "study." Anthropologists conduct long-term fieldwork and write ethnographies to describe and interpret forms of cultures in certain societies based on qualitative research methods, mainly participatory observations and semi-structured interviews. Thus, no one would oppose that Anthropology is a subject to study culture and that anthropologists try to understand meanings of culture in context.

In fact, there is no uniform definition of culture even among anthropologists, which should be partly because of its academic character respecting diversity, holism, and relativism. The most quoted definitions are by Tylor, Geertz, and Peacock. Tylor (1871, pp. 1–25) explains that culture and civilization, taken in its broad ethnographic sense, is that complex whole that includes knowledge, belief, art, morals, law, custom, and any other capabilities and habits acquired by man as a member of society. For Geertz (1973, p. 89), culture denotes a historically transmitted pattern of meanings embodied in symbols, a system of inherited conceptions expressed in symbolic forms through which men communicate, perpetuate, and develop their knowledge about and attitudes toward life. Finally, Peacock (1987, p. 7) emphasizes that culture is a name that anthropologists give to the taken-for-granted but powerfully influential understandings and codes learned and shared by members of a group. Through comparing the literature, he further analyses fundamental features of culture as to be learned (thus not genetic), social/shared, and invisible (taken for granted in certain societies), but strong (influencing all range of human codes of conducts, thoughts, and actions) (ibid.: 3–8). Summing the above arguments, culture can be defined as a system of recognition and practice encompassing the whole range of human activities and experiences learned and shared *posteriori* in certain societies, often habitual but influential.

Definitions of agency are also varied but much more united than the definitions of culture. According to the American Psychological Association, it is defined as "the state of being active, usually in the service of a goal, or of having the power and capability to produce an effect or exert influence (VandenBos, 2007)."

In the context of International Development, which is one of the main locations of case studies of this book, it is explained as "what a person is free to do and achieve in pursuit of whatever goals or values he or she regards as important" (Sen, 1985, p. 203) or "the ability to define one's goals and act upon them" (Kabeer, 1999, p. 437). In sum, agency can be defined as an individual's power/ability to produce an effect or exert influence on some issues in pursuit of specific goals and values in the context of International Development, which definition can be also generally and widely accepted in other related fields of studies. However, as an Anthropologist, the author would point out that definitions made by Sen and Kabeer, who are both development economists, are rather individualized and context-free, which are also pointed out in Drydyk (2008), Keane (2007), Ratner (2000) and Cornwall and Brock (2005).

Thus, culture can be a system of recognition and practice that humans can acquire posteriori, encompassing the complete range of human activities and experiences. Agency, in general, can be defined as individual's power/ability to produce an effect or exert influence on some issues in pursuit of specific goals and values. Technically speaking, no culture can exist without exercising agency as no activities and experiences, which are foundations of culture, can be realized. Philosophically speaking, no one can exercise agency without culture as it is necessary for people to have values or codes of conduct to set goals for exercising agency. Practically speaking, no individual, community, or society can operate smoothly if agency and culture are not related and function simultaneously. Therefore, culture and agency should be intertwined quite strongly in reality.

Thus, reflecting the above discussions, agency in the context of Anthropology can be defined as individual's or shared power/ability to produce an effect or exert influence on some issues in pursuit of specific goals and values, which is context-bound as influenced by culture. However, agency, in some occasions, can be also power/ability to transform culture.

2.2 Culture, Agency, and Its Development

If so, there should be a rich collection in Anthropology regarding agency and its development. In the field of Anthropology, agency is used rather commonly without defining the term in a precise manner. For instance, In the American Anthropological Association (AAA) annual meeting programs, there are many sessions and presentations that include agency in their titles and contents. However, unlike Sociology, which has a long history of discussing how to define agency (often in relation to structure), Anthropology has no strong drive for defining and redefining the term itself as far as research.

As an anthropologist, the author has always felt that it seems almost taboo to propose working theories on agency development based on fieldwork among anthropologists. In fact, the author has not been able to find ethnographies explicitly dealing with agency development, proposing hypothetical mechanisms. The author assumes that the main reason would be cultural relativism, one of the most fundamental features of Anthropology, which believes that culture should be equally respected and not be judged against the criteria of others. Thus, in Anthropology, "exercising agency" is a politically correct expression, but "developing agency" or "agency development" is not, as it means that anthropologists judge states of agency of certain people as others, applying outsider's criteria. Besides, ethnography is a descriptive and interpretive study of a particular human society, and thus it is not common for anthropologists to share working theories of agency development that can be applied into different contexts beyond specific case studies.

However, anthropologists should be those who have closely observed, researched, and sometimes worked with people in "developing countries" for the most extended periods, compared with scholars of other academic disciplines. Therefore, although having not explicitly elaborated, there should be specific literature that can contribute to discussions of agency and its development. Thus, in the following sections, the author explores selective anthropological studies related to agency and its development, both in academic and applied Anthropology, although their boundary has recently been becoming somewhat ambiguous.

3 Agency and Its Development in Academic Anthropology

One of the academic roots of Anthropology is associated with colonization in the Modern Era. For ruling colonies, it was necessary to understand their people and societies. From the 1870s to the 1920s, missionaries and colonial administrators produced a significant body of monographs, which inspired early modernist anthropological thinking (Pina-Cabral, 2018). Furthermore, the emergence of long-term data-gathering among non-European populations was made possible by the expansion of colonial administration and the establishment of ethnography (ibid.). Thus, Anthropology initially emerged and developed to study others in foreign, remote, and "primitive" societies.

This section explicates how academic Anthropology has discussed agency and its development in chronological manners, although it would be implicitly or metaphorically shown in the texts.

3.1 *Cultural Evolutionism in the UK: From the Mid Twentieth Century*

Cultural Evolutionism was a school of Anthropology influenced by Social Darwinism, a theory inspired by Charles Darwin's concept of selective biological evolution. It believes in *survival of the fittest*—the idea that certain people become powerful in society because they are innately "better."

In this school, no fieldwork was conducted, and only secondary information served as references. Three prominent scholars are recognized, all discussed how a society and people could be "developed" from uncivilized to civilized. Edward Tyler, who is considered the ancestor of English Anthropology, wrote *Primitive Culture* (1871). In the text, he expresses that civilization is stronger and more competent than the barbarian and that society is divided into three levels depending on forms of religions, which are animism, polytheism, and monotheism. Likewise, Luis Morgan, in *Ancient Society* (1877), divides the stages of societal development based on marriage systems; group marriage, polygamy, and monogamy. Finally,

Herbert Spencer (1857) links the development of society and children's growth and explains that "barbarians" are like children who grow into adults in stages.

Thus, people in "primitive societies" were considered "backward," and they were supposed to "develop" in the direction of where modern societies and people have already reached. If interpreting, it can be said that their agency was considered "inactive" and should be developed in the direction of where people in modern societies have already progressed. This discourse of "from underdeveloped to developed" is what current anthropologists find uncomfortable, and thus, those texts are usually not referred to positively these days. However, this ideology has been accepted in Modernization theory, which is still a common discourse of International Development, and this may explain why many anthropologists still do not feel favorable toward development policies and projects.

3.2 Modernist Anthropology in Europe: From the Early Twentieth Century

This school of Anthropology counter-argues Cultural Evolutionism and its imperialistic discourses. The scholars assert that people in primitive societies have their own logic, functions, and structures. Although they are precisely categorized into Functionalism, Functional Structuralism, and Structuralism, the author does not argue their differences and categorically calls them Modernist Anthropology.

From the early twentieth century, anthropological methods, such as long-term fieldwork, participatory observation, interviews, and ethnography, were gradually established. Moreover, through direct communications with "the natives," scholars noticed that they were not "savages" and had their own ways of living and maintaining their communities and societies. In this period, departments of Anthropology were also established in many universities in European countries, and secondary information based on fieldwork was accumulated. Some prominent scholars are Alfred Radcliffe-Brown, Bronislaw Malinowski, Marcel Mauss, and Cloud Levi-Strauss. However, the author mainly discusses literature by Mauss and Levi-Strauss as their arguments were more related to exercising agency and its development.

Radcliffe-Brown (1922) in *Andaman Islanders*, detailed information on various aspects of the indigenous cultures found on the Islands, with analysis of social organization, ceremonial customs, myths, legends, and religious beliefs.

Malinowski (1922) in *Argonauts of the Western Pacific* decodes detailed mechanisms of Kula ring in the Trobriand Islands from his long-term fieldwork, which were quite functional and organized but not entirely recognized or explained by the local people themselves. His study challenged images of savages as inferiors and contributed to the development of an anthropological theory of reciprocity.

In his famous text *The Gift: Forms and Functions of Exchange in Archaic Societies* (1924), Marcel Mauss eloquently discusses complex mechanisms of gift exchange exercised in primitive societies based on the extensive meta-review of secondary information by Malinowski and other scholars. He argues that the maintenance or prosperity of those societies is strongly linked with how the members effectively generate and develop gift exchange relationships among people through giving, receiving, and returning gifts. Mauss also distinguishes types of gift exchanges between limited (gift exchange between two parties) and general (gift exchange among more than two parties) and asserts that a society's prosperity is based on the latter.

In *Savage Mind* (1962), Levi-Strauss argues that natives have their own forms of intelligence and established two concepts, Bricolage and Totemism. Through his field research of the Indigenous peoples in Latin America and Native Americans in North America, he found that those people were quite capable of creatively inventing tools made of "leftovers" and "scraps," and named this mode of production bricolage, in contrast with the western mode of production engineering. Levi-Strauss further emphasizes that notions and practices of bricolage are also observed in modern societies and omnipresent beyond time, cultures, and forms of societies. Another concept is Totemism, which was inspired by Totem poles of Northern American Indian tribes. He analyses that each item carved into Totem poles represents each tribe's origins and legends that have been orally conveyed and thus represent each tribe's essential codes and social structures, differentiating it from others (ibid.). In other words, carved items are codes of their original logic and languages abstractedly expressed.

All scholars, especially Mauss and Levi-Strauss, explain how "archaic" or primitive cultures are maintained because of people's intelligence and are mechanisms to manage their societies through exercising agencies rooted in the culture. Besides, their status of agencies is understood to be more developed according to how to exchange gifts, and invent tools innovatively, and create totem poles and reinterpret the stories behind them.

Thus, although they have not directly used the term agency and its development, it can be said that their assertions are strongly associated with agency and its development.

3.3 *Cultural Relativism (from the Mid Twentieth–)*

During and after World War II, the center of Anthropology shifted from Europe to the United States because many Jewish scholars evacuated to the United States during wartime, and the United States won the war. As a result, conducting fieldwork and making ethnographies became a default setting of Anthropology, and many investigations on Native Americans were conducted and recorded.

Cultural Relativism was believed to be conceptualized originally by Franz Boas in his book *The Mind of Primitive* (1911). He emphasizes that a person's beliefs, values, and practices should be understood based on that person's own culture and not be judged against the criteria of others. Cultural Relativism differs from Modernist Anthropology in that it does not distinguish primitive from modern societies and asserts that they are just different societies with different cultures to learn from each other (Blackhawk & Wilner, 2018). In other words, while the former tends to discuss forms of civilizations through comparing and crystalizing features of modern and primitive societies, the latter often compares cultures of different societies without such boundaries. Boas taught many well-known scholars, including Ruth Benedict and Margaret Mead. Under him, "non-white scholars" such as Zora-Neale Hurston and Ella Cara Deloria were also produced, becoming renowned writers and researchers of their own cultures.

Mead's *Coming of Age in Samoa* (1928/2001) was based upon her research and study of primarily adolescent girls in the Samoan Islands. The book details the sexual life of teenagers in Samoan society in the early twentieth century. Mead theorizes that culture is a leading influence on psychosexual development. She observed and interviewed 68 girls between the ages of 9 and 20 living in three villages on the island of Ta'ū in American Samoa and concluded that the stable and sexually active nature of Samoan girls was due to cultural features and values such as education, extended family structures, social structure, and rules. Further, she concluded that personality and sexuality are also influenced and constructed by culture.

Benedict wrote *Patterns of Culture* in 1934 and asserts that each culture chooses from "the great arc of human potentialities" and that only a few characteristics become the leading personality traits of specific societies. The central case studies used in the book are the Kwakiutl of the Pacific Northwest based on Boas' fieldwork, the Pueblo of New Mexico based on her fieldwork, and the Dobu culture of New Guinea, which relied upon Mead's and Reo Fortune's fieldwork. Benedict asserts that personality and morality are relative to the values of the culture in which one operates.

Another prominent anthropologist who relates to the "agency of the poor" in this period should be Oscar Lewis, although not necessarily categorized in this school of Anthropology. In his *Five Families: Mexican Case Studies in the Culture of Poverty* (1959), by illustrating the daily life of five poor Mexican families in detail, Lewis claims that poverty is not only based on economic status but also sociocultural and phycological constructions that make poor people accept their situations as "destinies." They thus do not make an effort to improve their situations, which habitual patterns are passed to their children as cycles of deprivations.

Compared with Modernist Anthropology, cultural patterns of individual life were closely examined and interpreted under this school. The above literature examined linkages between culture and personality or poverty, but discussions on agency and personal actions and its development were seldom explicitly observed. Perhaps, discussions regarding agency (development) were absorbed into "personality" or "cycles of deprivation," and thus, debates on agency were seldom spotlighted. However, we can understand that those scholars deal with cases where people need to exercise agency and analyze patterns, how to exercise it was internalized deeply into one's personality or inherited over generations.

3.4 Postmodern Anthropology (from 1970–)

Until the 1970s, Anthropology studied primitive societies and cultures of ethnic and racial groups, either in developing countries or regions. However, such a mode of study was questioned from the 1970s because of the conceptual formation and academic rise of Postmodernism and Postcolonialism, which claimed that no one could have objective and neutral knowledge of others. Thus, postmodern Anthropology emerged under such academic trends.

Clifford Geertz published *The Interpretation of Cultures* in 1973, where he criticized that existing anthropological texts are searching too much for universal truths and theories beyond cultures (Geertz, 1973). Instead, he insists that anthropologists should write ethnographies with thick descriptions, describing physical behaviors and their contexts in detail so that they can be wholly understood. Furthermore, he advocates methodologies describing and interpreting details of a particular culture to deeply understand specific people's realities and experiences in particular contexts without comparisons (ibid.).

In 1978, Edward Said published *Orientalism* and criticized exaggerated differences or cliched representations of the East (the Orient) compared with the West, which is set as the standard axis from Postcolonial perspectives (Said, 1978). He further asserts that Orientalism functions as a powerful apparatus for dominating the East by the West.

In 1985, Clifford and Marcus published *Writing Culture* and asserted that anthropologists could not write about non-western cultures holistically because their texts are unconsciously written under asymmetric power relations between anthropologists and informant communities (Clifford & George, 1985). They insist that anthropologists intentionally or unconsciously select what is or is not to be written in their ethnographies (ibid.). Their assertions deeply concerned anthropologists, and consequently, extracting working theories beyond cultures has become politically incorrect.

Research directly dealing with agency under Postmodern Anthropology is referred to as Actor-Network Theory (ANT). ANT assumes that all entities in a network should be symmetrically described in the same terms (Aoyama, 2012). According to Gigi (2011), ANT challenges researchers to deconstruct dichotomies between nature/society and subject/object that are the foundations of western philosophy. Having agency is not a privilege entitled to "only human beings." Thus, it asserts that humans and non-humans both exercise agency equally, and everything in the social and natural worlds exists in constantly shifting networks of relationships (Latour, 1993, 2005). Their assertion influences many disciplines of the humanities and social science. The author also agrees that non-human things also affect human beings and their decisions and actions, which can be reflected more in social applications and projects. However, it is also true that only humans can observe, decode, and describe such networks of relationships, representing the "voices" of non-human beings. Additionally, they do not discuss how agency of humans and non-humans can be developed through intricately associating with one another.

Under Postmodern Anthropology, ethnographies have become denser, more interpretative, and context-specific. Thus, extracting patterns and working theories to serve other similar cultures became somewhat "out of mode". Moreover, as Postmodern Anthropology has tried to deconstruct and reshape its methodological approaches fundamentally, including its academic identities themselves, there have been perhaps no spaces open to discuss agency and its development, even implicitly.

3.5 Summation

Anthropology has radically transformed its shape from Cultural Evolutionism to Postmodern Anthropology throughout its doctrinal history. Its modes of study have shifted from judging natives as underdeveloped based upon the perspective of modern society towards describing each culture in dense detail and interpreting it in open-ended ways without judging the "cultural levels" of societies. In other words, Anthropology has been more "democratized" and "individualized" throughout its history, in search of fairness and political correctness. Thus, discussions about agency and its development are not explicitly found in its texts, especially after Cultural Relativism.

However, carefully looking into its history, anthropologists have also extracted patterns and hypothetical theories, which can be applied beyond specific settings. Especially under Modernist Anthropology, anthropologists propped up social theories beyond cultures through comparing societies and shared working theories on specific topics. Additionally, it is confirmed that what counts as Anthropology has shifted and transformed over time, reflecting its academic practitioners' openness to diversity and plurality.

4 Agency and Its Development in Applied Anthropology

After World War II, many colonies achieved their independence, and International Development has emerged both as an industry and academic field of study. Thus, "pre-modern societies" that were the focus for Anthropological research were newly called "Third World" or "developing countries." Gradually, willingly or unwillingly, Anthropologists began involving themselves in this new field, and gradually such Anthropology has been called *Development Anthropology*, a form of Applied Anthropology.

This section explores how Development Anthropology has defined and discussed agency and its development, especially the latter as the subject is applied. In this section, the author explores how anthropologists have or have not associated with International Development and agency development by loosely adopting the categorization of those anthropologists by Lewis (2005); (1) Anthropology of Development (antagonistic observer), and (2) Development Anthropology (reluctant participant, and engaged activists).

4.1 Anthropology of Development (Antagonistic Observer)

Anthropologists in this category are pure academicians who rather have an antipathy against development as local traditions seem to be destroyed by development projects and are not interested in improving development interventions. Thus, they are called antagonistic observers and characterized by taking critical distance and making criticisms to the ideas of developing the Third World and the interventions required to do so (ibid.). They have questioned that if a key development goal is to alleviate poverty, then why has poverty not been reduced, and why is development so externally driven rather than having an internal basis. In short, they inquire why so much planned development fails when so much money and time has been invested into it (Gow, 1996). Gardner and Lewis (2015, pp. 50–76) analyzed publications of this field of Anthropology and categorized them into three types; (1) sociocultural influences of economic changes, (2) sociocultural influences of development planning on local societies, and (3) discourse analyses on international development agencies and their cultures. Under the first category, Wilson (1942) worked in Zambia in the late 1930s. He showed how industrialization and urbanization processes were structured by colonial policies that discouraged permanent settlement and led to social instability, as massive levels of male migration took place back and forth between rural and urban areas. Long (1977) conceptualized actor-oriented approaches through his work in Peru. He explored local, small-scale processes of growth and challenged macro-level structural analyses by focusing on the complexity and dynamism of people's strategies and struggles. Geertz (1963) researched Indonesian agricultural change in the second category and raised practical concerns about technological change and land use. It showed how the adaptation of an increasingly complex system of wetland agricultural production reflected both cultural priorities and material pressures. Kilby (2019) analyzed three underlying principles that have guided green revolutions: the political environment in which they were set; how they contributed to both the successes and challenges the Green Revolution continues to face; and the systemic institutional barriers for access to these agricultural production advances, with a focus on how gender relations limit the inclusion of women even when they are the principal cultivators and farm managers. In the third category, Ferguson (1990), based on his fieldwork in Lesotho, drew on Foucault's work on power and discourse (governmentality) and showed how a World Bank project in Lesotho functioned primarily as a system to extend development agencies power instead of alleviating the poverty of the nation at all. Escobar (1995), also based on Foucault's conceptualization of power and knowledge, traces how development as an ideology has constructed and framed the concept of the Third World that is defined and acted upon by the West and advocates resistance against its domination. This publication has obtained increasing attention among anthropologists as it has eloquently asserted that development is something beyond the simple aggregation of agencies and experts attempting to make differences, but rather it is an apparatus of domination.

In sum, those publications focus on "what socioculturally went wrong with development interventions" or "what influences development interventions or modernizations have brought to local communities." As they take positions against development, they have not discussed how such interventions would influence agency and its development of local people at all, although resisting against or subverting development interventions surely do need exercising agencies very tactically.

4.2 Development Anthropology: Reluctant Participants and Engaged Activists

Gradual professionalization of the development industry from the 1970s onwards led to a growth of opportunities for anthropologists to work within development agencies as staff or consultants. In addition, under-funding of higher education institutions in the United Kingdom, which began to become severe during the 1980s, hit anthropology departments particularly hard (Lewis, 2005, p. 8). Under such contexts, anthropologists have commenced working for or in development agencies reluctantly or willingly.

One of the pioneers in this category is Michael Cernea, who introduced sociological and anthropological approaches to the World Bank. He worked for the World Bank from 1974 till 1997. In *Putting People First: Sociological Variables in Development*, Cernea (1985) introduces anthropological and sociological analysis on various development programs/projects. It addresses the sociocultural and practical considerations involved in designing and implementing effective rural development projects, indicating how to incorporate sociocultural variables into the development design. Another pioneer is Robert Chambers. In the 1980s, Chambers (1983) writes *Rural development: putting the last first*, contending that researchers, policymakers, and fieldworkers rarely appreciate the richness and validity of rural people's knowledge or the hidden nature of rural poverty, proposing a series of participatory rural appraisal (PRA) and People's Learning and Action (PLA) publications (such as Chambers 1997, 2005). In his books, Chambers repeatedly asserts that it is fundamental to count local people and their subjective realities first and that outsiders should only facilitate their development processes. Thus, he should have recognized that people in developing countries are active agents, and supporting their knowledge generation and problem-solving processes would possibly develop their agencies. However, perhaps because his focus is on shifting modes and paradigms of development research, he has not particularly crystalized any models or analyzed patterns of agency development or empowerment. Such a stage model can be only partly observed in the learning/action processes in the *Handbook of*

Community-led Total Sanitation written by Kamal Kar and Chambers (2008). Thus, if carefully analyzing his books, patterns of agency development could be more extracted.

From the 1990s, development agencies hired more anthropologists to work within development projects or accepted to conduct research in development projects. As a result, much research has been realized, especially in the health and sanitation sectors. For example, in Japan, Matsuyama (2011, reproductive health), Sugita (2008, water and sanitation), Shirakawa (2011, malaria), Sato (2008, adolescents reproductive health education) can be counted in this category. In the rural development sector, Lewis et al. (1996) would be an outstanding example that was researched in rural north-western Bangladesh during an Official Development Assistance (ODA) aquaculture project, identifying a complex range of hidden intermediaries within local fish production and marketing networks.

One of this category's best-known and encompassing works are the three volumes comprising the trilogy, *Voices of the Poor* (Narayan et al., 2000). They are the product of comprehensive research work on poverty published in connection with the *World Development Report 2000/2001: Attacking Poverty*. Chambers (2013), who did consultation work for the volume, reflected that four topics were identified by analyzing the voices of the explored peoples; 1. People's own words and concepts of wellbeing and ill-being, 2. People's priorities, 3. People's experiences with institutions and attitudes towards them, and 4. Gender relations. He concluded that there were striking findings such as the diversity and commonalities of people's concepts of wellbeing and ill-being, good and bad quality of life, and the importance of physical and mental health to poor people (ibid.).

From the 1990s till the beginning of the 2000s, anthropologists thus have associated social projects that aimed at people's participation and empowerment, and they have realized that their research could offer some influences on local people, and more research articles and books were published regarding this topic. Through such encounters, anthropologists have perhaps fully realized that people who were often labeled as "beneficiaries" of development projects were indeed actors and active agents of their communities. Long (2001), for instance, theorizes actor-oriented approaches based on social constructionism and asserts that researchers should understand local people as equal actors as development practitioners and that they have the knowledge, ability, and agency to judge the situation in question and make appropriate responses. He also points out that researchers should understand social relations beyond the binomial confrontation of internal and external and analyze the process of the interactive and complex interaction of people that was not taken up in the project (ibid.). However, he has not analyzed how this process could develop people's agencies. Likewise, Fujikake (2008) made a qualitative empowerment evaluation for development projects to measure levels of empowerment based on people's narratives but does not explicate how to facilitate empowerment itself.

During this period, critiques towards concepts and practices of empowerment have also become popular. For example, through analysis of case studies, Sato et al. (2005) assert that empowerment is merely a discourse over-utilized without standard definitions. Empowerment processes should be spontaneous and thus cannot be planned and achieved through external interventions so easily. However, comparing eight case studies in the book, he also identifies three factors of empowerment: personal agency development, capability development, and transformation of social relations that allows people to flourish their capabilities (ibid.). Likewise, Cornwall (2016) criticizes that women's empowerment focuses on instrumental gains and is treated as a destination reached through development projects, but clear pathways that women are taking for empowerment remain hidden.

In this period, some anthropologists have also noticed that their long-term fieldwork has dimensions to "empower" people and anthropologists themselves. For instance, Sekine (2007) points out that long-term anthropological research with local communities eventually includes emergent collaboration and strategic assentation beyond writing ethnographies. Oguni et al. (2011) also articulates that her fieldwork has gradually incorporated dimensions as a supporter from daily associations among the researched and researchers.

Thus, anthropologists have written about "empowerment" or admitted that their works are somehow related to it. However, they seldom examine or propose mechanisms, patterns, or stage models of agency development.

5 Beyond Aloof Cynicism: Anthropology on Engaged Activists for Making a Difference

From the 2000s till today, macro-economic and political reforms such as the Millennium Development Goals (MDGs) and Sustainable Development Goals (SDGs) have been promoted rather than contextualized and socially and culturally sensitive development interventions (Hagberg & Ouattara, 2012). This trend has reduced the number of anthropologists hired to work on development projects. Under such a trend, David Mosse (2013) analyses an academic shift from anthropological critiques of the discursive power of development toward the ethnographic treatment of development as a category of practice. In other words, anthropologists seem to return to their "original positions" or "comfort zones" as ethnographers. There are mainly two types of such ethnography. One is project ethnography, which makes densely detailed descriptions of specific development projects and policies or describes inter-linkages between them. For instance, Oguni (2003), through her experience as an extension worker for Japan Overseas Cooperation Volunteers in Indonesia between 1994 and 2001, wrote a project ethnography with the application of an actor-oriented approach, interface analysis, and process documentation. She describes in detail how people dynamically interact with one another and that she was also involved as an actor in the development process. Mosse (2005), through a development project in western India, makes detailed observations to understand the complex relationship between policy and practice in development. He reveals how the exigencies of organizations influence actions made by development workers and how hard the workers make efforts to maintain the coherence of their actions with official policy.

The other is aid ethnography, through which anthropologists observe and experience aid cultures in development institutions as insiders. The most prominent anthology could be *Adventures in Aidland* by Mosse (2011). They became staff at development agencies and made an intensive participatory observation as insiders, drawing critical attention to the global poverty and the social life of development professionals. Although their texts give readers academic thrills, the author feels that their academic stances are quite similar to those of the Anthropology of Development, keeping distance as observers, although they are practically involved in development projects as professionals.

It may be a fact that if anthropologists are committed as development practitioners to specific development projects or processes, it would perhaps become difficult for them to analyze objectively and reflectively what is going on. However, it is possible for anthropologists to observe and interpret what development practitioners, who are also "insiders" of development projects, are doing for promoting people's participation or empowerment, both encompassing exercising agency and its development. They often exercise practical knowledge habitually and do not connect what they are doing with more extensive theories to extract mechanisms. Thus, anthropologists can conduct research to describe, analyze, and crystalize their knowledge to extract working theories of agency development. The author would name this alternative approach the "Anthropology of development practices." As anthropologists have perhaps the longest and deepest associations with local people, including practitioners among all academic disciplines of International Development Studies, the author believes that "Anthropology of development practices" is an optimal alternative.

In the following chapter, the author will share an attempt of "Anthropology of development practices," through which one hopes to practice a form of emancipatory Development Studies and Anthropology to make a difference in the real world.

References

Aoyama, M. (2012). Ejenshiganen no Saikento: Jinkobutsu niyoru Ejenshi no dezain wo megutte. *Cognitive Studies, 19*(2), 164–174.
Benedict, R. (1934/1958). *Patterns of Culture*. (Original Work Published 1934).
Blackhawk, I., & Wilner, L. (Eds.). (2018). *Indigenous Visions: Rediscovering the World of Franz Boas*. Yale University Press.
Boas, F. (2018/1911). *The Mind of Primitive*. Forgotten Books. (Original Work Published 1911).
Cernea, M. (1985). *Putting People First: Sociological Variables in Development* (Revised and Expanded ed.). The World Bank.
Chambers, R. (1983). *Rural Development: Putting the Last First*. Longman.
Chambers, R. (1997). *Whose Reality Counts?: Putting the First Last*. Practical Action Publishing.
Chambers, R. (2005). *Ideas for Development*. Routledge.
Chambers, R. (2013). *'Voices of the Poor' and Beyond: Lessons from the Past, Agenda for the Future*. ISS.

References

Clifford, J., & George, E. M. (Ed.). (2010/1985). *Writing Culture: The Poetics and Politics of Ethnography*. University of California Press. (Original Work Published 1985).

Cornwall, A. (2016). Women's Empowerment: What Works? *Journal of International Development, 28*(3), 342–359.

Cornwall, A., & Brock, K. (2005). What Do Buzzwords Do for Development Policy? A Critical Look at 'Participation', 'Empowerment 'and 'Poverty Reduction'. *Third World Quarterly, 26*(7), 1043–1060.

Drydyk, J. (2008, September 10–13). *How to Distinguish Empowerment from Agency*. Paper presentation at the 5th Annual Conference of the HDCA, New Delhi, India.

Escobar, A. (1995). *Encountering Development: The Making and Unmaking of the Third World*. Princeton University Press.

Ferguson, J. (1990). *The Anti-Politics Machine: "Development," Depoliticization and Bureaucratic Power in Lesotho*. Cambridge University Press.

Fujikake, Y. (2008). Qualitative Evaluation: Evaluating People's Empowerment. *Japanese Journal of Evaluation Studies, 8*(2), 25–37.

Gardner, K., & Lewis, D. (2015). *Anthropology and Development: Challenges for the Twenty-First Century* (2nd ed.). Pluto Press.

Geertz, C. (1963). *Agricultural Involution: The Processes of change in Indonesia*. University of California Press.

Geertz, C. (2017/1973). *The Interpretation of Cultures* (3rd ed.). Basic Books. (Original Work Published 1973).

Gigi, F. (2011). Koishatosite no mono: Ejenshi no gainen no kakucho ni kansuru ichikosatsu. *Doshisha Review of Sociology, 15*, 1–12.

Gow, D. D. (1996). Review: The Anthropology of Development: Discourse, Agency, and Culture. *Anthropological Quarterly, 69*(3), 165–173.

Hagberg, S., & Ouattara, F. (2012). Engaging Anthropology for Development and Social Change. *Bulletin de l'APAD, 34–36*, 1–30. (online journal).

Kabeer, N. (1999). Resources, Agency, Achievements: Reflections on the Measurement of Women's Empowerment. *Development and Change, 30*(3), 435–464.

Kar, K., & Chambers, R. (2008). *Handbook on Community-led Total Sanitation*. Plan International.

Keane, W. (2007). *Christian Moderns: Freedom and Fetish in the Mission Encounter*. University of California Press.

Kilby, P. (2019). *The Green Revolution: Narratives of Politics, Technology and Gender*. Routledge.

Latour, B. (1993). *We Have Never been Modern*. Harvard University Press.

Latour, B. (2005). *Reassembling the Social: An Introduction to Actor-Network-Theory*. Oxford University Press.

Levi-Strauss, C. (1966/1962). *The Savage Mind*. University Chicago Press. (Original Work Published 1962).

Lewis, D. (2005). Anthropology and Development: An uneasy relationship. In J. G. Carrier (Ed.), *A Handbook of Economic Anthropology*. Cheltenham.

Lewis, D., Wood, G. D., & Gregory, R. (1996). *Trading the Silver Seed: Local Knowledge and Market Moralities in Aquacultural Development*. Intermediate Technology Publications.

Lewis, O. (1975/1959). *Five Families: Mexican Case Studies in the Culture of Poverty* (Rev. Version). Basic Books (Original Work Published 1959).

Long, N. (1977). *An Introduction to the Sociology of Developing Societies*. Tavistock Publication.

Long, N. (2001). *Development Sociology: Actor Perspectives*. Routledge.

Malinowski, B. (2014/1922). *Argonauts of the Western Pacific*. Benediction Classics. (Original Work Published 1922).

Matsuyama, A. (2011). Kokusaihokenkenkyu niokeru Iryojinruigaku no aprochi: Kansatsu to kijutsu ni motozuita shituteki kenkyu. *Journal of International Health, 26*(2), 81–92.

Mauss, M. (2001/1924). *The Gift: Forms and Functions of Exchange in Archaic Societies*. Routledge Classics. (Original Work Published 1924).

Mead, M. (1928/2001). *Coming of Age in Samoa: A Psychological Study of Primitive Youth for Western Civilisation*. William Morrow Paperbacks (Reprinted). (Original Work Published 1928).
Morgan, L. (1978/1877). *Ancient Society*. New York Labor News. (Reprint in 1978; Original work published 1877).
Mosse, D. (2005). *Cultivating Development: An Ethnography of Aid Policy and Practice*. Pluto Press.
Mosse, D. (2011). *Adventures in Aidland: The Anthropology of Professionals in International Development* (Vol. 6). Berghahn Books.
Mosse, D. (2013). The Anthropology of International Development. *Annual Review of Anthropology, 42*(1), 227–246.
Narayan, D., et al. (2000). *Voices of the Poor: Can Anyone Hear Us?* Oxford University Press for the World Bank.
Oguni. (2003). *Sonraku Kaitastu ha Darenotameka: Indoneshia no Sankagatakaihatukyoryoku ni miru Riron to Jissen*. Akashishoten.
Oguni, et al. (2011). *Shien no Fieldwork: Kaihatsu to Fukushi no Genbakara*. Sekaisishosha.
Peacock, J. (1987). *The Anthropological Lens: Harsh Light, Soft Focus*. Cambridge University Press.
Pina-Cabral, J. (2018). Social and Cultural Anthropology. In H. Callan (Ed.), *International Encyclopedia of Anthropology*. John Wiley & Sons, Ltd.
Radcliffe-Brown, A. R. (2013/1922). *The Andaman Islanders*. Cambridge University Press. (Original Work Published 1922).
Ratner. (2000). Agency and Culture. *Journal for the Theory of Social Behavior, 2,000, 30*, 413–434.
Said, E. (2003/1978). *Orientalism*. Penguin Modern Classics. (Original Work Published 1978).
Sato, H., et al. (2005). *Enjo to Empowerment: Noryokukaitastu to Shakaikankyohenka no Kumiawase*. IDE.
Sato, M. (2008). Hitobitono Kotoba to Kaihatsuno Kotoba wo Tsunagu Kokoromi: Kaihatsuenjo Jissen no Jinruigaku ni Mukete. *IDE World Trend, 151*, 20–23.
Sekine, H. (2007). Taiwasuru Field Kyodosuru Field: Kaihatsuenjo to JInruigaku no Jissen Style. *Journal of Cultural Anthropology, 72*(3), 361–382.
Sen, A. (1985). Well-Being, Agency and Freedom: The Dewey Lectures 1984. *The Journal of Philosophy, 82*(4), 169–221.
Shirakawa, C. (2011). Bunkajinruigaku to Kokusaiiryokyoryoku no Tsunagari. Hedatari: KAP survey wo megutte. In K. Sato & Y. Fujikake (Eds.), *Kaihatsuenjo to Jinruigaku: Reaisen, Mitsuzuki, Partnership* (pp. 84–103). Akashishoten.
Spencer, H. (2018/1857). *Progress: Its Law and Cause*. Hansebooks. (Reprint in 2018; Original Work Published 1857).
Sugita, E. (2008). Emic no shiten kara mieru toire no mondai. *IDE World Trend, 151*, 16–19.
Tylor, E. (1871). *Primitive Culture: Researches into the Development of Mythology, Philosophy, Religion, Art, and Custom*. Cambridge Library Collection. (Reprint in 2010).
VandenBos, G. R. (Ed.). (2007). *APA Dictionary of Psychology*. American Psychological Association.
Wilson, G. (1942). *An Essay on the Economics of Detribalisation in Northern Rhodesia. Part II. Livingston, Northern Rhodesia*. Rhodes-Livingstone Institute.

Chapter 3
A Psychological Perspective on Agency in the Context of Behavior Change

1 Introduction

This chapter will conduct a selective review on the psychological literature of agency relevant to the enactment and change of behavior, provide a definition of agency for the objectives of the chapters of this volume on psychology, and posit that autonomous motivation as defined by self-determination theory (SDT) is a central mechanism of agency and is the concept that is best suited for its research. However, as this is an interdisciplinary work and many readers may not be familiar with the field of psychology, we shall first make a detour and inspect the basic assumptions behind psychological research, for the understanding of these assumptions is crucial for the understanding of psychological theories and the interpretation of empirical research.

1.1 *Psychological Constructs*

One characteristic of most[1] psychological theories is that they posit psychological concepts, or *constructs*, such as intelligence, attachment, and motivation. What may be confusing to someone who has no specialized training in psychology is that constructs do not necessarily have any entity or substance. Instead, psychological constructs are concepts that, *if assumed to exist*, are useful in explaining individual differences in behaviors and attitudes.

---

[1] Behaviorist approaches, which have a significant influence upon contemporary psychology, do not assume such psychological constructs and view behavior as a function of only the interaction of environmental stimuli with physiological and social drives, and past experiences.

© The Author(s), under exclusive license to Springer Nature Singapore Pte Ltd. 2022
M. Sato et al., *Empowerment Through Agency Enhancement*,
https://doi.org/10.1007/978-981-19-1227-6_3

For example, intelligence is a construct that was put forth to explain why some individuals do better than others in academic achievement and problem-solving. Such differences are notable from early childhood: children who have higher academic performance and are good at problem-solving are assumed to have higher intelligence. However, we still do not fully understand the neurological bases of intelligence, nor do we know if there is any such base. Nonetheless, intelligence has been operationalized as is well known as intelligence tests which produce a quantitative intelligence quotient (IQ). IQ scores are an epitome of psychological measurement, or *psychometrics*. They have no unit but are a standardized score indicating the relative position of the person that has been measured within a given population. Typically, an IQ of 100 signifies that the person is of average intelligence of their age group, and the standard deviation is set at 15—thus, someone with an IQ of 115 is one SD higher than average of people the same age group in the population. It should be noted that IQ tests are not universal but are dependent upon contextual factors such as culture and historical period. As an example, one question on a Japanese IQ test from the 1930s displayed the illustration of a young woman and an elderly woman, and asked which figure was more beautiful (Sato, 2006). This would certainly not be considered a measure of intelligence now, not to mention that it is highly inappropriate. Current IQ tests are valid for examining the individual differences in intelligence within the context that they were developed in, but it is not appropriate to derive an IQ score from the same test under a different context. Furthermore, not many psychological scales have been standardized as IQ tests have (see Chap. 9 of this volume for further discussion). Perhaps relevant to many readers of this book, it may not be appropriate to simply translate psychological scales that were developed in a high-income country and administer them in a low-income country (Sayanagi et al., 2021).

That constructs do not necessarily have any entity contrasts from the assumptions of economics, where concepts such as social capital are assumed to be as if they are an entity (Yanagihara, Chap. 4 of this volume). Some recent studies have criticized the usage of psychometrics in economics studies (Laajaj et al., 2019; Sayanagi et al., 2021), and it can be said that these reprovals are rooted in the differences in underlying assumptions. Comparing absolute values of scores based upon concepts that have tangible substance may be meaningful, but not for intangible psychological constructs. To reiterate, psychometric scores merely are for comparing individual differences within a certain context: thus, the comparison of absolute values across contexts can often be misleading. See Chap. 9 of this volume for further discussion, especially the validity and reliability of in psychometrics. There also will be a review on the measurement of agency.

1.2 Agency as a Psychological Construct

While the co-authors of this volume each provide definitions of agency that are relevant to their respective fields, the common ground we have agreed upon is to begin with the *APA Dictionary of Psychology*'s entry on agency, "the state of being active, usually in the service of a goal, or of having the power and capability to produce an effect or exert influence" (VandenBos, 2007). Additionally, the title of this volume, *What Moves People to Take Initiatives* encompasses the assumption that such initiatives are taken to improve the situation that the person is in. Indeed, as many workers in fields such as aid and education will probably agree, there are individual differences to the degree that people take action to make their situation better: some fight tooth and nail for their progress, while others seemingly are resigned to their misfortunes or inabilities. Thus, agency can be formulated as a construct that explains these differences.

A more refined definition will be provided upon further discussion, but for the time being, agency shall tentatively be defined as *the ability and capacity to act towards the goal of improving one's environment and/or circumstances*. The clause "ability and capacity" indicates that agency is not exclusively an innate or learned ability, but the capacity to act can be enhanced or hindered by environmental factors as well. This is not particularly a novel definition, but it emphasizes the betterment of the person's situation. Additionally, while *agency* is a term that is commonly used in psychological literature, the construct itself has seldom been rigorously defined, operationalized, and investigated empirically, especially in the context of behavior change because other equivalent constructs have been advanced, as will be reviewed subsequently in this chapter.

2 Selective Review of Agency

2.1 A Brief and Selective History of the Term Agency

According to the New Oxford Dictionary, the English term *agency* originated in the mid seventeenth century from the medieval Latin prefix "agent-" meaning "doing." It was used in contexts such as chemistry, as in chemical agents that cause any given effect, or that flowers require "the agency of certain insects to bring pollen from one flower to another" (Darwin, 1862). Thinkers of this era also were writing about divine agency (e.g., West, 1794), that is, the will and actions of God, and their consequences.

The word was also applied to human beings and was often used to denote the will of human beings that cause action. In one example from the late eighteenth century, the American theologian Jonathan Edwards wrote a treatise titled *A Careful and Strict Inquiry into the Modern Prevailing Notions of That Freedom of Will Which Is Supposed to Be Essential to Moral Agency, Virtue and Vice, Reward and Punishment, Praise and Blame* (Edwards, 1790). Agency is one of the centerpieces to the thesis. As the title implies, there was a popular movement at the time in which free will was purported to be what enabled the moral agency of humans. This view was advocated by Arminianism, a school of theology. Edwards rejected this view, arguing that self-determination is not compatible with moral agency (pp. 31–35). His rejection was not a mere individual opinion: Calvinist theologians had declared Arminianism to be heretic in the early seventeenth century (Wynkoop, 1967). This has an interesting parallel with contemporary psychology. As will be reviewed later, there is controversy within psychology on the significance of free will and self-determination, and some researchers completely reject such notions.

The advent of psychology is considered as the late nineteenth century (Nolen-Hoeksema et al., 2009), but while a PsycInfo keyword search for "agency" produces several publications on institutional agencies, there are very few results of it being used as a psychological construct throughout the 1970s. For the years 1971–1975, 128 papers include "agency" as a keyword, but only 6 are on the construct agency. From 1976 to 1980, there are 173 papers, of which there are only 7. The number starts to increase from the 1980s, with 19 out of 284 in 1981–1985, and 68 out of 342 in 1986–1990. The number of papers with "agency" as a keyword are 666 in 2020 alone: for the sake of efficiency, the search was narrowed down to papers with full text availability, and 18 out of 21 papers refer to agency as defined in the APA Dictionary. This is a very coarse index, but it serves the purpose of illustrating that the study of the construct agency is a relatively recent development in psychology, and that it is now widely researched.

The reason for the past scarcity of studies on agency can be attributed to behaviorism, the dominant paradigm throughout the 1960s, where there is no room for a highly subjective construct such as agency. The subsequent increase in agency research coincides with the rise of cognitive psychology, which branched off from behaviorism in the 1960s and gained momentum in the 1970s. Cognitive psychology assumes, and its studies provide evidence, that subjective perceptions have a significant effect upon outcomes such as behavior and wellbeing.

The usage of the term *agency* predates the advent of psychology, and the psychological construct of agency is a recent development within the field, but the debate regarding its role in human behavior has been inherited. On one hand, there are researchers that reject agency and conscious will. This argument is rooted in the behaviorist tradition of psychology that eschews constructs, which are intangible, and some have presented neuroscientific evidence that conscious will can only be detected after the action has been initiated and thus conclude that conscious will is not the cause of behavior, as well as experimental evidence that the subjective sense of agency is illusory (e.g., Wegner, 2017). However, on the other hand several theories consider that it is given that agency predicts human behavior. Most theories of motivation fall into this camp, as does this chapter. As has been elaborated in the discussion of psychological constructs and definition of agency above, whether agency has any entity or not is not a problem insofar as the conceptualization meaningfully explains individual differences in behavior. It should be noted that the meaning of agency differs between the two camps. The former is used in a microscopic way, as to explain the precise moment that the subjective sensation arises; the latter is more macroscopic, encompassing the whole process of motivation including not just the spontaneous sensation but also the subjective regulation of goal-directed behavior.[2]

2.2 Contemporary Lines of Psychological Research on Agency

We shall begin with a brief and selective overview of research on agency that is *not* directly relevant to the enactment and change of behavior. Consequently, the meanings of the term in these fields are different than defined in this chapter.

One popular line of research on *sense of agency*, the subjective sense of being in control of one's own actions, apart from being used to provide evidence against the role of agency as described above, has demonstrated that it is an important factor in motor actions (e.g., Hemed et al., 2019) and speech production (e.g., Franken et al., 2021), is critical to mental health (e.g., Jennissen et al., 2021; Knox, 2011), among others (a recent issue of *Psychology of Consciousness: Theory, Research, and Practice* featured sense of agency: introductory article by Polito et al., 2015). One study demonstrated that monkeys perform discrimination tasks better when their self-agency was purportedly enhanced through an experimental procedure that effectively enhanced self-agency in humans (Smith et al., 2021).

Another influential conceptualization of agency is based on gender differences, with females considered to be relatively *communal* while males are *agentic* (Bakan, 1966). The theory evolved from biological-gender based concepts into social-gender based concepts, with communion focusing on others and forming connections, while agency focuses on the self and forming separations (Helgeson, 1994). The initial focus of communion and agency was their interaction for the well-being of humans, but other applications have emerged such as their relationship with morality (Frimer et al., 2011) and impact on effective leadership (Abele & Wojciszke, 2014).

Agency has also been increasingly used as an important keyword in qualitative studies on the disadvantaged (e.g., Barak & Barak, 2019; Guzman et al., 2020; Kang & Lee, 2021; Savard et al., 2021). The general implication of the term in these studies is that the disadvantaged person or persons are unable to act to improve their situation—a similar usage to the definition in this chapter—but a rigid definition is seldom provided. Indeed, the research points towards the importance of agency for these populations and has implications regarding how to support it, but without a rigorous definition the interpretation of the results of such studies are susceptible to cognitive bias in which only data fitting the loose definition are noted while data that does not gets ignored.

---

[2] The author of this chapter is not trying to imply that the former camp is irrelevant. Deciphering the neurological bases of agency is important for the advancement of the understanding of the human psyche and its relationship with behavior. Even if agency is determined to be illusory, the wealth of studies demonstrate that the association between the "illusion" and behavior are robust, so there probably will be a neurological explanation, too.

Agency as defined in this chapter has been most rigorously studied through the concept of *self-efficacy* (e.g., Bandura, 1977, 1982, 1989, 1997) and also to some extent through the motivational concepts proposed by SDT (e.g., Ryan & Deci, 2017). We shall review the two theories and their positions on agency in the following sections.

2.3 Self-Efficacy and Agency

No researcher has placed the spotlight on the concept of agency as much as Albert Bandura, one of the founders of the cognitive psychology movement and one of the most influential psychologists of the twentieth century (Haggbloom et al., 2002). Interestingly, while Bandura has written extensively on agency, he does not provide an explicit definition. However, he has stated, "To be an agent is to influence intentionally one's functioning and life circumstances" (Bandura, 2006, p. 164), and that "People have always striven to control the events that affect their lives. By exerting influence in spheres over which they can command some control, they are better able to realize desired futures and to forestall undesired ones" (Bandura, 1997, p. 1), which indicates that his conception addresses the ability and capacity to act to control and influence one's physical and psychological environment towards what is subjectively perceived to be better—which is in line with the definition of this chapter.

Bandura asserts that *self-efficacy* is the central mechanism of agency (e.g., Bandura, 1982, 1989, 2000). Self-efficacy is defined as the "beliefs in one's capabilities to organize and execute the courses of action required to produce given attainments" (Bandura, 1997, p. 3). Self-efficacy has been studied extensively, and has been shown to robustly predict motivation, affect, and action in diverse contexts (see Bandura, 1997 for an exhaustive review). Research on self-efficacy puts great emphasis on its predictive value.

It can be said that while agency (in Bandura's view) is a more generic and abstract concept, self-efficacy deals with specific actions. That is, humans have self-efficacy beliefs regarding each of the behaviors that they are engaged in: for example, a star football player at the peak of their career would probably have high self-efficacy regarding their football abilities, but not necessarily for their singing or academic skills. Some scholars have proposed a *generalized self-efficacy* in which people are assumed to have a predisposition to have a higher or lower degree of self-efficacy across the board (e.g., Schwarzer & Jerusalem, 1995). At first glance, generalized self-efficacy seems to be a good substitute for agency, but Bandura has explicitly argued against such a concept as such constructs generally have poor predictive value in empirical studies (e.g., Bandura, 1997, pp. 36–50). It can be speculated that Bandura did not operationalize the agency construct for this very reason, as he put great emphasis on predicting behavior.

While the rationale for not using a generalized conception of self-efficacy is reasonable, it creates a slight dilemma for agency research: if self-efficacy is based on specific behaviors, then who is to decide which behaviors work in the service of agency and which do not? Bandura (1997) asserts that enhanced self-efficacy for behaviors that effectively improve one's situation can lead to the self-regulation of goals, i.e., one can become able to self-determine the goals that are important to themselves, but the emphasis on behavior change in self-efficacy theory can lead to the paternalistic implementation of goals in which a party in power pushes what they deem to be important upon a disadvantaged person or population.

2.4 SDT and Agency

Another motivational theory that deals with agency is SDT (see Ryan & Deci, 2017 for a definitive overview of the theory). Little et al. (2002) state, "we define personal agency as the sense of personal empowerment, which involves both knowing and having what it takes to achieve one's goals. More broadly speaking, a well-adapted agentic individual *is the origin of [their] actions*, has high aspirations, perseveres in the face of obstacles, sees more and varied options for action, learns from failures, and, overall, has a greater sense of well-being" (emphasis added). The founders of SDT do not provide an explicit definition of agency, but it is used synonymously with *autonomy*, one of the most important concepts of SDT. Autonomy is defined as "act[ing] volitionally *with a sense of choice*" (Deci & Ryan, 2008, emphasis added). These definitions emphasize the subjective sense of self-determination, which contrasts from Bandura's position which puts emphasis on the intentional influence upon one's circumstances.

The term "self-determination" in SDT sometimes is confused in the sense that the theory asserts that one should be induced to conduct what can be objectively judged as a self-determined action that is independent from external influences. This is not the case, as SDT's main concern is the subjective experience of self-determination and volition. As Deci & Ryan (2008, p. 15) and Ryan & Deci (2017, pp. 342–348) assert, autonomy (and thus, agency also) as defined in SDT differs from independence, as one can be influenced by external factors and yet subjectively feel that they are acting on their volition.

It has been demonstrated that autonomous motivation predicts not just the enactment, but also resilience of behaviors under adverse conditions. The performance of achievement tasks is also positively correlated with the degree of autonomous motivation. Additionally, autonomous motivation is associated with the prevention of psychological ill-being and positively with well-being (for a definitive review SDT and the effects of autonomous motivation, see Ryan & Deci, 2017). These empiric findings indicate that autonomous motivation is also strongly associated with agency as tentatively defined.

One more potential benefit of an SDT-based approach of agency that it theoretically would promote *eudaimonia* (e.g., Ryan & Deci, 2017, pp. 612–614). Eudaimonia is a concept of happiness in the Aristotelean tradition, in which living well entails pursuing ends that are of inherent worth, and doing them well (Ryan et al., 2013). This contrast with the more common hedonic concept of happiness (e.g., Kahneman et al., 1999 for a psychological discussion), in which wellbeing is defined as the presence of positive affect and the absence of negative affect. Sayanagi & van Egmond (in press) argue that eudaimonia is especially relevant for international development and other vulnerable populations as it entails becoming able to identify and doing things that are meaningful to oneself—which also can be said to be a manifestation of agency as defined in this chapter.

2.5 Refined Definition of Agency

Both the self-efficacy and SDT definitions of agency are relevant to the aforementioned tentative definition of agency. However, this author argues that the SDT definition, which emphasizes volition and self-determination, are better suited for the theme of this volume, which is to discuss how to facilitate agency in populations that are initially low in agency. Such populations are typically disadvantaged and vulnerable to paternalistic interventions. However, such paternalistic interventions, which "push" a viewpoint that is endorsed by the advantaged with little regard for the viewpoint of the disadvantaged, can be problematic (e.g., Mill, 2010; Sayanagi & van Egmond, in press).

The definition of agency for the psychological chapters of this volume shall be *the ability and capacity to self-determinedly act towards the goal(s) of improving the environment and/or circumstances* (underlines denote amendments to the tentative definition). Self-determination in this case is based upon the SDT conception, that is, it is not the objective concept in which one decides independently of external influences, but rather the subjective experience of volition regardless of whether there are any external influences. Additionally, the clause "improving one's environment" has been revised to "improving the environment" to allow for agentic actions on behalf of others.

2.6 Autonomous Motivation as a Central Mechanism of Agency

As was with the case of self-efficacy, it is not easy to operationalize agency with the above SDT-based definition, as the number of possible self-determined actions are infinite. However, likewise to self-efficacy, limiting the focus to a single behavior allows for the empirical research of agency and its enhancement. Thus, the chapters on psychology in this volume will study autonomous motivation as the central mechanism of agency. A theoretical synthesis on enhancing agency through interventions to people who are low in agency will be presented in Chap. 6. Chapter 9 will address the issue of the measurement of agency, especially the challenges of psychometrics among such populations.

References

Abele, A. E., & Wojciszke, B. (2014). Communal and Agentic Content in Social Cognition: A Dual Perspective Model. *Advances in Experimental Social Psychology, 50*, 195–255.

Bakan, D. (1966). *The Duality of Human Existence*. Rand McNally.

Bandura, A. (1977). Self-Efficacy: Toward a Unifying Theory of Behavioral Change. *Psychological Review, 84*, 191–215.

Bandura, A. (1982). Self-Efficacy Mechanism in Human Agency. *American Psychologist, 37*, 122–147.

Bandura, A. (1989). Human Agency in Social Cognitive Theory. *American Psychologist, 44*, 1175–1184.

Bandura, A. (1997). *Self-Efficacy: The Exercise of Control*. W. H. Freeman and Company.

Bandura, A. (2000). Self-Efficacy: The Foundation of Agency. In W. J. Perrig & A. Grob (Eds.), *Control of Human Behavior, Mental Processes, and Consciousness: Essays in Honor of the 60th Birthday of August Flammer* (pp. 21–33). Lawrence Erlbaum Associates.

Bandura, A. (2006). Toward a Psychology of Human Agency. *Perspectives on Psychological Science, 1*, 164–180.

Barak, I., & Barak, A. (2019). Israeli Ethiopian Female Adolescents' Perspectives on Alliances with Social Workers: Agency, Power and Performing Identity. *American Journal of Orthopsychiatry, 89*, 77–85.

Darwin, C. R. (1862). *On the Various Contrivances by Which British and Foreign Orchids are Fertilised by Insects, and on the Good Effects of Intercrossing*. John Murray.

Deci, E. L., & Ryan, R. M. (2008). Facilitating Optimal Motivation and Psychological Well-Being Across Life's Domains. *Canadian Psychology, 49*, 14–23.

Edwards, J. (1790). *A Careful and Strict Inquiry Into the Modern Prevailing Notions of That Freedom of Will Which Is Supposed to be Essential to Moral Agency, Virtue and Vice, Reward and Punishment, Praise and Blame* (4th ed.). James Adams.

Franken, M. K., Hartsuiker, R. J., Johansson, P., Hall, L., & Lind, A. (2021). Speaking with an Alien Voice: Flexible Sense of Agency During Vocal Production. *Journal of Experimental Psychology: Human Perception and Performance, 47*, 479–494.

Frimer, J. A., Walker, L. J., Dunlop, W. L., Lee, B. H., & Riches, A. (2011). The Integration of Agency and Communion in Moral Personality: Evidence of Enlightened Self-Interest. *Journal of Personality and Social Psychology, 101*, 149–163.

Guzman, C. E. V., Hess, J. M., Casas, N., Medina, D., Galvis, M., Torres, D. A., et al. (2020). Latinx/@ Immigrant Inclusion Trajectories: Individual Agency, Structural Constraints, and the Role of Community-Based Organization in Immigrant Mobilities. *American Journal of Orthopsychiatry, 90*, 772–786.

Haggbloom, S. J., Warnick, R., Warnick, J. E., Jones, V. K., Yarbrough, G. L., Russell, T. M., et al. (2002). The 100 Most Eminent Psychologists of the 20th Century. *Review of General Psychology, 6*, 139–152.

Helgeson, V. S. (1994). Relation of Agency and Communion to Well-Being: Evidence and Potential Explanations. *Psychological Bulletin, 116*, 412–428.

Hemed, E., Bakbani-Elkayam, S., Teodorescu, A. R., Yona, L., & Eitam, B. (2019). Evaluation of an Action's Effectiveness by the Motor System in a Dynamic Environment. *Journal of Experimental Psychology: General, 149*, 935–948.

Jennissen, S., Huber, J., Nikendei, C., Schauenburg, H., & Dinger, U. (2021, December 30). The Interplay between Agency and Therapeutic Bond in Predicting Symptom Severity in Long-Term Psychotherapy. *Journal of Counseling Psychology*.

Kahneman, D., Diener, E., & Schwartz, N. (1999). *Well-Being: The Foundations of Hedonic Psychology*. Russell Sage Foundation.

Kang, H., & Lee, S. (2021, September 27). The Agency of Victims and Political Violence in South Korea: Reflection on the Needs-Based Model of Reconciliation. *Peace and Conflict: Journal of Peace Psychology*.

Knox, J. (2011). *Self-Agency in Psychotherapy: Attachment, Autonomy, and Intimacy*. Norton.

Laajaj, R., Macours, K., Hernandez, D. A. P., Arias, O., Gosling, S. D., Potter, J., Rubio-Cortina, M., & Vakis, R. (2019). Challenges to Capture the Big Five Personality Traits in Non-WEIRD Populations. *Science Advances, 5*, eaaw5226.

Little, T. D., Hawley, P. H., Henrich, C. C., & Marsland, K. W. (2002). *Handbook of Self-Determination Research*. E. L. Deci & R. M. Ryan (Eds.). Rochester University Press.

Mill, J. S. (2010). *On Liberty*. Penguin.

Nolen-Hoeksema, S., Fredrickson, B. L., Loftus, G. R., & Wagenaar, W. A. (2009). *Atkinson & Hilgard's Introduction to Psychology* (15th ed.). Cengage Learning.

Polito, V., Waters, F. A. V., & McIlwan, D. (2015). Sense of Agency: Theory, Methods, and Application. *Psychology of Consciousness: Theory, Research, and Practice, 2*, 207–209.

Ryan, R. M., Curren, R. R., & Deci, E. L. (2013). What Humans Need: Flourishing in Aristotelean Philosophy and Self-Determination Theory. In A. S. Waterman (Ed.), *The Best Within Us: Positive Psychology Perspectives on Eudaimonia* (pp. 57–75). American Psychological Association.

Ryan, R. M., & Deci, E. L. (2017). *Self-Determination Theory: Basic Psychological Needs in Motivation, Development, and Wellness*. The Guilford Press.

Sato, T. (2006). *IQ wo tou: Chino shisu no mondai to tenkai* [Questioning IQ: The Issues and Development of the Intelligence Quotient]. Brain Shuppan.

Savard, M., Badasu, M., & Recchia, H. (2021). Young Mothers of Northern Uganda: A Longitudinal Study of Individual and Collective Agency Within a Participatory Program. *Peace and Conflict: Journal of Peace Psychology, 27*, 588–596.

Sayanagi, N. R., Randriamanana, T., Razafimbelonaina, H. S. A., Rabemanantsoa, N., Abel-Ratovo, H. L., & Yokoyama, S. (2021). The Challenges of Psychometrics in Impoverished Populations of Developing Countries: Development of a Motivation Scale in Rural Madagascar. *Japanese Journal of Personality, 30*, 56–69.

Sayanagi, N. R., & van Egmond, M. C. (in press). SDT and International Development. In R. M. Ryan (Ed.), *The Oxford Handbook of Self-Determination Theory*. Oxford University Press.

Schwarzer, R., & Jerusalem, M. (1995). Generalized Self-Efficacy Scale. In I. J. Weinman, S. Wright, & M. Johnston (Eds.), *Measures in Health Psychology: A User's Portfolio. Causal and Control Beliefs* (pp. 35–37). NFER-Nelson.

Smith, J. D., Church, B. A., Jackson, B. N., Adamczyk, M. N., Shaw, C. N., & Beran, M. J. (2021). Launch! Self-Agency as a Discriminative Cue for Humans (Homo sapiens) and Monkeys (Macaca Mulatta). *Journal of Experimental Psychology: General, 150*, 1901–1917.

VandenBos, G. R. (Ed.). (2007). *APA Dictionary of Psychology*. American Psychological Association.

Wegner, D. M. (2017). *The Illusion of Conscious Will* (new ed.). MIT Press.

West, S. (1794). *An Essay on Moral Agency: Containing Remarks on a Late Anonymous Publication, Entitled, an Examination of the President Edwards's Inquiry on Freedom of Will* (2nd ed.). Unknown Publisher.

Wynkoop, M. B. (1967). *Foundations of Wesleyan-Arminian Theology*. Beacon Hill Press.

Chapter 4
Agency as Base for "Bounded Rationality", Core of "Human Capital", and Key to "Human Capabilities"

Context 1:	Rationality in decision-making—full/bounded rationality, Behavioral Economics
	Limited endowment of "cognitive and other elements of HC"
	Competing uses of "cognitive and other elements of HC"
Context 2:	Human Capital—physical, intellectual(cognitive), socioemotional, agentic elements
Context 3:	Capability Approach—functioning, capability, well-being, agency, achievement, freedom

1 Introduction

This chapter first puts forth the author's definition of the term "agency" and then proceeds to provide a selective review of literature in economics related to the theme of agency and its development. The exposition will be presented in three distinct contexts: (1) micro- and behavioral economics, (2) human capital theory, and (3) capability approach. The main features of (1) and (2) represent recent scholastic innovations in economics motivated by the desire to make economic research more empirically relevant by incorporating viewpoints and findings from psychology and neuroscience. By contrast, (3) reflects attempts spearheaded by Amartya Sen to bridge economics and philosophy (ethics, in particular). Interconnections among these three areas of research will be discussed with a view to identifying issues for possible cross-fertilization.

First, in a review of microeconomic theory, a contrast will be made on how agency is (implicitly) featured in the "full rationality" school and the "bounded rationality" school, with a view to identifying the place and role of agency in the decision-making by economic agents. This will be followed by a selective review of behavioral economics as elaboration and expansion of insights of the "bounded rationality" school and also as modification of preference specifications.

Second, a reformulation of the human capital theory will be undertaken with a view to incorporating recent studies on "personality capacity" as determinants of economic and social performances and also proposing to establish an "agentic" element as core part of human capital, thereby establishing a theoretical approach to the understanding of the role of agency and the process of agency development over time.

Third, in a review of the discussion of agency in the Capability Approach (CA), the critical role of agency in CA will be identified and examined. Attempts will be made to identify connections between this discussion and (i) that in micro- and behavioral economics as well as (ii) that in human capital theory.

It seems that many authors do not feel the need to define the term "agency," just as they seldom, if ever, define the term "agent." It is as if any human individual is simply assumed to be capable of making decisions and taking actions and that is all there is to be said about agent or agency. Here we refer to the definition of "agency" by the American Psychological Association as starting point of our discussion. It reads (VandenBos, 2007):

> the state of being active, usually in the service of a goal, or of having the power and capability to produce an effect or exert influence

It is immediately seen that this definition contains two usages of the term: first, description of a condition of an individual ("being active"); and the other, conceptualization of underlying factors beneath (successful) execution of actions. In both usages, the term (usually) implies the presence of a goal established prior to the action. There is a contrast between the two usages in that the first does not explicitly contain the evaluation of the action in terms of the achievement of the goal while the second clearly connotes success with the use of the words "effect" and "influence." There seems to be a gap between the two usages in the definition above insofar as "power" and "capability" may not be converted into an action in reality.

What is missing in the definition above is explicit attention to disposition, volition and intention. The present author believes that these internal orientations related to self-determination and self-management may better be included explicitly in the definition of "agency." Furthermore, it might be reasonable to consider these factors as essential constituents of agency.

Here we define "agency" of an individual as follows:

> disposition and capacity for self-determination and self-management of one's own actions and activities

In this definition emphasis is placed on the internal drive and orientation for action rather than action itself or the result of an action. Agency is postulated as a latent potentiality and something generic, with possibilities for application in a wide range of activities. (By contrast, "motivation" is understood to be "a factor or process by which agency is activated in a specific action or activity."). In a theoretical formulation, agency will be viewed as if it is an entity residing in human beings (and will be treated as a stock variable) that constitutes an element, indeed a fundamental element, of human capital, in that it generates the whole range of purposeful human actions and activities serving as the general foundation for human intentions and their actualization.

2 Agency in Microeconomics of Choice

2.1 Bounded Rationality

The concept of agency as defined here does not find its place in the lexicon of the standard microeconomics. It is because that discipline essentially deals with the response of economic agents to incentives external to them. In standard microeconomics, economic agents are postulated to take decisions rationally by engaging in the mental process of optimization under constraints, which could certainly be regarded as one way of formalizing human agency (i.e., being aware of one's own preferences as well as constraints and being able to select the best alternative from among all the feasible options). This is as far as it goes, however, and it does not treat agency or its development as a subject matter for investigation.

There is a school of thought in microeconomics, commonly referred to as the "bounded rationality" school, which questions the basic "rationality" premise of standard microeconomics and proposes instead the view of human decisions under (realistic) conditions of limited cognitive capacity for information processing. This school sheds a useful sidelight on human agency by highlighting internal constraints to rational decision-making and pointing to the roles of routines, heuristics, and subjective probabilities. The recognition of cognitive capacity as constraint to agency offers a new perspective for the study of varied recognition of and response to short- versus long-term outcomes as well as safe versus risky opportunities: in both comparisons the former choice requires less of cognitive capacity and thus tends to be preferred under the condition of the limited availability of it. In this view, agency is limited either by the lesser endowment or pre-emptive use of cognitive capacity. This school does not discuss the change over time of agency, however.

The "bounded rationality" school proposes to replace the standard optimization postulate by the "satisficing" postulate as basic theoretical hypothesis on human behaviour. Satisficing is a decision-making strategy or cognitive heuristic under circumstances in which a search for an optimal solution exceeds the constraints of information processing capacity. It entails searching through the available alternatives until an acceptability threshold is met. This may be viewed as "exercise of agency" under realistic conditions of limited cognitive capacity. Once chosen, the selected alternative becomes a routine procedure and continues to be in operation, thus economizing on the use of cognitive capacity. This situation will last unless and until the performance of the routine comes to fail to meet the acceptability threshold. In that eventuality, a search for a new alternative that satisfies the threshold will be started, constituting another occasion for exercise of agency. Once selected, such an alternative will be adopted as a new routine procedure to be followed.

It is opportune to note that our definition of agency is both about disposition and capacity, with emphasis on the former, if any, while the "bounded rationality" school is all about (limited) capacity for decision-making. That is presumably because the disposition/volition side of agency is simply taken for granted. We will explore this question in latter parts of the chapter.

2.2 Behavioral Economics

The "bounded rationality" view of decision-making and behavior has been elaborated on and expanded in the course of the onslaught of Behavioral Economics (BE). Over the last quarter century, behavioral economics has established itself as a powerful new approach to microeconomic theory of individual decision-making and behavior, supplementing, and oftentimes supplanting, the diagnoses and subscriptions of the standard microeconomic theory. The name "Behavioral Economics" reflects the incorporation of psychologically informed accounts of actual human behavior into microeconomics. Let us identify and discuss some of the implications of the "BE Revolution" in microeconomics for our view on agency and its determinants.

In an authoritative account of the purposes and orientations of BE, Mullainathan and Thaler (2000) identify and discuss three important ways in which humans deviate from the standard economic model: bounded rationality, bounded willpower, and bounded self-interest. According to the authors, bounded rationality reflects the limited cognitive abilities that constrain human problem solving; bounded willpower captures the fact that people sometimes make choices that are not in their long-run interest; and bounded self-interest incorporates the fact that humans are often willing to sacrifice their own interests to help others. (p. 1) The first of the three, as already argued by the "bounded rationality" school, focuses on the limitation of cognitive capacity for self-determination of goals and self-management of tasks, thus squarely related to our interest in agency. The second is also highly relevant to the extent that it could relate to "disposition and capacity" for both self-determination and self-management, the latter in particular. In this section we will focus on these two types of "boundedness."[1]

Datta and Mullainathan (2014) state that "[b]ehavioral economics can be understood as identifying a few more limited resources. In practice, we have found it helpful to think about the limits on four basic mental resources" and go on to

---

[1] Bounded self-interest, commonly labelled as "altruism" or "social preferences", also seems to relate to both the questions of what goals to be set and of how to manage the tasks, and as such may be importantly related to agency. We will touch upon this theme when we discuss personality in next section.

mention the scarcities of self-control, attention, cognitive capacity, and understanding (pp. 10–17).

Among these four factors, "self-control" is highly relevant for capacity for self-determination and self-management. The authors state that "[i]t takes self-control to identify, plan, and execute all the tasks that need to be done, all the while resisting the many temptations and distractions that surround us." (p. 10) "Attention" seems to be also relevant for capacity for self-management. People might be greatly helped by mechanisms that remind and prompt them for timely or regular actions.

As stated above, "cognitive capacity" sets a limit to information processing, undoubtedly a critical task in self-determination and self-management. In order to economize on cognitive capacity, boundedly rational agents draw on automatic choice procedures called "default rules"; under very predictable contexts, people prefer not to deliberate to choose and instead follow cue-based mental shortcuts or heuristics. There is a vast literature suggesting that economically relevant choices reveal the role of default rules in the explanation of actual behavior (Muramatsu & Avila, 2017).

In relation to "understanding", the key notion to be reckoned with is that of "mental model." Mental models determine what and how one sees and understands the surrounding world faced with the situations and events of daily life; and they also figure importantly shaping the long-term perspectives on life course. They seem to relate both to the disposition and capacity for self-determination and self-management by significantly influencing the "what" and the "how" of both.

One strand of behavioral economists follow the lead of Daniel Kahneman and Amos Tversky in modifying the specifications of the preference function, emphasizing the importance of "framing," i.e., sensitivity of choice judgements to contexts and perceptions of relative losses or gains. The most notable among the modified specifications of the preference function is the incorporation of "loss aversion" relative to a reference point. (Kahneman & Tversky, 1979; Kahneman, 2003). This is relevant for agency in that it points to the tendency toward inaction under the psychological inclination of loss aversion insofar as self-determination and self-management involves higher downside risks than accepting the status quo. This point deserves a thorough examination, both theoretically and empirically.

2.3 *Behavioral Economics of Poverty*[2]

Echoing the main tenet of the "bounded rationality" school, behavioral economists emphasize the importance of the limited endowment of cognitive capacity and competing demands on their uses (Mullainathan & Shafir, 2013, among others). The constant challenge of managing everyday minor emergencies affect very severely

---

[2] This section draws heavily on Kremer et al. (2019). Refer to it for relevant publications reviewed here.

people's time preference. This issue is particularly relevant for poor people. Under the hostile conditions of scarcity that characterize poverty, individuals are not capable of pursuing and achieveing what they want to be and do. Many of them fail to activate their agency effectively in planning and implementing desired courses of action for future gains in the face of ever-present urgencies and emergencies.

The growing field of behavioral economics has collected robust evidence that exercise of human agency is not only constrained by material and financial resources but also by psychological factors such as individuals' perception of decision tasks, default rules, self-control problems, and power of inertia (Datta & Mullainathan, 2014). The conviction that poor people face various external and internal constraints on decision-making and behavior that, under specific contexts, predictably prevent them from choosing or behaving in their best interests constitutes the core of the "behavioral economics of poverty" (Bertrand et al., 2004).[3]

A recent body of work suggests that living in poverty may directly affect cognitive function and economic behaviors, thus potentially exacerbating behavioral biases and deepening poverty (Haushofer & Fehr, 2014; Schilbach et al., 2016). Mullainathan and Shafir (2013) argue that poverty impedes cognitive function by capturing people's minds with thoughts of scarcity. This might imply that the poor pay more attention than the rich to price and cost.[4] However, according to Mullainathan and Shafir (2013), while some of this attention is intentional and productive, much of it is not, and since cognitive capacity is limited and money-related thoughts use up some of this capacity, mental capacity left available for other tasks is reduced. In this way, poverty itself impedes cognitive function among the poor, degrading the quality of decision-making.[5]

Poverty entails many other deprivations and potentially detrimental situations beyond lack of money (Schilbach et al., 2016). Another recent literature has documented that poverty and negative income shocks are associated with higher levels of stress (Haushofer & Fehr, 2014), although evidence on the effects of stress on decision-making is mixed at best. Moreover, poverty often entails stigma, shame, and social exclusion, which could all affect cognition and decision-making (Hall et al., 2014; Chandrasekhar et al., 2018).[6]

We now turn to positive psychological factors, particularly hope and aspirations. Aspirations are broadly understood as a hope or ambition of achieving something, which, it is believed, is closely related to agency, the disposition for goal setting for

---

[3] It may be noted that the psychological factors mentioned above go beyond the cognitive domain as commonly delineated but extends to the "non-cognitive" domain. However, we will not pay attention to the distinction between them in this section as we review salient features of the behavioral economics of poverty.

[4] Shah et al. (2015) provide examples in which lower-income individuals hew more closely to a rational model than the rich do.

[5] Mani et al. (2013) provide empirical evidence in support of this hypothesis.

[6] Dean et al. (2018) summarizes a rich literature in psychology, medicine, and other fields that has studied and often established impacts of adverse psycho-social conditions on cognitive function, decision-making, and health, mostly via experimental lab studies and observational data.

one's own actions in particular. Development economists have investigated the role of aspirations and hope in the lives of the poor at least since Sen (1985, 1999).[7] Genicot and Ray (2017) argue that aspirations moderately above the individual's present level provide incentives to invest, while avoiding frustration. Low levels of aspirations can limit social mobility and create a poverty trap.

A key empirical question related to this theme is whether aspirations are malleable and how different interventions might be able to affect them. Bernard et al. (2014) consider the impact of exposing individuals to documentaries showing similar individuals from their community who managed to escape poverty through their own efforts in agriculture or business. The authors find remarkably large five-year impacts on aspirations as well as investments in education, livestock, and agricultural inputs. Laajaj (2017) shows that an intervention providing input subsidies and a savings match to farmers in Mozambique increases their self-reported planning horizons. The author argues that the agent's planning horizon is endogenously determined by how bright their future prospects appear. The idea is that a gloomy future causes distress due to anticipatory utility, and the agent responds by avoiding thinking about the future, discouraging planning and reducing long-term investments. Aspirations for one's children could be particularly important for break the cycle of intergenerational transmission of poverty.

2.4 Nudges

Practical messages of Behavioral Economics are often referred to as "nudges." Nudges are designed to help ameliorate the deficiencies of human decision-making liable to be manifested under realistic psychological conditions (Thaler & Sunstein, 2009).

One type of nudges (called "noneducative") consist of modifications in environmental factors impacting on human decision-making. One notable example is a switch from an opt-in to opt-out in the setting of a default option. There is evidence that this modifies people's choices although they continue to have the same range of options to choose from. It is important to note that this type of nudges take the internal conditions of the decision-maker as given. One of the central proponents of nudges states as follows (Sunstein, 2017, p. 3):

> [Noneducative nudges] allow people to go their own way, but they do not teach them anything. They include default rules and strategic decisions about how items are ordered, as on a menu or at a cafeteria; these are designed to preserve the freedom of choice but without necessarily increasing people's capacity for individual agency (except insofar as they enable people not to think about certain problems).

There are the other type of nudges (called "educative") (ibid., p. 3):

> Educative nudges include disclosure requirements, reminders, and warnings, which are specifically designed to *increase people's own powers of agency*—perhaps by augmenting

---

[7] For discussions of the recent literature, see La Ferrara (2018) and Duflo (2012).

their knowledge and their capacities, perhaps by jogging their memories, perhaps by appealing to people's highest goals and aspirations, perhaps by making relevant facts salient….educative nudges easily fit within those aspects of the liberal tradition that emphasize *agency* and *autonomy*. By adding to people's stock of knowledge and by increasing their ability to figure things out, they can help them to become better choosers.

The grouping together of the three approaches mentioned under the single heading "educative" and treating them as measures that help to add to people's stock of knowledge and increase <u>their ability to figure things out</u> seems to be inappropriate from the perspective of this chapter. These are nothing more than technical aids to decision-making on the spot and do not involve any irreversible change in internal conditions of the individual.

3 Agency as a Core Component of Human Capital

3.1 The Concept of Human Capital

For the discussion of development of agency, the most appropriate reference in economics will be the human capital theory. In contemporary economics, the concept of Human Capital (HC) was proposed and formulated by Theodore Schultz and Gary Becker. The initial focus of attention was exclusively placed on human beings as resources in production processes and their productivity. Viewing humans as capital was justified in reference to the general capital theory consisting of two stages: investments build up capital stock (stage 1); and capital stock is activated and utilized according to demands for its service (stage 2). Until recently, investments in HC were almost exclusively concerned with augmenting "cognitive capacity" through education, training and experience. The conception of HC has since been expanded to incorporate "noncognitive capacity." In this chapter we will review that development and further present our own proposal to add another element, i.e., "*agentic* capacity," to the conception of HC.

In this chapter we propose to place agency as one part, a core part at that, of HC. As such, agency is postulated as a stock variable to be measured at a point in time. It is accumulated through investment and possibly as by-product of its utilization (analogous to "learning by doing"). It may undergo depletion with time and/or usage; or, as mentioned above, it may actually be enhanced by being exercised.[8]

---

[8] Physical capital stock is typically stipulated to deplete with time and/or use. There has been no explicit account of depletion in discussions of HC, in spite of a very likely possibility of obsolescence.

3.2 Cognitive and Noncognitive Capacities as Elements of Human Capital[9]

3.2.1 Human Capital as a Bundle of Capacities

Here we will review an attempt to incorporate viewpoints and findings of personality psychology into the human capital theory spearheaded by James Heckman in a series of works with his collaborators (both economists and psychologists). In this school, the nomenclature on 'noncognitive capacity' has evolved over time initially to "personality traits" and subsequently to "personality skills." This last step was taken to avoid the impression of fixity the term 'trait' gives and instead emphasize the malleability of personality as 'skill.' Concurrently, "noncognitive skills" also came to be called, more informatively, "socioemotional skills." It is important to note that the main interest of the Heckman school is to identify the dynamics of the formation of cognitive and noncognitive capacities over the life cycle.[10]

Heckman proposes a theoretical model of capability formation. Agents are assumed to possess a vector of capabilities at each age including pure cognitive abilities (e.g., IQ) and noncognitive abilities (patience, self- control, temperament, risk aversion, time preference). This reflects an emerging developmental literature in economics that demonstrates the importance of early environmental conditions on the evolution of adolescent and adult cognitive and noncognitive capacities. This literature documents critical and sensitive periods in the development of human capabilities. Evidence on the importance of early environments on a spectrum of health, labor market, and behavioral outcomes suggests that common developmental processes are at work.

Cognitive Capacity

Intelligence (or cognitive ability) has been defined by an official taskforce of the American Psychological Association as the "ability to understand complex ideas, to adapt effectively to the environment, to learn from experience, to engage in various forms of reasoning, to overcome obstacles by taking thought". Psychologists have postulated the general high-order factor 'g' for intelligence. There is ample evidence from economics and psychology that cognitive ability is a powerful predictor

---

[9] This and next sections draw heavily on the works by James Heckman and his collaborators cited in References.

[10] Here we take objection to this phraseology. A capacity is a latent potentiality of deploying resources and skills for the pursuit of a determinate action. An ability is the power to have a capacity actually realized in a specific context of an action. A resource is something, tangible or intangible, usable for the pursuit of a determinate action. It may be an operant resource relating to an operational capability of an agent or an operand resource to be worked on in an operation. A skill is the ability to have resources actually utilized for the pursuit of a determinate action.

of economic and social outcomes. IQ scores become stable by age 10 or so, suggesting a sensitive period for the formation of cognitive capacity below age 10.

There is less agreement about the number and identity of lower-order factors. Cattell (1971, 1987) proposed one of the more widely accepted distinction contrasting two second-order factors: "fluid intelligence" (the ability to solve novel problems) and "crystallized intelligence" (knowledge and developed skills). It has been found in psychological studies that many measures of executive function do not correlate reliably with IQ. However, measures of one aspect of execution function—working memory capacity in particular—correlate very highly with measures of fluid intelligence.

Noncognitive Capacity

Recent developments in the study of noncognitive capacity provide useful inputs to the discussion of the development of agency, conceived here as element of human capital. Here we review relevant studies on the formation and development of noncognitive capacity over the life cycle based on a series of studies conducted by James Heckman and colleagues.

The power of noncognitive capacity for success in life is vividly demonstrated by the Perry Preschool study. This experimental intervention enriched the early family environments of disadvantaged children with subnormal intelligence quotients (IQ). Both treatments and controls were followed into their 40s. On a variety of measures of socioeconomic achievement, over their life cycles, the treatment group was far more successful than the control group although IQ did not exhibit any lasting difference between the two groups. Something besides IQ was changed by the intervention. Borghans et al. (2008) called that something "personality traits."

There is evidence that adolescent interventions can affect noncognitive skills. On average, the later remediation is given to a disadvantaged child, the less effective it is. The available evidence suggests that for many skills and human capabilities, later intervention for disadvantage may be possible, but it is much more costly than early remediation to achieve a given level of adult performance.

Interdependence between Cognitive and Noncognitive Capacities

It is common to distinguish between the concepts of "cognitive capacity" and "noncognitive capacity." Heckman cautions that the conceptual contrast should not be taken to imply that they are functionally separated. Schulkin (2007) reviews evidence from neuroscience that cortical structures associated with cognition and executive functions play an active role in regulating motivation, a function previously thought to be the exclusive domain of sub-cortical structures. Conversely, Phelps (2006) shows that emotions associated with noncognitive capacity are involved in learning, attention, and other aspects of cognition.

The problem of conceptually distinguishing cognitive and noncognitive capacities is demonstrated in an analysis of "executive function" which is variously described as a cognitive function or a function regulating emotions and decision, depending on the scholar. The APA Dictionary defines "executive function" as "higher level cognitive processes that organize and order behavior, including logic and reasoning, abstract thinking, problem solving, planning and carrying out and terminating goal-directed behavior." Executive function may be understood not as a trait but, rather, a collection of behaviors thought to be mediated by the prefrontal cortex. Components of executive function include behavioral inhibition, working memory, attention, and other so-called "top-down" mental processes whose function is to orchestrate lower-level processes.[11]

3.2.2 Mechanisms of Changes in Cognitive and Noncognitive Capacities

Given the impact of cognitive and noncognitive capacities on life outcomes, it is important to know how much they can change, and if they indeed change, to what extent environments and investments influence the developmental trajectories of those capacities. Many economists and psychologists assume that preference and personality parameters are fixed early in life. The evidence suggests otherwise. Recent research shows how cognitive and noncognitive capacities are affected by parental investments and life experiences. They both evolve over the life course, albeit at different rates at different ages.

Both cognitive and noncognitive capacities can be affected by parental investment and schooling. Sensitive periods for cognitive skills come earlier than those for noncognitive capacities. Sensitive periods are periods in which investment has especially high productivity for a capacity (Cunha & Heckman, 2007). Cognitive and noncognitive capacities cross-fertilize each other with high stocks of each at one age improving the productivity of investments at later ages. The evidence of cross-fertilization from noncognitive to cognitive capacities is stronger than evidence for the cross-fertilization of cognitive to noncognitive capacities. Both cognitive and noncognitive capacities affect adult outcomes but they have different relative importance in explaining different outcomes.

Early interventions, such as enriched childcare centers coupled with home visitations, have been successful in alleviating some of the initial disadvantages of children born into adverse conditions. While these interventions were originally designed to improve the cognitive capacity of children, their success has mostly been in boosting noncognitive capacity, as demonstrated, for example, by the Perry Preschool Program, where an enriched early childhood intervention evaluated by random assignment where treatments and controls are followed to age 40, did not boost IQ but did raise achievement test scores, schooling, and social skills.

---

[11] We concur with Heckman that "[t]hese components are so distinct that it is odd that psychologists have bundled them into one category."

3.2.3 Main Findings

Heckman (2007) summarizes main findings of the studies by his group in the following nine points:

1. Ability matters. A large number of empirical studies document that cognitive ability is a powerful determinant of wages, schooling, participation in crime and success in many aspects of social and economic life.
2. Abilities are multiple in nature. Noncognitive abilities (perseverance, motivation, time preference, risk aversion, self-esteem, self-control, preference for leisure) have direct effects on wages (controlling for schooling), schooling, teenage pregnancy, smoking, crime, performance on achievement tests, and many other aspects of social and economic life.
3. The nature versus nurture distinction, although traditional, is obsolete. The modern literature on epigenetic expression and gene environment interactions teaches us that the sharp distinction between acquired skills and ability featured in the early human capital literature is not tenable. Abilities are produced, and gene expression is governed by environmental conditions. Behaviors and abilities have both a genetic and an acquired character. Measured abilities are the outcome of environmental influences, including in utero experiences, and also have genetic components. Some adverse early effects are more easily compensated than other effects. The concepts of remediation and resilience play prominent roles in economic analysis.
4. Ability gaps between individuals and across socioeconomic groups open up at early ages, for both cognitive and noncognitive skills.
5. There is compelling evidence of critical and sensitive periods in development. Some skills or traits are more readily acquired at certain stages of childhood than other traits. Different types of abilities appear to be manipulable at different ages.
6. Despite the low returns to interventions targeted toward disadvantaged adolescents, the empirical literature shows high economic returns for remedial investments in young disadvantaged children.
7. If early investment in disadvantaged children is not followed by later investment, its effect at later ages is lessened. Investments at different stages of the life cycle are complementary and require follow up to be effective.
8. The effects of credit constraints on a child's adult outcomes depend on the age at which they bind for the child's family. Recent research demonstrates the quantitative insignificance of family credit constraints in a child's college-going years in explaining a child's enrollment in college in the US.
9. Socioemotional (noncognitive) skills foster cognitive skills and are an important product of successful families and successful interventions in disadvantaged families. Emotionally nurturing environments produce more capable learners.

3.3 Integrating Cognitive and Personal Psychology with Economics

Heckman and his collaborators focus their analysis on personality, defined as patterns of thought, feelings, and behavior. Personality psychologists have developed measurement systems for personality traits, of which the most prominent is the "Big Five" personality inventory. Heckman and his collaborators (Borghans et al., 2008) examine these measurement systems and their relationship with the preference parameters familiar to economists. Based on their work, here we will examine the concepts captured by the psychological measurements and the stability of the measurements across situations in which they are measured.

3.3.1 The Evidence on Preference Parameters

Many economists and some psychologists estimate the traditional preference parameters in economics: time preference, risk aversion and preference for leisure. More recently, altruism and social preferences have been also studied. In this section, we review the evidence from the group of psychologists and economists who directly measure these preferences.

Time Discounting

Evidence from animal and human experiments suggests that future rewards are discounted non-exponentially as a function of delay. There is some consensus in psychology that hyperbolic functions fit data from these experiments better than do exponential functions, although, as noted by many economists, the evidence for hyperbolic discounting is far from solid.

Several economists have used observational data to estimate discount rates. In real life, one must not only choose delayed gratification but also maintain this choice in the face of immediate temptation. A meta-analysis of 24 studies in which both IQ and discount rates were measured shows the two traits are inversely related ($r = -0.23$). The complexity entailed by comparing the present and future values of rewards suggests that the inverse relationship between discount rates and intelligence is not just an artifact of measurement. An individual with poor working memory and low intelligence may not be capable of accurately calculating or even perceiving the value of a deferred reward. At the least, making such calculations is more effortful (that is, costly) for individuals of low cognitive ability. If the cost of making calculations exceeds the expected benefit of such deliberation, the individual may choose by default the immediate, certain reward. Here the line between preference and constraint blurs—is this individual's behavior best explained as a constraint on cognition or a preference?

Risk Preference

The risk preference parameter (also referred to as "risk aversion" or "risk tolerance") represents the curvature of the utility function. As discussed above in relation to time preference, the effects of numeracy and intelligence may not simply constitute methodological artifacts, but are root explanations for behavior in the face of uncertainty. There appears to be an inverse relationship between cognitive ability and risk aversion, where higher IQ people have higher risk tolerance. Risk preference also varies with socioeconomic characteristics. However, there is no general consensus on the direction of such differences.

Preference for Leisure

There is a large literature on estimating leisure preferences. Most omnibus measures of personality include scales closely related to preference for leisure or, more frequently, the obverse trait of preference for work. The widely used Big Five includes an Achievement Striving subscale of Conscientiousness, which describes ambition, the capacity for hard work, and an inclination toward purposeful behavior.

Altruism and Social Preferences

There is a large literature on altruism and an emerging literature on social preferences in economics.

A recent literature explores social preferences which are distinct from altruism per se. Altruism is based on the assumption that the preferences of one agent depend on the utility of other agents. Social preferences are preferences that depend on agent's evaluations of a social condition (inequality, for example) or the intentions of other agents. Fehr and Schmidt (2006) summarize the theory and empirical support for social preferences. Their research suggests that social preferences distinct from pure altruism may play an important role in shaping individual behaviors.[12]

3.3.2 Frameworks for Integrating Personality and Economics

This section attempts to integrate the main lessons summarized in the preceding sections into formal economic models. As was noted before, preference anomalies have attracted a lot of attention in the recent literature in behavioral economics. However, choice is generated by preferences, expectations, and constraints, and psychology has something to say about each of these aspects of agent decision making.

---

[12] This corroborates the behavioral economics' claim of "bounded self-interest."

The evidence from personality psychology suggests a more radical reformulation of traditional choice theory than is currently envisioned in behavioral economics which tinkers with conventional specifications of preferences. Cognitive ability and noncognitive capacities impose *constraints* on agent choice behavior. More fundamentally, conventional economic preference parameters can be interpreted as consequences of these constraints. As discussed above, high rates of measured time preference or risk aversion may be produced by the inability of by the inability of agents to imagine the future or uncertain outcomes.

Most economists are unaware of the evidence that certain personality skills are more malleable than cognitive ability over the life cycle and are more sensitive to investment by parents and to other sources of environmental influences at later ages than are cognitive traits. Social policy designed to remediate deficits in achievement can be effective by operating outside of purely cognitive channels.

Heckman and collaborators believe that conventional economic theory is sufficiently elastic to accommodate many findings of psychology, but at the same time they opine thar their analysis suggests that certain traditional concepts used in economics should be modified and certain emphases redirected. Some findings from psychology cannot be rationalized by standard economic models and could fruitfully be incorporated into economic analysis. Much work remains to be done in synthesizing a body of empirical knowledge in personality psychology into economics.

3.3.3 Cognition and Personality as Constraints

Capacities may be physical, cognitive (abstract reasoning), and related to personality. Capacities determine, for example, how effectively persons process information, cope with uncertainty, adjust to setbacks, envision counterfactual states, project into the future as well as their sense of pride in their work. These capacities affect learning, social engagement and even the definition of self. They are in part acquired, and there is evidence that aspects of these capacities are heritable.

Individual differences in cognition and personality shape the constraints of individuals and hence their choices. Depending on how the constraints are determined, one can capture a variety of aspects of choice behavior. A shy person may limit her options in a way an extravert does not. Individuals who are more intelligent or more open to experience (that is, more intellectually curious and motivated to learn) may acquire information more easily. Other personality capacity may affect the basic attribute spaces perceived by agents. An intelligent person may have a much richer choice set, and revise it more frequently over time, not only because of greater earnings capacity but also because of more information and greater imagination he/she possesses.

Uncertainty and risk are essential aspects of life. Economists have devoted much attention to the specification of the preferences of agents and the effect of uncertainty on choice. Observed negative relationship between IQ and risk aversion may be due, in part, to the greater resolution of reality (removal of components of uncertainty) by the more intelligent. Applied to intertemporal settings, this framework captures the phenomenon of high time preference as an inability of an agent to imagine future states or as an inability to accurately assess future states.

It is true, as stated above, that cognitive capacity has important bearing on an individual's decision making. At the same time, it seems likely that personality capacity play an important role in decision making under ambiguity. Individuals may differ in their capacities to deal with poorly defined situations. Greater intelligence may help define situations in a more precise manner, but person with greater self-control, openness to experience, lower levels of anxiety and those who seek excitement may better cope with ambiguity.

Over time, persons may also accumulate assets and skills, and may change their personality characteristics and cognitive traits. Preference parameters affect asset and skill accumulation. Cognitive and personality capacity can be changed. Both are influenced by experience and current stocks of the characteristics and other determinants. Interventions can affect preferences, information, opportunity sets, and the formation of skills and preferences. Personality and cognitive ability evolve over time through investment, through learning by doing or through other life experiences.

3.4 Reflections: Agency as Personality Trait?

The central question to be addressed in relation to personality is whether we can see 'agency' as personality trait consisting of/supported by a set of resource/skills. Recent interest in Social-Emotional Skills and Social Emotional Learning at OECD and as also promoted by the Collaborative for Academic, Social, and Emotional Learning (CASEL) gives us a useful entry point to this question.[13]

Social-Emotional Skills (SES) relate to capacities to "understand and manage emotions, set and achieve positive goals, feel and show empathy for others, establish and maintain positive relationships, and make responsible decisions." Of these items mentioned, "set and achieve positive goals" and "make responsible decisions" directly relate to our conception of agency.

Corresponding to these five items, five "core competencies" are defined as follows:

Self-awareness: The ability to accurately recognize one's emotions and thoughts and their influence on behavior. This includes accurately assessing one's strengths and limitations and possessing a well-grounded sense of confidence and optimism.

Self-management: The ability to regulate one's emotions, thoughts, and behaviors effectively in different situations. This includes managing stress, controlling

---

[13] For CASEL, see https://casel.org/.

impulses, motivating oneself, and setting and working toward achieving personal and academic goals.

Social awareness: The ability to take the perspective of and empathize with others from diverse backgrounds and cultures, to understand social and ethical norms for behavior, and to recognize family, school, and community resources and supports.

Relationship skills: The ability to establish and maintain healthy and rewarding relationships with diverse individuals and groups. This includes communicating clearly, listening actively, cooperating, resisting inappropriate social pressure, negotiating conflict constructively, and seeking and offering help when needed.

Responsible decision-making: The ability to make constructive and respectful choices about personal behavior and social interactions based on consideration of ethical standards, safety concerns, social norms, the realistic evaluation of consequences of various actions, and the well-being of self and others.

Among these "core competencies," "Self-management" and "Responsible decision-making" seem to have direct relevance to agency, "setting and working toward achieving personal and academic goals" in the former and "the realistic evaluation of consequences of various actions" in the latter in particular.

Insofar as agency is related to SES, development of agency is related to SEL as process/mechanism of acquisition/enhancement of SES. However, we find the interest and focus of these conceptions essentially situational rather than developmental and transformative. In contrast, we see 'agency' a layer beneath these "core competencies," as deeper human disposition and capacity supported by conviction and volition.

3.5 Agency as the Core of Human Capital

We believe that there is good reason to define and treat 'agency' as element of human capital that is distinct from personality trait or socioemotional skills. The reason is that we see 'agency' as fundamental driver of human actions and not only as factors that influence choices. In this sense we place and emphasize agency as the core part, or fundamental layer of human capital.

We believe that agency has both intrinsic and instrumental value: exercise of agency is, in and of itself, a fulfilling experience; at the same time, one will obtain better results from actions chosen and taken on one's own. Without agency, one's cognitive and socioemotional capacities just constitute human resources to be employed and utilized for somebody else's purpose. With agency, one uses one's own human capacities in such ways that could contribute to the achievement of your own goals and in such manners that suit your own mode of execution. We believe that this perception could be related to such human values as "integrity" and "dignity."

In closing our discussion on agency, it will be useful to remind ourselves of an important conceptual distinction between "agency in existence (AE)" as core part of human capital and "agency activated (AA)" as mobilization and utilization of that capital in a specific context or activity. We postulate that AE, which is latent, is mobilized and utilized up to the level of AA, depending on the extent that an individual is "motivated" to direct and exert AE to carry out a specific activity. The level of AA exhibited in a certain activity is thus a function of the level of AE and the intensity of motivation applied toward the activity in question.

The level of "agency in existence (AE)" at any point in time may be stipulated to be determined by the following three factors: the initial level of AE, the level of "agency activated (AA)" over time, and external influences affecting the level of AE.

In the case of agency, there might not be any decay in AE with the passage of time, and its use (AA) might exert a positive effect on AE if, as is imaginable, the exercise of agency leads to an enhanced state of AE rather than a depleted state (analogous to social capital). Positive influences and supports from external sources will be the functional equivalents of tune-ups in the case of an engine (as discussed below). In real-world situations, positive influences may come from inspirational stories or beliefs and positive supports may be provided by someone intimately related or by some professionals like social workers.[14]

4 Agency in the Capability Approach

4.1 *Amartya Sen's Conception of Agency*[15]

This section aims to provide an overview of the conceptual and normative foundations of the idea of agency within Amartya Sen's capability approach. The focus is placed on the nature, value, and role of agency in the capability approach as Sen developed his arguments over years.

4.1.1 Functioning and Capability

For Amartya Sen, the normative premise of the Capability Approach is that people ought to have the freedom "to choose the lives they value and have reason to value." (Sen, 1992, p. 81) The approach's two main concepts are "functioning" and "capability." A person's well-being, for Sen, consists not only of her current states and activities ("functionings"), which may include the activity of choosing, but also of her freedom or real opportunities to function in ways alternative to her current

---

[14] On this point, our understanding of agency seems to intersect with the general discussion on factors determining the level of resilience of the individuals in the face of adversities.

[15] This and next sections draw heavily on Crocker and Roybens (2009).

functionings. Sen designates these real opportunities or freedoms for functioning as "capabilities." The distinction between functionings and capabilities is between the realized and the realizable, or in other words, between achievements, on the one hand, and freedoms or valuable options from which one can choose, on the other.

According to the Capability Approach, the ends of well-being, justice, and development should be conceptualized, *inter alia*, in terms of people's capabilities to function, that is, their effective opportunities to undertake the actions and activities that they want to engage in, and be whom they want to be. These "activities ... or states of existence or being," and the freedom to engage in them, together constitute what makes a life valuable. (Sen, 1985, p. 197)

Capabilities are the freedoms which allow "persons to lead the kind of life they value—and have reason to value" (Sen, 1999, p. 18). Capabilities are the opportunities and potential to achieve. In Sen's view, due to the complementarity between individual agency and social arrangements, it is crucial "to give simultaneous recognition to the centrality of individual freedom and to the force of social influences on the extent and reach of individual freedom." (ibid., pp. xi–xii) Development itself, as a metric, should be evaluated insofar as it effectuates "the removal of various types of unfreedoms that leave people with little choice and little opportunity of exercising their reasoned agency." (ibid., p. xii).

4.1.2 Well-being and Agency

In his works before *Development as Freedom* (1999) Sen usually discusses "agency" in comparison with "well-being." For example, Sen speaks of an aspect of agency as the "moral power to have a conception of the good" (Sen, 1984, p. 186) as well as of an aspect of well-being that would be the maximization of self-interest, the standard utilitarian idea of well-being (choice, desire or happiness). (ibid., p. 187) When he speaks of the agency aspect of a person as being the power that allows the formulation of a conception of the good, he is describing a subjective mechanism of value formation and choice of goals that will not necessarily be harmonious with choices that would maximize personal well-being.

In explicating Sen's concepts of well-being and agency, it is useful to attend to a cross cutting distinction, namely, achievement and freedom.

A person's position in a social arrangement can be judged in two different perspectives, i.e., (1) the actual achievement, and (2) the freedom to achieve. Achievement is concerned with what we accomplish, and freedom with the real opportunity that we have to accomplish what we value. The two need not be congruent (Sen, 1992, p. 31). Table 4.1 shows Sen's two cross-cutting distinctions: (i) well-being and agency, and (ii) achievement and freedom.

With regard to well-being, Sen uses the term "functionings" to designate "well-being achievements," or "the state of a person—the various things one manages to do or be in leading a life," and "capabilities" to refer to "well-being freedoms," or "the freedoms to design, manage and choose from possible alternative states, or sets

Table 4.1 Cross-cutting distinctions: (i) well-being and agency, and (ii) achievement and freedom

	Well-being	Agency
Achievement	Well-being Achievements (Functionings)	Agency Achievements
Freedom	Well-being Freedoms (Capabilities)	Agency Freedoms

Source: Compiled from Crocker and Roybens (2009)

of functionings, to lead the kind of life one values and has reason to value," as stated above.

Agency, like well-being, has two dimensions, namely, "agency achievements" and "agency freedoms." According to Sen, a person's "agency achievement" is "the fact of deciding and acting on the basis of what one values and has reason to value," and a person's "agency freedom" is "the freedom to exercise one's power to decide and to act and be effective." As agents, persons individually and collectively decide and achieve their goals in the world, and as agents they have more or less power and freedom to exercise their agency. Not only do people have more or less power to decide, act, and make a difference in the world but social arrangements can also extend or limit the reach of agency achievements and agency freedom, as agency "is inescapably qualified and constrained by the social, political, and economic opportunities available to us" (Sen, 1999, pp. xi–xii).

4.1.3 The Value of Agency

Sen believes that agency is valuable in three ways. It is *intrinsically* valuable: we have reason to value agency for its own sake (although the exercise of agency may be used for trivial or nefarious actions). Some agency-theorists seek additional justification by explaining agency's intrinsic value in relation to our conception of persons as morally responsible (Sen, 1999, p. 288), worthy of respect (Berlin: "a somebody, not nobody"), or having the capacity to "have or strive for a meaningful life" (Nozick, 1974, p. 50).

Agency is also *instrumentally* valuable as a means to good consequences. If people are involved in making their own decisions and running their own lives, their actions are more likely to result, when they so aim and act, in achievement of their well-being freedoms, such as being able to be healthy and well-nourished. Moreover, when individuals are agents in a joint enterprise rather than mere "patients" or pawns, they are more likely sustainably and loyally to contribute to the joint action.

Finally, agency is, what Sen calls, *"constructively"* valuable, for in agency freedom the agent freely scrutinizes, decides on, and shapes its values. Included in the constructive value of agency is agent's selecting, weighing, and trading-off capabilities and other values.

4.1.4 Development as Agency Freedom

One reason that development, conceived as good social change, is important for Sen is that it provides a variety of social arrangements in which human beings express their agency or become free to do so. The responsibility-sensitive analyst evaluates policies and practices—in both rich and poor countries—in the light, among other things, of the extent to which these policies and processes enhance, guarantee, and restore the agency of individuals and various groups (Sen, 1999, pp. xii–xiii).

One challenge for Sen and others is to give an account of how democracy, including public discussion, provides procedures for *collective* agency, procedures in which many agents can reason together to arrive at policy that is wise and action with which most can agree. For Sen, groups as well as individual persons can and should be authors of their own futures. Public deliberation and democratic decision-making are arguably defensible ways in which citizens and their representatives both exercise their agency and forge good policy.

Without agency freedom, without "the liberty of acting as citizens who matter and whose voices count," people run the risk of "living as well-fed, well-clothed, and well-entertained vassals" (Drèze & Sen, 2002, p. 288). At the same time, without an adequate level of well-being freedom and achievement, people are unable to realize their potential as agents. Because of the important linkages between well-being and agency, there is good reason to advocate an "agency-focused capability approach."

4.2 Examination of Sen's Conception of Agency

We follow Crocker and Roybens (2009) and present the following interpretation of Sen's conception of agency.

A person (or group) is an agent with respect to action X to the extent that the following four conditions hold:

1. *self-determination*: decides for oneself rather than someone or something else making the decision to do X;
2. *reason orientation and deliberation*: bases one's decisions on reasons, such as the pursuit of goals;
3. *action*: one performs or has a role in performing X; and
4. *impact on the world*: thereby brings about (or contributes to bringing about) change in the world.

Rather than make each one of these four conditions necessary and together sufficient for agency, it will be more instructive to see that the more fully an agent's action fulfills each condition the more fully is that act one of agency. Agency is a matter of degree rather than "an 'on/off' capacity or condition." Brief commentary on each of these four components follows:

Self-determination
Even though an agent gets what she wants, she has not exercised agency unless she herself decides to perform the act in question. When external circumstances cause the agent's behavior or when other agents force or manipulate her, the person does not exercise agency even if she gets what she wants: "There is clearly a violation of freedom [i.e., agency freedom]" when an agent "is being forced to do exactly what she would have chosen to do anyway" (Sen, 2004, p. 331). Sometimes Sen says "free" or "active" agency to characterize internally-caused behavior that is freely self-determined.

Reason-Orientation and Deliberation
Not just any behavior that an agent "emits" is an agency achievement, for acting on whim (let alone compulsions or addictions) is behavior not under the agent's control. Agency takes place when a person acts on purpose and for a purpose, goal, or reason. Such activity Sen and co-author Jean Drèze sometimes call "reasoned agency" (Drèze & Sen, 2002, p. 19) or "critical agency" (ibid., p. 258) because it involves more or less scrutiny of and deliberation about reasons and values: "What is needed is not merely freedom and power to act, but also freedom and power to question and reassess the prevailing norms and values" (ibid., p. 258).

Action
Agency achievement involves more than the freedom to act, more than deciding, and more than scrutiny of reasons and norms for action. People lack full agency if they decide (on the basis of reasons) to act and either take no action or utterly fail to realize their goals.

Impact on the World
The more an agent's actions make a difference in the world the more fully does the agent exercise agency. Not only does one's exercise of agency include a doing and not merely an intention, the doing must have a larger or smaller impact. When, by her action, the agent intentionally achieves her goal, she is in this instance an agent, the author of her own life. What is true of individuals is also true of groups who engage in joint actions: "The basic approach [of Drèze & Sen, 2002] involves an overarching interest in the role of human beings—on their own and in cooperation with each other—in running their lives and in using and expanding their freedoms." (ibid., p. 33). To realize an individual's or a group's goals and to change the world, to have an ability to do the things we value (ibid., pp. 17–20), requires that the individual or collective agent has agency freedom and effective power: "Greater freedom enhances the ability of people to help themselves and also to influence the world, and these matters ["the 'agency aspect' of the individual"] are central to the process of development" (Sen, 1999, p. 18).

4.3 Discussion

As summarized above, "agency" occupies a central position and plays a crucial role in Sen's assessment of human conditions. From the perspective of this book and its central question of "What makes people take initiatives?" the Capability Approach makes an important contribution in that it offers a way to discuss enabling/constraining factors that impinge on people's ability to exercise agency ("agency freedom"), or make decisions and take actions. However, it does not discuss the determinants of agency as inner capacity or the process of development of agency. We will squarely focus on these issues in later chapters.

5 Reflections and Concluding Remarks

The first word "disposition" in our definition of agency may seem to suggest that agency could be seen as a personality trait, while the second word "capacity" represents enabling/constraining conditions posed by factors internal to individuals. In this chapter we have reviewed the two recent strands of scholastic innovation in microeconomics of choice and behavior and also the capability approach to the evaluation of life conditions.

Behavioral Economics (BE) has broadened and modified our understanding of human decision-making and behavior with the elaboration of the limited cognitive capacity and the revised formulations of time discounting and risk aversion. BE, informed by psychology and neuroscience, provides new hypotheses and formulations of preferences and constraints in human decision making and behavior. Given the preferences, BE pays almost exclusive attention to the external environment ("choice architecture") in which decisions are made and actions are taken. Nudges are classical cases of BE subscriptions incorporating minor changes in external environments.

The attempted integration of personality traits into microeconomics of human capital dynamics by James Heckman and colleagues has enriched our views on human development and determinants of socioeconomic outcomes. With its recent emphasis of social emotional skills and learning, it has provided a useful conduit to the establishment of "agency" (as defined in this chapter) as a separate, foundational layer of "human capital." Thus established, "agency" can be seen as the core of "human capital" and could be related to such human values as "integrity" and "dignity." We believe that our emphasis of disposition, volition and purposefulness as core internal condition of an individual in the definition of the term "agency" is highly relevant and useful in making it conceptually and empirically insightful and constructive.

This belief has been further strengthened in our attempt to relate our conception of agency to the central themes of the capability approach proposed by Amartya Sen. In that approach, the value of any doing and being is derived from reasoning in the process of selection from among possible alternatives, which corresponds directly our conception of agency as "disposition and capacity for self-determination and self-management." And, as with Sen, we see both intrinsic and instrumental value of agency in leading fulfilling life and promoting human well-being.

Heckman points to the lack of discussion on the determinants of internal capabilities as a critical weakness of the Capability Approach and puts forth his theory of skill formation as a way to fill that gap. He argues as follows: "Skills provide agents with *the power to act* in multiple capacities. Preferences can be understood as providing the desires and wants to choose which of the available actions agents choose to take." (Heckman & Corbin, 2016, p. 352; italics in original) In this formulation, "agency," a term Heckman does not use, may be identified with the combined working of "skills" as determinants of available options for action and "preferences" as source of "desires and wants to choose" from among those options. This is in line with the traditional microeconomic theory of consumer choice, and for that matter, essentially in accordance with the role of "agency" (or "the act of choosing") in the capability/functioning setup of the Capability Approach.

An important question remains in relation to the central theme of this book: "What moves people to take initiatives?" The authors of this book decided to build our academic discussions on this theme around the concept of "agency." From this perspective, "agency" cannot be reduced to "the act of choosing from among available options." Nor is it sufficient to identify "agency" as "the act of planning and execution for the purpose of expanding available options." What matters most fundamentally in addressing the question "What makes people to take initiatives?" is the underlying desire and capacity to act in such a way.

We believe that "agency" should be discussed at this fundamental level. In this chapter, in an attempt to place "agency" in the tradition of Economics, we have decided to see it as an aspect of human capital, in fact as the deepest layer of it. This decision allows us to discuss "empowerment," a key concept in clinical psychology, social work and development practice, as activation or enhancement of "agency" as human capital. We will squarely take on this task in later chapters.

References

Bertrand, M., Mullainathan, S., & Shafir, E. (2004). A Behavioural Economics View of Poverty. *American Economic Review, 94*, 419–423.

Borghans, L., Duckworth, A. L., Heckman, J. J., & ter Weel, B. (2008). The Economics and Psychology of Personality Traits. *Journal of Human Resources, 43*(4), 972–1059.

Cattell, R. (1971). *Abilities: Their Structure, Growth, and Action*. Houghton Mifflin.

Cattell, R. (1987). *Intelligence: Its Structure, Growth and Action*. Elsevier.

Chandrasekhar, A., Golub, B., & Yang, H. (2018). Signaling, Shame, and Silence in Social Learning. *NBER Working Paper No. 25169*.

Crocker, D. A., & Roybens, I. (2009). Capability and Agency. In C. W. Morris (Ed.), *Amartya Sen*. Cambridge University Press. Chapter 3.

Cunha, F., & Heckman, J. J. (2007). The Technology of Skill Formation. *American Economic Review, 97*(2), 31–47.

References

Datta, S., & Mullainathan, S. (2014). Behavioral Design: A New Approach to Development Policy. *The Review of Income and Wealth, 60*(1), 7–35.

Dean, E., Schilbach, F., & Schofield, H. (2018). Poverty and Cognitive Function. In C. Barrett, M. Carter, & J. Chavas (Eds.), *The Economics of Poverty Traps*. University of Chicago Press.

Drèze, J., & Sen, A. K. (2002). *India: Development and Participation* (2nd ed.). Oxford University Press.

Duflo, E. (2012). Human Values and the Design of the Fight against Poverty. *Tanner Lectures*, 1–55.

Fehr, E., & Schmidt, K. M. (2006). The Economics of Fairness, Reciprocity and Altruism-- Experimental Evidence and New Theories. In S.-C. Kolm & J. M. Ythier (Eds.), Handbook of the economics of giving, altruism and reciprocity (Vol. 1.) Foundations (pp. 615–691). Elsevier Science.

Genicot, G., & Ray, D. (2017). Aspirations and Inequality. *Econometrica, 85*(2), 489–519.

Hall, C., Zhao, J., & Shafir, E. (2014). Self-affirmation among the Poor: Cognitive and Behavioral Implications. *Psychological Science, 25*(2), 619–625.

Haushofer, J., & Fehr, E. (2014). On the Psychology of Poverty. *Science, 344*, 862–867.

Heckman, J. (2007). The Economics, Technology, and Neuroscience of Human Capability Formation. *PNAS, 104*, 13250–13255.

Heckman, J., & Corbin, C. (2016). Capabilities and Skills. *Journal of Human Development and Capability, 17*(3), 342–359.

Kahneman, D. (2003). Maps of Bounded Rationality: Psychology for Behavioral Economics. *The American Economic Review, 93*, 1449–1475.

Kahneman, D., & Tversky, A. (1979). Prospect Theory: An Analysis of Decision under Risk. *Econometrica, 47*, 263–291.

Kremer, M., Rao, G., & Schilbach, F. (2019). Beavioral Development Economics. In B. Bernheim, S. DellaVigna, & D. Laibson (Eds.), *Handbook of Behavioral Economics, Volume 2*. North-Holland.

La Ferrara, E. (2018). Aspirations, Social Norms and Development. European Economic Association Presidential Address.

Laajaj, R. (2017). Endogenous Time Horizon and Behavioral Poverty Trap: Theory and Evidence from Mozambique. *Journal of Development Economics, 127*, 187–208.

Mani, A., Mullainathan, S., Shafir, E., & Zhao, J. (2013). Poverty Impedes Cognitive Function. *Science, 341*, 976–980.

Mullainathan, S., & Shafir, E. (2013). *Scarcity: Why Having Too Little Means So Much*. Times Books/Henry Holt and Co.

Mullainathan, S., & Thaler, R. H. (2000). Behavioral Economics. *Working Paper 7948*. National Bureau of Economic Research (NBER).

Muramatsu, R., & Avila, F. (2017). The Behavioral Turn in Development Economics: A Tentative Account through the Lens of Economic Methodology. *Brazilian Journal of Political Economy, 37*(2), 363–380.

Nozick, R. (1974). *Anarchy, State, and Utopia*. Basic Books.

Phelps, E. A. (2006). Emotion and Cognition: Insights from Studies of the Human Amygdala. *Annual Review of Psychology, 57*, 27–53.

Schilbach, F., Schofield, H., & Mullainathan, S. (2016). The Psychological Lives of the Poor. *The American Economic Review, 106*, 435–440.

Schulkin, J. (2007). Effort and Will: A Cognitive Neuroscience Perspective. *Mind and Matter, 5*, 111–126.

Sen, A. (1984). *Rights and Capabilities in Resources, Values and Development*. Harvard University Press.

Sen, A. (1985). Well-being, Agency and Freedom: The Dewey Lectures 1984. *The Journal of Philosophy, 82*(4), 169–221.

Sen, A. (1992). *Inequality Re-examined*. Clarendon Press.

Sen, A. (1999). *Development as Freedom*. Oxford University Press.

Sen, A. K. (2004). Elements of a Theory of Human Rights. *Philosophy & Public Affairs, 32*(4), 315–356.

Shah, A., Shafir, E., & Mullainathan, S. (2015). Scarcity Frames Value. *Psychological Science, 26*(4), 402–412.

Sunstein, C. R. (2017). *Human Agency and Behavioral Economics. Nudging Fast and Slow.* Palgrave Macmillan.

Thaler, R., & Sunstein, C. (2009). *Nudge: Improving Decisions about Health, Wealth and Happiness.* Penguin Books.

VandenBos, G. R. (Ed.). (2007). *APA Dictionary of Psychology.* American Psychological Association.

Part II
Enhancing Agency: Its Plausible Mechanisms and Influential Factors

Chapter 5
What Is Done for Facilitating Agency Development in Practice?: Documenting and Crystallizing an Unsung Practical Knowledge of a Third-Country Expert

1 Introduction

The theoretical contributions to discussions on development policy and practice have, since the 1980s, seen attempts to adopt a bottom-up development model for poverty alleviation (Sen, 1985, 1999; Dreze & Sen, 1989). This approach supports the importance of will and ownership amongst community members in relation to the initiatives and actions taken by them to improve or maintain their quality of life, instead of the application of a top-down development model in which outsiders diagnose the problems of insiders and impose solutions.

One of the most important bottom-up schools related to this theme is undoubtedly empowerment. The arguments of this school have been present from the 1980s in international development theory. There is still widespread agreement that the empowerment process can enable people living in poverty, and those who are marginalized, to participate meaningfully in shaping their own futures (Alsop et al., 2006), and how participation can quickly become a token exercise or even a means of maintaining unequal power relations without genuine empowerment (Hickey & Mohan, 2008). Thus, empowerment is still an evergreen agenda in international development, both for practitioners as well as academics, but especially for the former.

However, as its conceptual framework is related to terms such as agency, autonomy, self-direction, self-determination, liberation, participation, mobilization, and self-confidence (Narayan-Parker, 2005), empowerment has been defined in a number of different ways in the literature, and this has caused confusion. For instance, Kabeer (1999) defines empowerment as the process by which those who have been denied the ability to make strategic life choices acquire this ability. Narayan-Parker (2002) defines empowerment as the expansion of the assets and capabilities of poor people that allows them to participate in, negotiate with, influence, control, and hold accountable institutions that affect their lives. And Rowlands (1997) asserts that empowerment is more than participation in decision making; it must also include the processes that lead people to perceive themselves as able and entitled to make decisions.

To make the concept more concise and understandable, from the 2000s, scholars have tried to reframe empowerment by using the term agency and its development. Malhotra and Schuler (2005), through reviewing the mainstream literature on empowerment, concludes that enhancing agency probably comes closest to capturing the concept that the majority of writers are referring to as empowerment. Narayan-Parker (2005) points out that there are two dimensions of empowerment: (1) the expansion of agency; and (2) the increases in opportunity structure that provide what might be considered preconditions for effective agency. As for the definition of agency, Sen (1985, 1999) defines this as what a person is free to do and achieve in pursuit of whatever goals or values he or she regards as important, and an agent as one who acts and brings about change. By contrast, structures are defined as those influencing factors (such as social class, religion, gender, ethnicity, customs, institutions etc.) that determine or limit agency and the ability to make decisions (Barker, 2003). According to Anthony Giddens (1984), agency is critical to both the reproduction and the transformation of social structures and society, as it signifies an ability to deploy a range of causal powers, including that of influencing those deployed by others.

From the aspects of monitoring and evaluation, Ibrahim and Alkire (2007) also suggest that empowerment can be equivalently understood as expansion of personal agency and be divided into four types of power based on definitions by Rowlands (1997). These indicators are power over (ability to resist manipulation),[1] power to (creating new possibilities), power with (acting in a group), and power from within (enhancing self-respect and self-acceptance). Thus, when empowerment is reframed as expanding or developing agency, it becomes more intelligible and connectable with major development theories such as the capability approach, and more measurable by the indicators provided by academic contributions.

Nevertheless, some concerns remain with the integration of empowerment with agency development, which might cause discrepancies between the two schools. One is the individualization of the concept. Empowerment is a concept originally born out of social movements that has been adopted also in international development policymaking (Rowlands, 1997). It is thus historically associated with processes as well as with results achieved collectively. In comparison, the term agency seems to be defined as being more individualized. Agency, in Sen's definition, refers to *a person's* scope for achieving that *person's* valued goals (Drydyk, 2008).

The second problem is de-contextualization. Related to the first issue, when individual agency and its development are focused this tends to omit the fact that each empowerment or agency development process happens in specific contexts and

---

[1] "Power over" in Rowlands (1997, p. 13) is defined as controlling power, which may be responded to with compliance, resistance or manipulation. This, however seems slightly different from the definition by Ibrahim and Alkire (2007). The author however does not argue this topic, as it is not the main purpose of this article.

1 Introduction

social relations. In the literature of agency/agency development, there are fewer in-depth case studies than in that of empowerment. As Cornwall and Brock (2005) warns, this underscores the historical lesson that, ironically, one-size-fits-all development solutions that ignore context do violence to the very hope of a world without poverty.

The third problem is the lack of applied research on how to assist the promotion of empowerment/agency development processes, which are also well-connected to academic theories. On the one hand, the above-mentioned literature focuses on explaining what empowerment or agency (development) is and how to measure it, not on how to promote empowerment or agency development. On the other hand, there are countless reports written by development practitioners working for NGOs and development agencies. These witness the changes (in the case of empowerment) as results of their interventions, but are often not connected to theories or macro data, or use the word *agency* at all. Thus, the gap between explanation and practice, representing the gap between the two schools, is a persistent reality. An alternative approach for conducting research should be intended to make knowledge situated (Haraway, 1988).

Given the intention to respond to the above issues and concerns, this paper tries to understand what is being done to facilitate empowerment or agency development in practice by connecting research (academic theories) and practice (development projects) with clarifying context specific factors. Through analyzing and crystalizing a case study, the paper tries to frame a hypothesis (a supposition made on the basis of limited evidence as a starting point for further investigation) on plausible dynamics for enhancing agency divided into the four types/dimensions.

In the following section, the author first reviews the main literature on empowerment and agency to develop a theoretical framework for the agency development process and identifies black boxes of the theories. The author also clarifies the three critical factors for analyzing a case study. Subsequently, a development project is described in detail, one that was implemented with the particular purpose of enhancing the agency of community people. Thirdly, the case is analyzed to understand the black boxes in the theoretical framework, focusing on the following three aspects for analysis: (1) context specific factors, (2) development of an agency development project, and (3) the possible mechanisms in the agency development of community members for enhancing each type of power (power from within, power with, power to, and power over). This is further related to plausible theoretical frameworks adapted from academic disciplines related to human resource development.

The author takes this research approach with the intention to reframe development researches for making a difference: theories can, for instance, explain "*what* empowerment, people's participation, or gender equalities are or should be," but cannot answer the question of "*how* to realize or promote them in each context", which can be only crystalized through case studies in detail. Thus, this paper is not written to prove the validity of certain theories, but to suggest plausible mechanisms of empowerment or agency enhancement in practice, which can be shaped into a development model through further investigation Thus, the paper does not give a rigorous impact analysis of the power and power relations in the case study, or focus on women's empowerment.

In this paper, the two terms empowerment and agency development/enhancement are used compatibly. The author defines empowerment as enhancing or developing agency, which is a process within particular domains, contexts and social relations that leads people to perceive themselves as being able to make decisions, and act upon these to make differences (mainly referring to Rowlands, 1997 as well as Ibrahim & Alkire, 2007). Agency is defined as the will and ability to deploy a range of causal powers in pursuit of identified goals or values (Sen, 1999; Giddens, 1984). Although there are a variety of definitions of these terms, the author adopts the above definitions, because they are among the most quoted definitions used by both practitioners and researchers in promoting international development.

2 Research Framework, Methods and the Case Selection

2.1 Research Framework: Identifying Black Boxes of Current Theories

What is then an alternative way to connect the discussions regarding empowerment and agency, as well as their explanation and practice, so that development studies and development practices can altogether work for the poverty alleviation that should be the shared goal beyond their differences? To answer this, the discussion now turns into the two classic references on empowerment, read and referred to widely in both schools (Kabeer, 1994; Rowlands, 1997).

First, regarding the core of empowerment/agency development processes, in *Reversed Reality*, Kabeer (1994), by analyzing the practices of non-profit organizations, strongly emphasizes that power within, such as self-respect, aspiration and sense of agency, is the foundation of the empowerment process. In this way, people can feel entitled to analyze their current situation, and identify their own needs in the pursuit of well-being. Second, with regard to types of power, in *Questioning Empowerment*, Rowlands (1997), divides them into four; power over, power to, power with and power from within (identical to power within for Kabeer), emphasizing the importance of understanding the generative side and types of power (power to, power with and power from within). Her typology is adopted by Ibrahim and Alkire (2007) in their development of indicators of agency development. The following table shows each power type as developed by both parties (Table 5.1).

Third, with respect to the dimensions of empowerment/agency development, Rowlands (1997), reflecting upon her NGO works in Honduras as well as referring to related literature (including Kabeer), divides the dimensions of empowerment into three processes: personal, relational and collective, each of which is interrelated. In the discussion of agency development, Narayan-Parker (2005) divides dimensions of empowerment into two, though these are co-influencing: (1)

Table 5.1 Types of power

Type of power	Rowlands (1997)	Ibrahim and Alkire (2007)
Power from within	The spiritual strength and uniqueness that resides in each one of us and makes us truly human. Its basis is self-acceptance and self-respect, which extend, in turn, to respect for and acceptance of others as equals.	Enhancing self-respect and self-acceptance
Power with	A sense of the whole being greater than the sum of the individuals, especially when a group tackles problems together	Acting in group
Power to	Generative or productive power (sometimes incorporating or manifesting as forms of resistance or manipulation) which creates new possibilities and actions without domination	Creating new possibility
Power over	Controlling power, which may be responded to with compliance, resistance (which weakens processes of victimisation) or manipulation	Ability to resist manipulation

Elaborated by the Author based on Rowlands (1997), Ibrahim and Alkire (2007, p. 11)

Table 5.2 Dimensions of empowerment

Dimension (1997): Process explanation	Dimension (Narayan-Parker, 2005): Focus on the process
Personal: Developing a sense of self and individual confidence and capacity, and undoing the effects of internalized oppression	Expansion of agency
Relational (Close relationship: Family and Small groups): Developing the ability to negotiate and influence the nature of a relationship and decisions made within it	Expansion of agency/ Increase of opportunity structure
Collective (Community): Where individuals work together to achieve a more extensive impact than each could have had alone	Expansion of agency/ Increase of opportunity structure
Social: where a collection of communities (society) as a whole try to transform current structures/institutions as an ends and means of empowerment.	Increase of opportunity structure

Elaborated by the author based on Rowlands (Rowlands, 1997, p. 15) and Narayan-Parker, 2005, p. 5)

expansion of agency; and (2) increases in opportunity structure for effective agency. Table 5.2 is an attempt to bring together both arguments, adding the fourth dimension of "social" into Rowlands' typology. The main difference between collective and social is that while the former represents a community where one physically or mentally resides, the latter represent a collection of community and institutional transformations.

Combining the two tables, it is perhaps possible to generate a further table as a research framework for this paper (Table 5.3). Although each type of power and its exercise are often interrelated in real situations, the author intentionally divides the process into four to make the argument intelligible. The table explains how a person develops her/his personal agency from within (power within) that is the foundation of the agency development process. Then, or at the same time, through relations

Table 5.3 A process model of agency development of community members

Type	Dimension	Explanation of status of agency at each process
1st Power from within	Individual (Expansion of Agency)	S/he develops sense of agency (self-respect and self-acceptance) and undoing the effects of internalized oppression.
2nd Power with	Relational (Expansion of agency/Increase of opportunity structure)	S/he develops a sense of the whole being greater than the sum of the individuals, especially when a group tackles problems together as well as foster the ability to negotiate and influence the nature of a relationship within family and small groups
3rd Power to	Community (Expansion of agency/ Increase of opportunity structure)	S/he experiences generative power that creates new possibilities and actions through working as a community to achieve a more extensive impact than each could have had alone.
4th Power over	Social (Increase of opportunity structure)	S/he as develops the ability to resist manipulation, where a society as a whole tries to transform current power structures.

Elaborated by the author through combining Table 5.1 and 5.2

within small groups, such as with families, and neighbors, how we experience the ability to negotiate and influence a relationship, and decisions made within it, as well as experiencing a sense of the whole being greater when a group tackles problems together (power with). Such social relations may be experienced at a higher level, that of community (a collection of groups), where we experience generative or productive power from the creation of new possibilities and actions through working as a community to achieve a more extensive impact than individuals could have had alone (power to). Additionally, we develop the ability to resist manipulation, allowing a society as a whole to transform current power structures and institutions (power over).

The table theoretically explains *what* the status of agency at each process is. However, as discussed above, it does not explicate *how* agency development can be exercised or facilitated at each process. Thus, it is necessary to carefully analyze an appropriate case study and fill the black boxes of the theories.

2.2 Research Methods and the Case Selection: Two Dimensions and Three Factors for Analysis

As a research method, the author adopts case studies to understand how agency development is attempted in development practice. The author tries to crystallize a unique development project through documenting how such initiatives are taken, developed and accepted, as well as interpreting the mechanisms involved through plausible explanations. This approach is taken for contesting to the third concern discussed above—the lack of applied research that is well-connected to academic theories.

Likewise, reflecting the first and second concerns (individualization and de-contextualization of the concept), the author pays special attention to the following two dimensions: first it looks at the specific socio-cultural contexts of each process of change and external intervention; second it covers the "making of" a development project exercised collectively; how and who have taken initiatives, developed ideas, and made these into projects. To look into the case study, the following three factors are covered; context, promotion of agency through making a development project, and the dynamics of agency enhancement through application of the project.

As the case study, the author chose the MMO training program (*Metodologia de Motivacion y Organizacion*: Training for motivation and organization, edited by Instituto Nicaraguense de Tecnología Agropecuaria [INTA], Unión Nacional de Agricultores y Ganaderos de Nicaragua [UNAG], & Japan International Cooperation Agency [JICA] in 2004, 2005, 2007, and 2012), created and implemented over a decade primarily in Nicaragua by a third-country specialist Tetsuo Nohara, a *Nikkei* (Japanese-descended) Brazilian. There are some reasons for this selection. First, this training program is carried out before PRA (Participatory Rural Appraisal, a collection of people-centered participatory research methods) and seems to deal with agency development, although the term agency development or empowerment is not utilized in the program. After MMO, the majority of the villages in this project have conducted PRA, through which over forty participatory community projects have been planned, more than half implemented (Kuzasa, 2013). The author thus assumes something had to be done to facilitating empowerment processes. Besides, the titles of the training, such as "Self-respect and commitment", "Synergy", and "Social Capitals and Leadership" seem to be strongly related. Second, this training was not elaborated by external actors, but instead its knowledge was created in a specific context by local ownership and social relations on site over ten years. Third, this training has been recognized, well-accepted, and diffused in the country. It was incorporated in a JICA development project known as *Alianza Comunitaria*,[2] held from March 2009 to March 2013, and in addition it has been used not only in the target project area, but also in employee training seminars in counterpart organizations and lectures in some national universities, transcending social strata. Fourth, though anecdotal and rather self-reported, the impacts of the MMO are reported in several project documents (Yamaguchi, 2011; Hanawa, 2011; Kuzasa, 2013). Fifth, the author wants to pay special respect to wisdom and knowledge of third-country specialists, whose achievements are often unsung in the framework of bilateral international cooperation.

The research was conducted over three years between 2012 and 2015, structured around literature reviews, individual and group interviews both online and on site, and participant observation of training sessions. In the following discussion, after overviewing the initial context, the author traces the process of MMO through each

---

[2] Details can be found at http://www.jica.go.jp/project/nicaragua/003/index.html.

stage from its conception to diffusion so that the contents can be understood. After this discussion, Sect. 4 analyses the factors that supported the development of the MMO and its diffusion, as well as elaborates the possible mechanisms of agency development based on power from within. Concluding remarks follow.

3 Documenting the Process: The Conception, Development, Execution, and Diffusion of the MMO

This section traces the MMO process in detail; how the MMO was conceived, developed, executed, and diffused stage by stage, after introducing the rural sector and living conditions in Nicaragua. Over twenty years have passed since the end of the civil war in Nicaragua, but although steady economic growth raised per capital national income above 1500 US dollars,[3] it is the second most impoverished nation after Haiti in the region. The Ortega administration of the Sandinista National Liberation Front (FSLN), which began its second term in January 2012, is strengthening relations with left-wing governments internationally and domestically implementing social policies (education, health, etc.) focused on the poorest strata of society. The poverty rate has been steadily declining, but 42% of citizens are reported to be still in poverty,[4] and the poverty gap between urban areas (26.6%) and rural areas (63.3% in poverty, 26.6% in extreme poverty) is striking (Medina & Bernales, 2009, pp. 207–209). Among Nicaragua's primary development policies is the National Development Policy (PNDH, 2009–2011),[5] and beneath this is a rural development-specific program, called the Sector-wide Productive Rural Development Program (PRORURAL-Incluyente 2010–2014).[6] The former suggests a shift from a top-down free market economics model to a bottom-up citizen participation model (*Participacion Ciudadana*). The latter promotes "increased organization, participation, and ability in residents of rural communities," striving for efficient and sustained development through collaboration between residents and municipal authorities. However, this has yet to see realization, so it was under the above conditions that JICA dispatched Nikkei-Brazilian expert Mr. Nohara for several months every year during 2001–2007 for the purpose of "rural organizational leadership," training (MMO training) at administrative bodies, and to foster a sense of self-reliance and collaboration in the same communities.

---

[3] Data retrieved from http://data.worldbank.org/country/nicaragua.
[4] Details can be found at http://www.jica.go.jp/project/nicaragua/003/index.html.
[5] Gobierno de Reconciliación y Unidad Nacional de Nicaragua (2009), Plan Nacional de Desarrollo Humano 2009–2011, Managua, Nicaragua.
[6] MAGFOR (2010), Plan Sectorial PRORURAL Incluyente, Managua, Nicaragua.

3.1 Training Conception Stage (–2000)

Although the MMO training program itself was created after 2001, the development of its conceptual base dates back to a much earlier time. Thus, the author positions the life history of Mr. Nohara, who was the key person of MMO development.[7] Mr. Nohara, who turns 80 years old in 2021, was born and raised in a Japanese-descent community on the outskirts of São Paulo, Brazil. At age 17 he began to attend a seminary to become a pastor. At age 20, due to the recommendation of a bishop, Mr. Nohara advanced to the School of Philosophy of the University of São Paulo. During his time in university, he participated in a "literacy in 48 hours" program, part of Paulo Freire's *Consientizacion* (consciousness-raising methodologies and movement), working in the favelas. However, in 1964, General Branco undertook a large-scale purge of student movements, and Mr. Nohara was caught in its net and imprisoned for ten months. Afterwards, he sought asylum in Uruguay, being invited to Bulgaria from 1965 to 1970 on a scholarship, where he studied agriculture. In 1971 he returned to Brazil, and from 1972 to 1994 he worked at the Cotia Agricultural Cooperative, São Paulo branch.[8] Mr. Nohara's primary responsibility there was to administer the youth clubs and women's groups of the union members' families. He was engaged every day in the trial-and-error process of determining "how to encourage people to voluntarily take actions."

In 1985, the cooperative headquarters held an investigative analysis of the reasons why some producers were successful, and from the results of this decided to invite a compost specialist to begin training and research & development relating to soil amelioration. However, those producers who received the training felt compost-making was a bother and produced none of it, resulting in all the invested funds going to waste. Feeling keenly that producers must identify problems, and learn and act with their ownership to solve them for any progress to be made, Mr. Nohara started reading books on psychology and sociology, while actively receiving training in self-reliance and collaboration so he could understand how an individual and community as a whole would take initiatives and promote actions in pursuit of identified goals. After the dissolution of the Cotia Agricultural Cooperative in 1994, he joined the national Federation of Agricultural Workers branch in São Paulo[9] as a consultant, and held training programs on local citizen organization. In 1997, Mr. Nohara participated in a sustainable local development program conducted by the union headquarters and Ministry of Labor, leading to his involvement in municipal development projects. The program was meant to raise awareness among civilians, but there was question as to whether it would amount to more than one-way

---

[7] This section was written in consultation with Mr. Nohara in reference to the following website: http://www.jica.go.jp/brazil/office/information/articles/2010/20101216.html.

[8] This agricultural union was founded in 1927 with 89 members, and at its peak reached a total of 14,470 members (1986); however, due to a decline in business it disbanded in 1994. http://www.ndl.go.jp/brasil/column/nokyo.html.

[9] Federacion de Trabajadores en la Agricultura del estado de Sao Paulo.

instruction resulting in no change. From his experiences as recounted above, it is clearly understood that knowledge generated without ownership or the exercise of agency does not encourage people to voluntarily take actions or lead to empowerment.

3.2 Training Development Stage (2001–2007)

In 2001, Mr. Nohara was for the first time dispatched to UNAG (*Unión Nacional de Agricultores y Ganaderos de Nicaragua*), the National Union of Farmers and Ranchers, Nicaragua) at the request of the Ministry of Farming and Forestry [MAGFOR], (2010). Building on his experience in Brazil, he conducted three different types of training programs in five prefectures. At the core of these activities was the development of the MMO training program.

One participant, UNAG Managua representative Dolores Roa, reflects on the time as follows. "When I met Mr. Nohara the first time in 2001, I was told the 'crocodile story'; the brokers and middlemen are like crocodiles, and as long as the farmers are not united, they cannot sell their goods at a just price and cannot be economically independent.[10] This story left an impression on me. The next day, the 35 of us from management at UNAG attended the ten-day training seminar. This dealt with the meaning of self-respect and organization, subjects I had had never heard discussed before, such as: 'What is the most important thing in your life?' 'What is the real nature of humans?' and other topics—I was repeatedly asked questions that I had never considered before. Up to that point we had received training seminars on topics such as how to care for the soil or poultry, and I realized that we had been neglecting to care for our very souls. The topics of the training program were modified to our needs and increased every year." Thus, the training program has made its participants think and reevaluate themselves, and the whole process of making more functional contents situated in knowledge making in practice.

From 2001 to 2003, the training program was simply called "Nohara's training". There was no textbook or other organized material. However, in 2004, INTA (*Instituto Nicaraguense de Tecnología Agropecuaria*, the Nicaraguan Institute of Agricultural Technology) was invited to attend the program, which led to the seminar's contents being transcribed for publication as training material. The text has seen four publications over the years to the present day. Maria Eugenia Cruz, who has been involved in development since the beginning, shared her reflections as well: "I attended the training seminar for a week in 2004. The handouts we received at the seminar were in a mixture of Portuguese and Spanish. I corrected the grammar and retyped them at home. No one requested this, but I felt that I had to make a record of it for some reason." Thus, she documented the training contents purely with her own ownership without being told by anybody, so that the training contents

---

[10] This was confirmed by Mr. Nohara as being an extract from Peter Senge's *The Fifth Discipline* (1990).

would become shared knowledge. Her work, done free of charge, was stored in a document that became the first edition of the text.

The second edition was written with illustrations in 2005, when Mr. Nohara returned to Nicaragua to conduct a seminar. The reputation of the seminar has spread gradually by word of mouth, and in 2007 the third edition was produced by 17 members who had voluntarily participated in the program, coming from INTA, UNAG, JICA, and UNAN (*Universidad Nacional Autónoma de Nicaragua*, the National Autonomous University of Nicaragua). This was the first time the book came printed with something like a table of contents. At this time, the members of the group began to create fables as well, leading to the production of a thin textbook containing only fables for the use of training program participants in villages and towns. This was also distributed, photocopied, or hand-copied to read at home, because people wanted to reread and share, without any instructions from aid workers or village leaders.

3.3 Training Execution Stage (2009–2013)

Between 2009 and 2013, the development project *Alianza Comunitraria* began supported by JICA, with the MMO at its core, and held in three prefectures and twelve villages. The poverty indicators of the three prefectures are given in Table 5.4. It is noticeable that Matagalpa Prefecture's poverty ranking and rate is much higher than the national average, while those of Managua and Masaya are not. However, the selected villages' poverty rates are higher than the average (Hanawa, 2011). No data was taken to measure the status of life and agency before the project. From the domicile visits in 2014 and 2015, it seemed that the majority of the village facilitators were not categorized into the poorest of the poor in the communities, and were rather of the lower-middle classes, while the majority of the village training participants were from poor families.

Table 5.4 Poverty Indicators of the three cities

Prefecture	City	World Bank (2008) Poverty ranking among 153 cities	Extreme poverty rate*	Below poverty Line**	INIDE (2008) Poverty ranking among 153 cities	Extreme poverty rate***	Poverty rate****
Matagalpa	Matagalpa	43/153	24%	57%	91/153	37.1%	64.4%
Managua	Tipitapa	139/153	5%	34%	122/153	29.2%	63.1%
Masaya	Masatepe	144/153	4%	36%	123/153	29.0%	60.9%

Source: Hanawa (2011, p. 25)
*Population lived at average daily consumption of $1.25 or less
**Population lived at or below *$1.90 a day*
***Population lived at average annual consumption below US$334.79
****Population lived at average annual consumption below US$568.65

Regarding the "levels" of their agencies before involvement in the training, it can be seen that there were few participants in the first training sessions, that some people had serious drinking and domestic violence problems (but did nothing), that there were no leaders or occasions in the communities to discuss common issues, that members of the agricultural cooperatives were working with cooperation, and that very few women participated in village meetings (Sato, 2015). Thus, it can be assumed that the status of agency before the training implementations was not good at all.

In the initial stage, 17 members received training from Mr. Nohara, and they then became the core facilitators who expanded the training out into the 12 target communities. Some reports suggest that the project resulted in noticeable impacts for such a short period of implementation, and the small numbers of Japanese experts (basically two). In the twelve villages, 60 local volunteer facilitators were trained, and these organized 151 training sessions for free with 756 participants, and 42 mini projects were planned. 27 projects were implemented in a self-reliant way, and most participants shared the training contents at home and beyond at their own discretion (Yamaguchi, 2011; Hanawa, 2011; Kuzasa, 2013).

3.4 Training Diffusion Stage (2009–)

Since the arrival of Mr Nohara, but more pronounced after the commencement of the JICA project *Alianza Comunitaria*, the training contents have been shared among villagers through mouth-to-mouth means, especially through children and university students as part of their classes, and public and private organizations through having some training units adopt the staff training methods of the project counterpart institutions. Trained village facilitators have been invited to share the training in other villages, which they voluntarily accepted and travelled sometimes at their own cost. Similarly, the core facilitators were invited to organizations such as city councils, NPOs and universities, in which they have held training sessions for free. In 2014, the facilitators still held training sessions, a year after the termination of the project. Also, Mr. Nohara, back home in Brazil, holds MMO workshops occasionally, a service that has been also known among members of some agricultural unions.

3.5 Current MMO Training: Structure and Contents (2012–)

In 2012, the latest edition of the manual was published. This edition is more structured compared to the third edition, and features a new chapter based on the lectures of a professor of psychology at UCA (*Universidad Centro America*, the Central American University). However, the text has various issues; there is no introductory chapter; the purpose of the program and the relationship between chapters are not necessarily explicitly stated; it is unclear how the references are reflected in the text; and various other problems. To offset these, this study conducted participant observation on-site, interviewed related parties, and attended the organization of the actual contents of the training program rather than rely on the manual.

The goal of the training program is that "every participant becomes a protagonist so as to build a foundation for realizing self-reliant and collaborative community development". The table of contents lists 15 chapters, but in the actual seminar only 10 chapters are covered. Through analyzing the contents, the main contents can be divided into three sections excluding Methodology; chapters on Self-Reliance, and chapters on Collaboration and Application, which is shown as in Table 5.5.

There are 4 Chapters on Self-reliance, which are intended to affirm the "power from within" of self to commit to self and others. In regard to "Self-identity", it is explained that the existence of each and every person is itself a miracle, and that every individual is a special and important presence. Anecdotes are used here, such as the story of Viktor Frankl's experiences at a concentration camp. In "Self-respect and commitment," it is learned that every person's existence has value, every person is the protagonist of his or her own life, and that therefore one can commit to oneself and others. In "Body, mind and spirit," participants learn about differences among reason, emotion, and instinct, so that they may consider why, if human beings are such a sacred and valuable existence, they suffer setbacks, and what is at the origin of human activity. This includes a didactic story about a truck driver who, driven by emotion, smashed his son's hand. This is followed by a discussion in which participants share their experiences with anger and jealousy and ways to deal with and prevent such emotional outbursts. The "Self-Reliance" chapter is a summary of the preceding sections, asserting that self-reliance is indeed "being *not dependent*" and includes the ability to "stand up by oneself." Participants often share experiences on what it is to be independent, when someone offers support to others to enable them to "stand up" by oneself.

The second section is about Collaboration, and consists of two chapters, which affirm "power with" through working together with others. In "Synergy," they learn that even when an independent person decides to take actions, working in groups is necessary for efficiency and effectiveness. Stories like collaboration among migratory geese are used here to illustrate collaboration. The content of the second

Table 5.5 Structure of the MMO training: Categorizing the training chapters

Category	Chapters on Self-reliance: For affirming "power from within"	Chapters on Collaboration: For affirming "power with"	Chapters on Application: For affirming "power to" and "power over"
Name of chapters	2. Self-identity 3. Self-respect and commitment 4. Self-Reliance 5. Body, mind and spirit	6. Synergy 7. Mental health	8. Social Capitals and Leadership 9. Agrobusiness 10. Soil

Elaborated by the author based on INTA, UNAG, JICA (2012)

chapter "Mental health" is about the fact that it is human nature to cooperate to survive, and hence collaboration yields mental stability and health.

The final section containing three chapters is about Application; how to apply the knowledge acquired in training sessions in agricultural activities, which are for affirming "power to" and "power over" through working in environment and alternating power structures. In the "Social capital and leadership" chapter, the importance of looking to their environment as a source of capital and resources, categorized into natural, material, economic, personal, and social capital, shows participants how to make use of other capitals/resources effectively. They also recognize that the most important traits of a leader are to understand deeply the nature of capital (including human capital), and to find how to utilize its potential and special qualities. The example used here is a case study of an innovative union that illustrates both self-reliance and synergy. The main messages of "Agribusiness" are that in agricultural product sales there are three parties, the sellers, the brokers, and the producers, that producers must organize or they will have difficulty seeing profits, and finally that the specifics of the flow of goods from the producer to the consumer must be understood. Here, there are two fables taken from Peter Senge's *The Fifth Discipline:* "The Lukewarm-water Frog" (producers) and the "The Crocodiles" (brokers). In the final chapter "Soil," the nature of soil is studied, referring to knowledge of soil science that will allow effective utilization of soil resources.

The training methods in all the sessions are quite simple. Each training session consists of ice-breaking, questions and answers, reading fables or anecdotes associated to the theme, the sharing of experiences from participants, and a summary by the facilitator. The basic progression of the seminar is simple: that all participants answer the same questions, while all other participants listen closely.

4 Analysis: Context Specific Factors and Plausible Mechanisms of Agency Development

This section analyses three of the structural processes in MMO, which are: (1) context; (2) promotion of agency through making a development project; and (3) the dynamics of agency enhancement. This is achieved through application of the project to the understanding of the mechanisms of agency development in contextualized situations also connected with academic theories. The author first clarifies the context specific factors that have influenced the development of the MMO (4-1). Second, the processes of agency development of core facilitators (project counterparts) and village level facilitators (community leaders) are explained and connected with academic theories when appropriate (4-2, 4-3). Finally, the mechanisms of the agency development of village level participants (community members) are analyzed to fill the black boxes of the theoretical framework outlined in Table 5.3 (4-4).

4.1 Context Specific Factors Behind the Process

As expressed in the previous section, the MMO process has been influenced by context specific factors. The first is Mr. Nohara's background and personality. He has rich experience in "human development" as he has been involved in social movements and purged, exiled and then welcomed back to his home country, working in agricultural cooperatives to support farmer livelihoods. Additionally, he has a wide range of academic backgrounds and interests, such as theology, philosophy, agriculture, psychology and organizational management, which are all strongly related to human nature and well-being. Thus, it is perhaps his life work to explore what it means to live well, and how we can support others to pursue their own well-being by themselves. His background and experience richly support the contents of training programs as well as the selection of episodes/stories utilized in the texts. Then there is Mr. Nohara's personality, which generates overwhelming trust and respect. From the on-site investigation, it was understood that that he is respected and trusted far and wide, not only by his counterparts in training program-creation, or in the JICA project and other projects, but also by local women in the villages as well as the Minister of Agriculture and Forestry. His background and personality can thus be linked to the reasons why the training sessions have been implemented so widely within and beyond the project villages.

The other context specific factors are rather more associated with Nicaraguan socio-cultural specificities. First is the social acknowledgement of volunteer activities and cooperative works in Nicaraguan history. Of those interviewed during the investigations, several had also volunteered under the Sandinista administration in the 1980s, or volunteered at some other NGO, or were members of the producers' unions, and so on. Nicaragua has a relatively long history of socialist government and, combined with the influence of Christian culture, it can be said that a foundation for volunteerism and benevolence toward others already existed. Nicaragua has also experimented with social movements such as literacy training based on Freire's methods and liberation theology that have socialist aspects. Second, judging from comments received from people in the villages, such as "I had never heard the word 'self-respect' before," it is likely that the training program has a strong novelty and freshness for those leading information-limited lives. In reality, however, in those target villages that were located near cities or villages in which many people went to work at sewing factories and received their wages in cash, there was not much analysis of the training program's effectiveness. Third, reading through reports, it was found that residents can probably receive external support when necessary (though not sufficiently), helping them not to become demotivated.

4.2 Agency Development of Core Facilitators (2002–2007)

In 2001, Mr. Nohara went to Nicaragua for a few months for training content development. Although the inspiration and major ideas of MMO were from Mr. Nohara, the program has been developed based on the needs and knowledge of the Nicaraguan core facilitators, who are staff of the government or NGO members working at central or municipal-level branch offices. This is due to the fact that Mr. Nohara had no intention of creating a textbook for his training program, and hence he did not know the sources of the fables, anecdotes, and concept maps that were created through exchanging dialogue during training sessions. The Nicaraguan core facilitators have mainly edited the training text, though they have not been paid extra for this task. Nevertheless, it can be confirmed that Mr. Nohara is very much respected, and that, through MMO training program development, a good relationship of trust has been built among the core facilitators in the twelve years of its existence.

One of the possible academic theories explaining the strong ownership held by the core facilitators is self-determination theory, a major school of psychology. According to this theory, individuals have three innate needs to be motivated: a need for autonomy (the desire to be the source of one's own actions); a need for competence (the desire that one's actions have an effect on others or one's environment), and a need for interpersonal connections (the desire to build connections with others). Many experimental studies suggest that the circumstances in which these needs are to a certain extent fulfilled facilitates autonomous motivation (i.e., the will to commence and continue identified actions) (Deci & Richard, 1999). This theory, when applied to the MMO case, seems to explain the observed phenomena well. First, the Nicaraguan core facilitators chose and determined the MMO training program content, editing, and projects that satisfied the need for autonomy. Second, he program contents had a favorable effect on themselves, those around them, and their environment and satisfied their need for competence, and finally, through executing and editing the training programs, good personal relationships were established that satisfied their desire to build connections with others. In this way, the Nicaraguan members can be thought to have fostered a sense of agency and a trust relationship through developing the contents of MMO.

4.3 Agency Development of Village Level Facilitators (2009–2013)

Between 2009 and 2013, the JICA project *Alianza Comunitaria* was implemented in twelve village communities within three cities in three prefectures, and the local facilitators selected from village level communities were trained. These executed MMO training sessions not only in their own communities, but also in neighboring communities, including at schools and city councils. On observing the training sessions being carried out, it was confirmed that they have digested and internalized the contents quire well and are able to handle the sessions with confidence. It was also witnessed that training methods have been quite simple, and that providing MMO training sessions has contributed to their confidence levels.

Although these phenomena can be explained through the use of self-determination theory, there could be also other explanatory frameworks, given the fact that village level facilitators have not necessarily been able to handle the training content at the beginning. For instance, their education level is relatively low. The author noticed that many of them could not write grammatically correct Spanish phrases. Through domicile visits, it was also observed that they were not necessarily the better off people in their communities.

It is worth thinking about what enables people without much money and formal education to handle the training contents confidently. The following reasons possibly explain this phenomenon, backed up by some academic theories. The first is probably the loose application of Freire's theory of *concientizacion* (raising consciousness or critical consciousness) in this context, which itself is a representative of classic individual and social transformation theory. Though the phrase itself does not directly appear in the MMO training program textbook, it does appear repeatedly in interviews with Mr. Nohara. He explains the concept as "over coming oppressive conditions and fostering thoughts and behavioral patterns that create better conditions for individuals' lives and society's future." Freire and Macedo (1998) suggests that it is a process of developing an awareness of one's social reality through reflection and action, which is a sociopolitical educative tool that engages learners in questioning the nature of their historical and social situation, or "reading the world". In the training itself, the theory is applied by the simple method of "answering a question by each participant", "question-driven discussions" and "the interpretation and application of stories/tales (fables and anecdotes) to real life."

The second is the use of stories (anecdotes and fables) for raising conciseness through reflections. There are seventeen stories printed in the current textbook. In fact, in the textbook that participants carry back to their homes, there is nothing but anecdotes and fables. This method of expression and transmission of social messages by story rather than direct explanation has been used in mythology and folklore since antiquity to deliver social messages (Nakazawa, 2002). There are a couple of reasons why this method is supportive of agency development for MMO. The first is familiarity. The participants can feel an association with the stories that are commonly heard in their daily life, as well as understanding that story telling is a common way to deliver messages. For example, biblical stories or in novels in the text are based on stories that they also listen to in churches that they go to.

The third reason is accessibility. Given that stories are told colloquially and in relatively easy to understand words, or are easy to ask somebody to read aloud even if they cannot read well, the recipients can understand the contents without feeling intimidated. Children without much education can also understand the contents. The fourth follows from this fact, and is the flexibility to allow interpretation by storytellers, which facilitates knowledge creation with ownership leading to agency development, as well as internalization of the social messages. One of the main features of storytelling is that, although the stories are easy even for children to understand and remember, they allow many varied and complex interpretations and versions or retellings. Even in the actual MMO training seminar, a story in the training textbook was re-interpreted frequently, or even fashioned into a brand-new story. Storytelling is an ancient but also contemporary method applied in the field of business management studies, and utilized in various companies for product ideas or to share values, to train employees, and/or to sell products (Nakahara & Nagaoka, 2009).

The fifth factor is the strategies for increasing replicability through making the training program content as simple as possible. The core of the MMO seminar consists of three parts: questions (all participants answer a question written on a card), storytelling and reflection (volunteer participants read aloud the stories of life experiences related to them so that they are shared among participants), and the summary of the sessions given by the facilitator. The tools necessary for the training program include easily acquired items like markers, paper (simili or imitation vellum), cards (cut to easily usable sizes), and masking tape. To prevent the content of the program from diverging too widely across villages and central areas though, municipal-level members serve a liaison function, participating in training sessions at both central and village levels to alleviate discrepancies in contents and to share information relating to all sessions.

The point that is consistent throughout the above methods is that the theory, language, and tools utilized are quite simple but profound, and are familiar or close to the people's everyday lives. Therefore, it is easy for village facilitators to convey the content of the training program to others, which likely leads to increased self-confidence as well. On the topic of raising consciousness, in the course of the program, facilitators are not asked to have complicated skills to lead the training, but to "just listen carefully" to each and every participant's experiences and opinions, treating them as valuable knowledge. Regarding the usage of stories and their interpretation and application in the daily lives of participants, a wide variety of interpretations may be given though a simple method, and this can be said to grant the interpreter creative space or self-expression as a protagonist. Further, because liaisons are in place, which mean that some core facilitators are stationed at local levels, local facilitators can always ask for inquiries on the training as well as discussions on the contents, and this creates a sense of solidarity and security that can be interpreted as fostering relationships of trust.

4.4 Agency Development of the Village Level Training Participants (2009–)

"MMO is my second bible. I have become able to live with pride. It taught me ways to be both independent and also collaborative with others", and "I am sharing the training contents at home and beyond" were the most heard comments at the village level training participants throughout the field research. From this impact research

4 Analysis: Context Specific Factors and Plausible Mechanisms of Agency Development   83

Table 5.6 A process model of agency development of MMO participants

Process of agency development	Corresponding chapters of MMO training sessions	Explanations of how agency development is facilitated at each process
First process: Affirming "power from within" of self to commit to self and others	Chapters on Self-Reliance 2. Self-identity 3. Self-respect and commitment 4. Self-Reliance 5. Body, heart, and mind	By repeatedly receiving the message through content and attitude in training sessions that "your existence itself is valuable 'bundle of potential,'" a participant recursively recognizes her/himself as an existence with full of potentialities. This feeling is strengthened by the experience of "Self-Reliance" through acting upon others and one's environment.
Second process: Affirming "power with": working together with others	Chapters on Collaboration 6. Mental health 7. Synergy	The participants learn that it is more effective and efficient to cooperate with others for solving problems, which is also "natural" for human beings and understand that they can affirm "power from within" of others and rely on them.
Third process: Affirming "power to" and "power over": working to environment and alternating power structures	Chapters on Application 8. Social capital and leadership 9. Agribusiness 10. Soil	The participants learn and practice collective resource management; seeing into what exists in their surrounding as resources and understanding their natures and act upon them. They also learn alternating power relations through working together.

Elaborated by the author combining Table 5.3 and 5.5

(Comunitaria, 2010), it was also found that more than 95% of training participants have talked about the training contents at home. In this section, three hypothetical process mechanisms or dynamics of agency development incorporating training participants that have been attempted by the MMO, to fill the black boxes in the research framework of Table 5.3, are formulated to aid in the understanding of how it is intended to enhance several types of agency in practice; a task that is not easily explained by existing theories (Table 5.6).

4.4.1 The First Process (Chapters on Self-Reliance): Affirming "Power from Within" of Self

The work on Self-Reliance consists of four chapters: "Self-identity" (everyone is a special presence no matter the circumstances), "Self-respect and Commitment" (every person is the protagonist in his or her own life when committing to oneself and others), "Body, mind and spirit" (how setbacks happen and how to avoid to be caught up in them), and "Self-Reliance" (a summary of the preceding points sharing participants' experiences of becoming independent physically and mentally). In process terms, the most important defining feature of the MMO training program is that, unlike typical self-development seminars, it begins not with raising awareness of self-reliance but with a fundamental affirmation of one's existence itself. In the training program itself, the first chapter that precedes "self-esteem and commitment" and "independent" is a chapter named "self-identity". Here the message, oft-repeated by program organizers and directed at the participants, is that "the very existence of each and every individual is a miracle, precious, and full of potential." This message is emphasized through the seminar policy of letting all participants express their own opinions, which are listened to carefully and with respect.

What do the participants start perceiving after they receive the message again and again via words and actions? Perhaps it is possible to imagine them thinking the following: first, they recognize the message that "my presence is considered important and valuable by others;" next, perhaps they start thinking, "if I am considered important to others, perhaps it is also possible for me to consider my presence important." This is the beginning of a recursive realization of the value of one's own presence (feeling of self- affirmation), and also of a relationship of trust with oneself (self-confidence). This feeling is strengthened through experiences of commitment to oneself or others through daily actions, and when this commitment being appreciated the participant develops a sense of self-efficacy in that s/he believes that they can now act in the same way on his/her surrounding environment. Gradually, the continuous experience of committing to others leads to increased self-confidence, which helps participants to affirm the "power from within" of oneself. It is important that such affirmation is not generated in vacuum, but in relationships with others in a process like that espoused by the MMO. Voices from the training participants such as "I could feel that I am the protagonist of my life for the training especially through learning the first few chapters," or "most of the aid agencies, political parties or church organizations have proposed that, in the context of their own interests such as agriculture, children's wellbeing or importance, people have faith in God. But the comment that "training truly taught me how to live every moment of everyday of my life fully with much pride and without any flags," bears witnesses to their change with respect to agency during this stage.

4.4.2 The Second Process (Chapters on Collaboration): Affirming "Power with" Working Together with Others

The second set is about Collaboration, and consists of three chapters: "Synergy" (working in groups and divisions of labor are necessary for efficiency and effectiveness); "Mental health" (it is human nature to cooperate to survive, which is also good for mental stability and health); and "Social capital and leadership" (acknowledging their environment as capitals/resources so they can make best use of them, which is also a necessary skill for leaders). Through a collaborative development process within this stage the participants learn that it is more effective and efficient to cooperate with others in solving problems, which is also a "natural" function for human beings in facing real episodes. They also learn that they can affirm "power with" by working together with others, and by relying on them through shared experiences and the learning case studies of successful cooperatives, as well as by reflecting on their daily work in cooperatives. As positive relationships among participants have already been established in the first stage, it can be assumed that they can relatively understand the contents of the sessions. Many participants also suggested that they started talking to and listening more to their own family members, as well as learning that they could do things more effectively in the cooperatives they belonged to when they collaborated more closely.

4.4.3 The Third Process (Chapters on Application): Affirming "Power to" and "Power over": Working to Environment and Alternating Power Structures

The final three chapters are about the application of this model to rural and agricultural development, about "Social capital and leadership" (the importance of looking at their surrounding environment to provide the capital and resources to enhance its potentialities, which is a must for leaders), "Agribusiness" (producers must organize themselves and understand how products are best distributed for profits), and "Soil" (producers must understand the nature of soil scientifically to best utilize it as resource). Through the process based on this stage, the participants learn and practice "collective resource management," and understand the "power to" work upon environment collectively. This enables them to see what exists in their surroundings as resources, to understand their nature, and to act upon them collectively to best develop them. They share their own bitter or positive experiences of agriculture and its business, and how to make plans how to improve their resource management so that they can obtain sustained profits. They also stop relying on brokers and try bringing their own products to the market, as well as holding their own market on the roadside collectively to avoid being exploited by brokers. This can be counted as the experience of "power over".

During the project, there were 27 community and agricultural mini-projects run by community volunteers mainly with their own resources, some of which are still active today. People started to sell vegetables directly on the side of main roads, built a pre-school and water tanks at schools, developed bee-keeping in groups, and facilitated fruit cultivation for home consumption and for selling. Such changes reflect "exercising agency" at this level.

5 Concluding Remarks

The purpose of this paper was to understand factors and elaborate plausible dynamics of agency development in practice by connecting research (academic theories) and practice (development projects), with and clarifying context specificities. For this purpose, the author first reviewed the literature on empowerment and agency development, to comprehend issues and develop a theoretical process model of agency development, identifying their black boxes. Second, the following three parameters of the analyses were identified to truly understand agency development in practice; the black boxes of the theoretical model, the context of an agency development project (stories of practitioners' experiences), and the actual mechanisms used in the agency development of "stakeholders" or "community members". Subsequently, a case study was conducted to analyze the three parameters in detail. A program instituted in Nicaragua called MMO was selected, and the process of its inspiration, development, execution and diffusion was documented. Finally, the case was analyzed to advance understanding of the conditions as well as the mechanisms of agency development in practice, with further reference to related theories.

Regarding the conditions of agency development, what is understood from the case study is that no particular training package can be developed in vacuum and applied to foster the growth in the agency of individuals, no matter where and who these might be. But rather, it was found that the whole process of developing and executing such training programs matters in multilayer structures. First, there are context specific factors influencing the whole process, such as the upbringing and experience of the key personnel, and the socio-cultural and economic features of Nicaragua. Second, it was confirmed that there is a process of agency development experienced by the core facilitators as well as village level facilitators, that can be explained by self-determination theory as well as by explanatory frameworks relating to social communication, such as *concientizacion*, storytelling, and devices that increase the replicability of simple training contents and the experience of liaison staff.

Third, in regard to the mechanisms enhancing the agency development of community members, the processes in this change were explained to fill the black boxes of the theoretical framework, thus allowing understanding of what is actually done in practice to foster the four types of power or agency; "power from within", "power with", "power to" and "power over". It was confirmed that each block of MMO training chapters fosters different types of power/agency in a loosely incremental manner.

In conclusion, it should be noted that some issues have been identified through this research. The first is a methodological constraint. The author wrote out the practical knowledge "as is" in field notes to the greatest extent possible, and then interpreted these to build the hypothetical model; but it is difficult to judge with absolute certainty that the specific academic fields quoted in the interpretation were the most appropriate, given the limits to possible proof and demonstration. Additionally, in listing the factors that made the case study a "success story," it was not in fact possible to understand how far context specific factors are fundamental and indispensable, when attempting to assess the likely replicability of the training program in other countries. Third, the impact of the training cannot be rigorously measured unless panel data is taken and analyzed.

This is perhaps an indispensable part of the process by which development studies will mature as an empirical science and make a difference to the assessment of context-bound reality. Indeed, this conclusion may mean that "the social sciences that call themselves empirical sciences ought not to aim for rapid growth within specific academic disciplines, but instead consider deeply how a real empirical science can be formed, one faltering step at a time (Uchida, 2000)".

References

Alsop, R., Bertelsen, M. F., & Holland, J. (2006). *Empowerment in Practice: From Analysis to Implementation*. World Bank Publications.
Barker, C. (2003). *Cultural Studies: Theory and Practice*. Sage.
Comunitaria, A. (2010). *Estudio de Impactos y cambios a través de la capacitación de Motivación y Organización*. Alianza Comunitaria, Mimeograph.
Cornwall, A., & Brock, K. (2005). What Do Buzzwords Do for Development Policy? A Critical Look at 'Participation', 'Empowerment 'and 'Poverty Reduction'. *Third World Quarterly, 26*(7), 1043–1060.
Deci, E., & Richard, F. (1999). *Why We Do What We Do: The Dynamics of Personal Autonomy*. Shinyōsha. (Japanese translation).
Dreze, J., & Sen, A. (1989). *Hunger and Public Action*. Clarendon Press.
Drydyk, J. (2008). *How to Distinguish Empowerment from Agency*. Paper presentation, 5th Annual Conference of the HDCA, New Delhi, India, September 10–13.
Freire, A. M. A., & Macedo, D. (1998). *The Paulo Freire Reader*. Cassell and Continuum.
Giddens, A. (1984). *The Constitution of Society: Outline of the Theory of Structuration*. University of California Press.
Gobierno de Reconciliación y Unidad Nacional de Nicaragua. (2009). *Plan Nacional de Desarrollo Humano 2009–2011*. Nicaragua.
Hanawa, N. (2011). *Nikaraguakoku nouson kaihatsu no tame no komyunitii kyouka keikaku houkokusho (sankagata kaihatsu/chihou gyousei)*. Rural Development Institute.
Haraway, D. (1988). Situated Knowledges: The Science Question in Feminism and the Privilege of Partial Perspective. *Feminist Studies, 14*(3), 575–599.
Hickey, S., & Mohan, G. (2008). *Participation: From Tyranny to Transformation* [Participation: From Tyranny to Transformation: Exploring New Approaches to Participation in Development]. Akashi Shoten.
Ibrahim, S., & Alkire, S. (2007). Agency and Empowerment: A Proposal for Internationally Comparable Indicators. *Oxford Development Studies, 35*(4), 379–403.
INIDE. (2008). *ENDESA 2006–2007*. Instituto Nacional de Información de Desarrollo.
Instituto Nicaraguense de Tecnología Agropecuaria, Unión Nacional de Agricultores y Ganaderos de Nicaragua, & Japan International Cooperation Agency. (2004, 2005, 2007, 2012). *Metodologia de Motivación y Organización*. Nicaragua.
Kabeer, N. (1994). *Reversed Realities: Gender Hierarchies in Development Thought*. Verso.
Kabeer, N. (1999). Resources, Agency, Achievements: Reflections on the Measurement of Women's Empowerment. *Development and Change, 30*(3), 435–464.
Kuzasa, I. (2013). *Senmonka shuryoji houkokusho*. JICA.
Malhotra, A., & Schuler, S. R. (2005). Women's Empowerment as a Variable in International Development. *Measuring Empowerment: Cross-Disciplinary Perspectives, 1*(1), 71–88.
Medina, F., & Bernales, M. (2009). *Encuesta de Hogares Sobre Medición del Nivel de Vida 2009. (EMNV 2009). Principales resultados: Pobreza, Consumo, Ingreso*. Instituto Nacional de Información de Desarrollo (INIDE), Managua (Nicaragua).
Ministry of Farming and Forestry. (2010). *Plan Sectorial PRORURAL Incluyente*. Nicaragua.
Nakahara, J., & Nagaoka, K. (2009). *Daiaroogu: Taiwa suru soshiki*. Diamond Sha.
Nakazawa, S. (2002). *Jinrui saiko no tetsugaku—kaie sobaaju I*. Kodansha.
Narayan-Parker, D. (2002). *Empowerment and Poverty Reduction: A Sourcebook*. World Bank Publications.
Narayan-Parker, D. (2005). *Measuring Empowerment: Cross-Disciplinary Perspectives*. World Bank Publications.
Rowlands, J. (1997). *Questioning Empowerment: Working with Women in Honduras*. Oxfam.
Sato, M. (2015). *Evaluación de impactos y sostenibilidad en la autogestión individual y colectiva de comunidades atendidas por el proyecto Alianza Comunitaria: Logros, dificultades, cambios y perspectivas*. Alianza Comunitaria.

Sen, A. (1985). Well-Being, Agency and Freedom: The Dewey Lectures 1984. *The Journal of Philosophy, 82*(4), 169–221.
Sen, A. (1999). *Development as Freedom*. Anchor.
Uchida, Y. (2000). *Ikiru koto, manabu koto*. Fujiwara shoten.
Yamaguchi, Y. (2011). *Nikaragua-koku nouson kaihatsu no tame no komyuniti kyouka purojekuto shuuryouji hyouka chousaji hyouka chousa (hyouka bunseki)*.

Websites Consulted

Japan International Cooperation Agency. (n.d.). *Project Overview*. Retrieved July 23, 2021, from http://www.jica.go.jp/project/nicaragua/003/outline/index.html
The World Bank. (n.d.). *Nicaragua*. Retrieved July 23, 2021, from http://data.worldbank.org/country/nicaragua

Chapter 6
Breaking the Poverty Trap: A Psychological Framework for Sustainably Facilitating Agency and Behavior Change in Development Aid Beneficiaries

1 Introduction

1.1 The Focus of This Chapter

This chapter will propose a theoretical framework based on self-determination theory (SDT) to facilitate agency, especially for people who face difficulties such as extreme poverty, through the enhancing of autonomous motivation. The explicit focus of the chapter will be poverty reduction among beneficiaries of development aid projects, but the theory can be applied to other populations as well, including those who are not necessarily facing such difficulties as poverty. The latter part of this chapter will examine some selective development aid schemes through the lens of the proposed theory.

1.2 The Fight Against Poverty

In recent years, the fight against poverty has seen significant progress. The United Nation's Millennium Development Goals (MDGs) of halving the proportion of people who live on less than $1.25 a day in developing countries between 1990 and 2015 was met 5 years ahead of the target date (World Bank & International Monetary Fund, 2012, p. 2). Some optimistic predictions claim that extreme poverty can be eradicated by 2030 (World Bank, 2013). With several notable leaders and celebrities advocating for the issue, and the Sustainable Development Goals (SDGs), the scheme succeeding the MDGs, presenting "No Poverty" as the first among its 17 goals, global awareness of the topic is increasing.

This chapter is an updated revision of Sayanagi (2017a, 2017b) that has also been edited for consistency with the other chapters of this volume. Significant revisions will be denoted with footnotes.

© The Author(s), under exclusive license to Springer Nature Singapore Pte Ltd. 2022
M. Sato et al., *Empowerment Through Agency Enhancement*,
https://doi.org/10.1007/978-981-19-1227-6_6

However, there is still much to be understood, and many misconceptions regarding poverty and the poor. As Banerjee and Duflo (2011, p. viii) remind us, "the field of anti-poverty policy is littered with the detritus of instant miracles that proved less than miraculous." It could be said that these failed policies are based on misunderstandings of the complexities of how those living in poverty behave, and how their subjective experiences influence their behavior.

One pioneering work on the subjective experience of poverty is Oscar Lewis' (1966) classic ethnographic study of Mexican families. Lewis asserted that when people fall into poverty, they form attitudes and behaviors to cope with the economic deprivation. While these attitudes and behaviors may help them get by on a day-to-day basis, oftentimes they decrease their long-term chances of escaping from poverty. It could be said that such attitudes and behaviors could be seen as a lack of agency from an outsider, as they do not lead to the improvement of living conditions. Additionally, these attitudes and behaviors are passed on through socialization to subsequent generations, causing a vicious cycle that has come to be known as the poverty trap (e.g., Pick & Sirkin, 2010; Sachs, 2005).

Lewis' (1966) assertion that poverty is a culture has been frequently criticized. The crux of these criticisms is that his depiction of the characteristics of poverty, including alcoholism, domestic violence, and inability to delay gratification or plan for the future, encourages thinking that poverty is due to cultural inadequacies of the poor (Tuason, 2002), and "[do] not envision any room for dynamic self-improvement" (Carr, 2013, p. 17). In fairness, Lewis did note the positive and adaptive characteristics of the poor, and stressed that they should also be taken into account. Nonetheless, many policies and projects based on his thinking indeed only focused on "remedying the pathological traits" of the poor (Goode, 2010), rather than building on their strengths. This kind of victim-blaming, based on the notion that poverty is self-inflicted, makes it difficult to garner public support for the funding and implementation of anti-poverty projects and policies. There is a tendency of humans, known as the classical social psychology concept of the *fundamental attribution error* (Ross, 1977), to overestimate the internal characteristics of an agent and underestimate contextual factors regarding the causes of another person's behavior. That is, people are predisposed to perceive that a poor person's behavior is a result of their character even when the reason for the behavior is due to context of their environment. This bias itself makes it difficult to rally support for the poor. It could be said that the "culture of poverty" thesis (Lewis, 1966) inadvertently exacerbated this underlying human bias towards those who are impoverished.

The victim-blaming view of poverty is problematic in several other ways, too, but this chapter will focus on two of such. First, as Lott (2002) asserts, even well-meaning efforts on behalf of low-income people can be predicated on assumptions about their inferiority and can ultimately hinder their advancement (p. 108). In other words, to provide support effectively and ethically for those who are poor, it is important to understand their subjective experiences and their strengths and preferences. The second, and perhaps more important reason that victim-blaming is detrimental, is that it flies against the body of evidence which supports the current dominant thinking that the major cause of poverty is the lack of opportunity rather

1 Introduction

than faulty cultural or personality traits (see Sen, 1999 for a comprehensive review and thesis). For anti-poverty policies to be effective, they must address the root cause of poverty (i.e., lack of opportunity) rather than its artifacts (i.e., the so-called pathological cultural/personality traits).

But would simply implementing policies that provide the poor with plenty of opportunities be enough to alleviate poverty? In his treatise on the Capability Approach, Sen (1999) gives a strong and convincing argument for the necessity of providing opportunities to the poor, but he is not clear whether *simply* providing opportunities would also be sufficient; he does not directly address the issue, and the lack of attention to the matter gives the impression that simply providing opportunities would indeed alleviate poverty. However, Pick and Sirkin (2010), who have done extensive field work with the extremely impoverished, point out that "objectively having opportunities is not sufficient: the individual must perceive having access. In other words, a person must emotionally and cognitively see the opportunities and understand that he has the right to access them, that he need not feel ashamed, fearful, or guilty for making use of them" (p. 6). That is, there are *psychological* barriers even when "objective" barriers have been removed. Additionally, there is evidence that even when all barriers, whether objective or psychological, have been taken down, such opportunities are not well used. For example, Neuman and Celano (2012) showed in a series of studies that due to differences in parental supervision and other habitual factors, poor children are not able to gain as much information capital from libraries as their peers from more affluent families, even when they are able to use facilities that were on par with their more privileged peers. This study's subjects were children, but it would be reasonable to assume that the same would apply to adults living in poverty.

The ultimate goal of many anti-poverty policies is to change the behavior of the poor in a manner that would help them break the vicious cycle of poverty: in the context of this book, this could be paraphrased as "anti-poverty policies aim to enhance the agency of the poor." However, the fact that many policies have failed is a testament to the difficulty of changing the behaviors of the poor, even if ample opportunities are provided to change in a way that would help them escape from poverty. Furthermore, studies such as Neuman and Celano (2012) suggest that simply providing accessible opportunities may not be enough, and additional measures may be necessary for the poor to be able to fully utilize them.

Some behavioral patterns of the poor indeed keep them at a socioeconomic disadvantage, and in many cases those behavioral patterns are passed on to their children, as Lewis (1966) asserted. While this chapter will desist from calling the behavioral patterns of the poor a "culture," it will hold that there are certain behavioral and habitual patterns of the poor that make it difficult for them to improve their livelihoods, and that such patterns are difficult to change. One speculation as to why such change is hard to achieve is that when people are born and grow up in a certain environment, they have little opportunity to learn of lifestyles and habits beyond those prevalent in their surroundings. Thus, even when presented with more rational but novel choices, such as would happen when a development aid program is introduced to an impoverished region, the beneficiaries would rather retain the ways that they are used to.[1]

1.3 The Literature on Poverty in Psychology

While there has been interest in issues regarding poverty in the field of psychology (e.g., American Psychological Association, 2000), there are still relatively few studies, and a former president of the American Psychological Association has called for more psychologists to join the cause (Davis & Williams, 2020). Many of the studies that have been conducted have been in the context of health and education, especially on the detrimental impact of poverty on developmental, cognitive, and educational outcomes and how to alleviate such impacts in children (e.g., Brown et al., 2013; Keiffer, 2008; McWayne et al., 2016; Reynolds et al., 2019; Yoshikawa et al., 2012). Few studies examine the psychological experiences of poor adolescents and adults with the objective of identifying factors that could potentially enhance agency and lift them out of poverty. Psychological studies on the prevention and reduction of poverty would complement and enhance the body of knowledge on anti-poverty policy. As Carr (2013) points out, in the past "most of the thinking about poverty has been relatively macro in kind, and level of analysis" (p. 10), and psychology can meet the deficit in micro needs. The existing anti-poverty studies conducted from the viewpoint of policy and administration focus on *what* we should do to fight poverty. From a psychological viewpoint, however, that is only part of the question: *how* the projects and policies are conducted is also critical for their success. Instead of asking which approach works better, as seems to be the prevailing question in development aid circles, psychology could provide means to explore how each respective approach could be improved to work better, and perhaps more importantly examine *why* each approach does or doesn't work.

In any case, there have been few psychological studies on poverty reduction. Below we shall review the handful of approaches that take a poverty-reduction stance.

In a series of studies, Tuason (2002, 2010, 2013) conducted interviews with people who had lived in poverty in the Philippines. The studies compared the experiences of those who were able to escape poverty and those who remained poor. Both groups were very similar in their subjective experiences, which included not having basic needs met, persisting negative emotions, attributing their poverty to family circumstances, and methods of coping with poverty. The differences were the occurrence of chance events that provided opportunities for education and emigration, underscoring the importance of opportunities.

---

[1] Irrational decision-making is by no ways limited to the poor. Countless studies in social psychology and behavioral economics have demonstrated that it is a hallmark of human beings in general, and whole books have been dedicated to the topic (e.g., Ariely, 2008). Additionally, it has been indicated that living in poverty further strains cognitive capacities, hindering rational decision-making (Dean et al., 2017; Haushofer & Fehr, 2014).

1 Introduction

In the field of development aid, Carr and colleagues have accumulated several studies which have been reviewed in several volumes focusing on psychological issues relevant to anti-poverty and aid, including the fundamental attribution error against the poor (discussed above), the importance of the culturally sensitive attitudes of aid workers and donors, community organization, and aid systems (e.g., Carr, 2013; Carr et al., 1998; Carr & Sloan, 2003). These views are indeed important in planning and implementing aid projects, but Carr and colleagues' main focus is the psychology of the aid providers, and there are few data on the psychology of the beneficiaries.

Pick and Sirkin's (2010) Framework for Enabling Empowerment (FrEE), which is based on their fieldwork and aid work with the poor and thus reflects the subjective viewpoint of those living in poverty, offers a more direct approach to providing support for beneficiaries. Their person-centered and culturally sensitive approach is based on the theory of planned behavior (TPB: Ajzen, 1991) and is informed by the Capability Approach (Sen, 1999). FrEE was originally developed through sexual health education for young women in Mexico, and has since been adapted to other educational programs such as domestic violence prevention, parental education, and community development. Pick and colleagues developed their approach through fieldwork spanning three decades, and also provide evidence that their approach is indeed effective. FrEE is certainly informative, and in fact is in many ways similar to the framework to be presented in this chapter, as will be discussed in detail later.

That there are few other bodies of psychological studies on development aid and poverty reduction is somewhat surprising, as specialists in the field of development aid have long been aware that the psychology of aid subjects is a critical factor in whether programs will succeed or not. Alkire (2005, 2007) has asserted that the psychological dimension of the lives of the poor needs to be brought to the foreground along with the other well-studied dimensions. Kukita (1996) has gone as far as to propose the creation of a field for the psychology of development aid. More recently, the 2015 issue of the *World Development Report* (World Bank, 2015), one of the most influential publications in development aid, was subtitled *Mind, Society, and Behavior*, obviously an allusion to psychological factors. In 2021, the United Nations Innovation Network (2021) released the *United Nations Behavoural Science Report*, asserting that understanding the psychology of beneficiaries is essential for aid to be effective. However, most of the empirical studies cited in these reports are from economics journals, and there are few publications from psychology journals. This seeming lack of interest on the side of psychology is perhaps partially because there are few theoretical frameworks that have been shown to be viable for both practice and research in the context of development aid, and consequently, few empirical psychological measures have been developed (see also Chap. 9 of this volume) to readily allow quantitative research—the preferred mode of study in psychology—in the field. Providing methods for empirical evaluation are crucial in psychological research, and the lack of such is probably another reason that inhibits psychologists, who work in a discipline where there is much pressure to publish in quantity, from entering the field of development aid.[2]

1.4 The Aim of This Chapter

The main goal of this chapter is to present a theoretical framework regarding the psychology of the beneficiaries of development aid that would be helpful in understanding their behaviors and motivations, and that could potentially guide anti-poverty policies to be more effective. The framework would also pave a path for empirical psychological research to be systematically conducted in the field of development aid.

The theoretical framework will be developed based upon SDT (Ryan & Deci, 2000, 2002, 2017), but will also be informed by behavior modification approaches (which as implied by the name are based in behaviorism). To one who is familiar with motivational theories, this combination may seem puzzling: behavior modification is based on operant conditioning techniques, that is, using incentives to induce changes in behavior; SDT was developed for the most part by demonstrating the adverse effects of such rewards. Also, behavior modification is generally mechanistic and relatively reductionist, while SDT is humanistic and relatively holistic. However, as will be discussed in detail later, both approaches have their limitations. In a nutshell, the biggest limitations of SDT is that it has been developed mostly through studies with "normative" subjects[3] such as university students and suburban American schoolchildren, where indeed the negative effects of rewards have been robustly demonstrated. There has been little focus, however, on underprivileged subjects, and as a result there is a lack of evidence on whether the theory holds, especially regarding behavior change, for this group. Furthermore, some studies imply that the autonomy-supporting approaches prescribed by SDT are somewhat ineffective in bringing about behavior change in subjects who are at a disadvantage. In contrast, the limitation of the behavior modification approaches is that the inducing of behavior change, which has been shown to be effective with subjects of diverse socioeconomic backgrounds but especially with those with difficulties, seems to be mostly temporary. It will be argued that these two seemingly contradicting approaches in fact are complementary in terms of predicting and promoting

---

[2] It should be clarified that the author also strongly endorses qualitative research methods, especially for the initial stages of researching a new field. However, while qualitative research is important, it is inherently time consuming. Providing a systematic framework that would more easily allow quantitative research would lower the hurdle for psychologists aspiring to enter the field of development aid.

[3] The term "subject," while used ubiquitously in psychology, may be unfamiliar in development aid literature. The term simply denotes the people who are the focus of any given study. The term "normative," also commonly used in psychological literature, denotes that there is no significant deviance from the majority of a given population.

sustainable behavior change, and consequently agency, especially in subjects facing adversities such as extreme poverty.

Next, the chapter will examine existing aid paradigms using the new theoretical framework. Needless to say, anti-poverty approaches in the field of development aid are diverse and abundant. This chapter does not aim to conduct an exhaustive examination of the full catalogue of such approaches. Instead, it will focus on a few selective programs that aim, whether explicitly or implicitly, to change the behavior of their beneficiaries. Many of these programs are so-called *capacity development* approaches that aim to enhance the aid beneficiaries' abilities to work themselves out of poverty. Thus, this chapter will not investigate programs such as infrastructure building, which certainly are important in improving the lives of the inhabitants of impoverished regions but do not aim to induce specific behavior changes. The anti-poverty programs that this chapter will examine will be conditional cash transfers (CCTs) (e.g., Cecchini & Madariaga, 2011; Levy, 2008), the life improvement approach (LIA: Kozaki & Nakamura, 2017; Tanaka, 2011), the smallholder horticulture empowerment project (SHEP) approach (Aikawa, 2013), and the aforementioned FrEE (Pick & Sirkin, 2010). These approaches were selected because (1) they all explicitly aim to foster behavior that will help the beneficiaries escape poverty, (2) they are all regarded to be relatively successful, and (3) they are all well-defined and administered in multiple areas/projects. Even under these criteria, the four approaches are not an exhaustive list, but for the purpose of this chapter, which is to demonstrate the application of the proposed theoretical framework, it should be sufficient. Through this demonstration, this chapter will attempt to identify potential factors in capacity development programs that are key to sustainable behavior change.

Finally, the chapter will discuss methods to empirically validate and systematically research the theoretical framework. Such a framework would provide a comprehensive theory that encompasses operable antecedents that are necessary for sustainable behavior change, specific guidelines on how to promote such change, and criteria to evaluate the changes in motivation and behavior. Additionally, this framework will be applicable not just to a specific approach, but to any aid paradigm.

2 An Outline of the Theoretical Framework

This section will present outlines of SDT and behavior modification, the two respective theoretical approaches that the framework will be based upon, and following each outline, will discuss the shortcomings of each approach. Finally, a modified SDT framework and approach that would be useful in promoting sustainable behavior change, especially in subjects with challenges such as extreme poverty, will be proposed.

2.1 An Outline of Self-Determination Theory (SDT)

SDT is a relatively new theory in psychology. Its beginnings were studies on intrinsic motivation published in the early 1970s. In his classic study, Deci (1971) demonstrated that giving rewards that are contingent with performance on an initially interesting task *decreases* the amount of subsequent free-choice engagement in the absence of rewards. This phenomenon, the *undermining effect*, is counterintuitive and also contrary to what behaviorist theory would predict. Nonetheless, these findings are robust, having been replicated time and again (e.g., see Deci et al., 1999 for a meta-analytic review). When a person is intrinsically motivated, he or she is driven by interest or enjoyment in the task itself, rather than aiming to attain an outcome that is extrinsic to the task. Motivation to attain such outcomes, such as to gain a reward or to avoid punishment, is called extrinsic motivation. It is important to note that in SDT, the motivation behind a given behavior is not necessarily single: a student may study to pass an upcoming exam (extrinsic motivation), but at the same time be studying because they enjoy studying the topic (intrinsic motivation).

SDT studies in the 1970s through the early 80s primarily focused on the conditions that undermine intrinsic motivation: these studies showed that such conditions include not only performance-contingent rewards, but also punishment, deadlines, quotas, surveillance, competition, and evaluation (see Deci, 1975; and Deci & Ryan, 1985, for reviews). During this period, intrinsic and extrinsic motivation were treated somewhat dichotomously, with a trade-off between the two (i.e., that the increase of extrinsic motivation would undermine intrinsic motivation).

Since the 1980s, SDT has moved beyond the intrinsic versus extrinsic dichotomy. Extrinsic motivation is now considered to have more autonomous and heteronomous states. For example, a student may study because the subject is important for their chosen career, or they may study because they do not want to be scolded by their demanding parents. Both reasons are extrinsic in the sense that they aim to attain an outcome that is not inherent to the activity itself: however, in the case of the former, the student personally endorses the value of the activity, while in the latter, they are merely complying to an external demand. The former is a relatively autonomous state of extrinsic motivation, while the latter is relatively controlled. As Ryan and Deci (2000) point out, the former would be "the type that is sought by astute socializing agents" (p. 71). Indeed, it has been shown that autonomous motivation is generally associated with a wide range of more desirable outcomes than controlled motivation, including more engagement, better performance, greater persistence, lower dropout rates, and enhanced psychological well-being. These findings have been replicated in a diverse range of domains, including education, health care, religion, physical exercise, political activity, and intimate relationships (for reviews, see Deci & Ryan, 2008; Ryan & Deci, 2000; Ryan & Deci, 2002; Ryan & Deci, 2017). Although there have been no studies that follow up on behavior maintenance in terms of years, there have been several longitudinal studies that span months, and autonomous motivation has been shown to predict sustained behavior (e.g., Kosmala-Anderson et al., 2010; Williams et al., 2006; Wilson et al., 2012).

Autonomy in SDT is defined as a state in which one *perceives* that their own action is self-determined, as opposed to prodded by external forces, and in which one self-endorses that action. Note that the subjective experience of the agent is the key: even if someone seems to be prodded by external forces from the viewpoint of an observer, as long as the agent believes that they are the origin of her action, the action is considered autonomous (see Ryan & Deci, 2006 for a detailed discussion on the SDT concept of autonomy, especially in regard to its distinction from the concept of independence). Intrinsic motivation is a highly autonomous form of motivation and represents the prototypical instance of self-determination (Ryan & Deci, 2000). As discussed in Chap. 3, it can be said that the SDT concept of autonomy is deeply associated with the psychological definition of agency posited in this volume.

Autonomous extrinsic motivation is facilitated through the taking in, or *internalization*, of values related to the task. When a value is internalized, it is assimilated to the self and personally embraced, as opposed to being impersonal and foreign to the self. The more internalized a value is, the greater the degree of autonomy. Internalization may progress incrementally over time, but not necessarily: the values of a new behavior can be internalized relatively deeply from the onset depending on prior experiences and current situational factors (Ryan, 1995).

SDT posits that intrinsic motivation and internalization are facilitated through the support of three basic psychological needs, namely, the needs for autonomy, competence, and relatedness (for a detailed commentary on the basic needs in SDT, see Deci & Ryan, 2000; Ryan & Deci, 2017).

The *need for autonomy* is the existential desire to act in congruence with one's sense of self. When individuals act in congruence with the self, they perceive that they are the originators of their own behaviors and self-endorse the actions. The conceptualization of this need is based on de Charms' (1968) theory of personal causation. Behavior- and performance-contingent rewards cause people to feel as if they are being coerced to act in a certain way, thus thwarting the perception that they are the originator of the action, which in turn causes the decline in autonomous motivation.

The *need for competence* is the desire to interact effectively with one's environment, based on White's (1959) concept of competence. Note that the meaning of *competence* here is not equivalent to the commonly used term but has a much broader connotation. If people feel that their action has a meaningful effect on their environment, they will be motivated to continue the action. Contrarily, if one cannot perceive the desirable effects of their action, they will not be motivated to continue. Take for example a child who is struggling with schoolwork: if they sit in class but do not feel that they understand anything, they probably will not see the value in continuing to sit in class. In order to be motivated to continue to sit in class, they need sufficient support to understand, and thus feel the effects (i.e., learning new and meaningful things) of sitting in class and studying.

The *need for relatedness* is associated with Bowlby's (1969) concept of attachment and represents the need for secure relationships. The importance of relatedness can be seen in an infant's exploratory behavior, which is typically observed when the baby feels secure with the people around.

These three needs are considered to be—and to some extent have empirical support indicating that they are—universal regardless of culture (see Chirkov, 2014; Ryan & Deci, 2011; Ryan & Deci, 2017, for reviews). This chapter mainly addresses the conditions that facilitate behaviors in adult participants of aid projects that would increase their likelihood to work themselves out of poverty, but the theoretical framework could also be applicable to children, for example, who are struggling in school. It is important to note that these needs are of a different nature than physiological drives such as hunger, which would motivate behavior to satisfy the need when there is a deficiency of nutrition. Instead, when these needs are thwarted, internalization would be hindered and thus subsequent behavior would decrease, and additionally psychological well-being would deteriorate.

Among the three needs, autonomy is currently considered to be the most important in SDT, and most research focuses on the effects of environmental contexts that facilitate autonomous motivation focus on the issue of autonomy versus control. Approaches that support the need for autonomy, or *autonomy supportive* approaches, are considered to be the modus operandi to facilitate autonomous motivation and consequently sustained behavior. Autonomy support is typically provided by someone who is in a supervising role regarding a certain task, such as a teacher or parent. While there is no clear definition of autonomy support, the literature generally agrees that it entails encouraging self-initiation, providing choices, minimizing controlling language, providing meaningful rationale, and accepting emotions, thoughts, and reactions regarding the task including resentment and resistance (e.g., Deci et al., 1994; Grolnick et al., 1997; Ryan & Deci, 2017). This may intuitively seem to be a rather "weak" approach to inducing a desired behavior compared to more forceful means, but it has been shown to be effective especially in producing autonomously motivated, and thus sustainable, behavior, as well as other positive outcomes (e.g., Grolnick & Ryan, 1989; Weinstein & Ryan, 2012; Ryan & Deci, 2017).

2.2 *Limitations of SDT's Autonomy Supportive Approach*

While the positive effects of autonomy support have been widely reported (see Deci & Ryan, 2008; Núñez & León, 2015; Su & Reeve, 2011; Vasquez et al., 2016 for reviews and meta-analyses), the majority of these studies have been conducted with "normative" subjects in high-income nations. It could also be said that the target tasks involved in these studies, such as schoolwork and exercise, would not be considered to be particularly novel or extraordinarily difficult or uninteresting to such subjects. In the context of these studies, the proposition that autonomy support is an effective approach for inducing desirable behavior holds well. Note that there is a parallel between this assumption and that of Sen's Capability Approach (Sen, 1999), that just providing opportunity is sufficient for the beneficiaries to utilize their own agency.

However, there are two studies (Deci et al., 1994; Joussemet et al., 2005) that examine uninteresting and novel tasks and indicate that autonomy support is not effective in bringing about behavior change in such contexts.

Deci et al. (1994) conducted an experiment with university students using Deci's (1971) free-choice experimental paradigm, using a boring task in place of an interesting one. The task was to sit in front of a computer and press the space key whenever a dot appeared on the screen. Also, instead of using reward versus no-reward conditions, a 2 × 2 × 2 three-way ANOVA design was employed, with each factor being a component of autonomy support: (1) providing rationale (the activity improves concentration) versus no rationale, (2) acknowledgement of the subjects' possible disinterest versus no acknowledgement, and (3) using no controlling language versus using controlling language such as "should," "must," and "have to." While no main effects or interactions on engagement time were significant, the main effects for each condition approached significance in the predicted direction, i.e., that autonomy support would facilitate engagement. The study also investigated the effects of the three conditions on self-reports of perceived choice, perceived usefulness, and interest/enjoyment. The main effects were significant for all conditions, as well as some interactions, indicating that the scores in the autonomy supportive conditions were higher. Taken together, these results imply that autonomy support facilitates both behavior enactment and internalization. However, analyses on the engagement time were conducted *only* with subjects that performed the task during the free-choice time: out of 192 subjects, 133 did *not* engage in the task. That is, the autonomy supportive conditions failed to change the behavior of almost 70% of the subjects.

Joussemet et al. (2005) replicated these results, this time with elementary school students, using a task almost identical to Deci et al. (1994). Of particular interest is their second study, where the effects of autonomy support versus controlling instructions versus rewards and controlling instructions were compared. It was found that children in the autonomy support condition valued the task more than those in the control conditions, indicating that they had internalized the value of the task more. However, there was no significant difference in free-choice engagement. Additionally, only 30% of the subjects engaged in the task in the free-choice time. The task was a tedious one in which the children had to concentrate in front of a monitor screen for 15 minutes. Again, autonomy support was not effective in altering the behavior of the subjects.

While internalization is purported to facilitate behavior enactment in the long term, it is doubtful that the subjects of these studies actively sought to continue the experimental tasks, even if they perceived their value. Although the authors of these studies (Deci et al., 1994; Joussemet et al., 2005) do not discuss these results in depth, it would be reasonable to conclude that autonomy support does not effectively facilitate behavior change in tasks where the need for competence is not sufficiently satisfied.

An uninteresting task can be considered one in which the underlying value is hard to perceive and thus difficult to internalize. There are two reasons why a task could be uninteresting to a certain person: the task may be inherently boring and thus difficult to be valued by a large majority of people, or the person may be unable to see the value of the task due to personal or contextual factors. Whether the reason lies in the task or the person, it is difficult to facilitate autonomous motivation and sustained behavior change in either case, and as we saw in the two studies, it seems difficult to induce *any* behavior change. This is especially relevant to people with challenges such as those who would be participants of capacity development projects. While the behaviors promoted by such aid projects may not be inherently uninteresting, being novel, they may seem strange or "wrong" within the beneficiaries' cultural context, making the underlying value even more difficult to perceive. Additionally, the effects of the behavior change may not be immediately apparent in capacity development projects such as farming and education. In such cases, autonomy support alone would not be sufficient, and it would be important to provide support for competence so that the subjects would be able to acknowledge the effects of their actions for the value of the action to be internalized.

Theoretically, Ryan and Deci (2002) have asserted that a behavior will not be enacted unless one can perceive the effect of their action and thus feel competent. Sayanagi (2007) also found that autonomy support is not effective in facilitating autonomous motivation in subjects with low perceived competence. In his study on schoolchildren in grades 4–6, he examined the relationship between teacher autonomy support and academic motivational styles while controlling for perceived academic competence. Teacher autonomy support was associated with autonomous motivational styles for schoolchildren with high perceived competence, but not for children with low perceived competence. Also, teacher autonomy support was negatively associated with controlled motivational styles for schoolchildren with high perceived competence, but not for those with low perceived competence.

In sum, there is some evidence that for those with low perceived competence, as participants of development aid projects would be, autonomy support alone is not an effective approach. Next, we will look into behavior modification approaches, which are commonly used with such subjects.

2.3 *An Outline of Behavior Modification*

Behavior modification has its roots in the well-established classical school of behaviorism, which posits that all volitional behavior is the result of operant conditioning. The principles of operant conditioning, while very straightforward (vis-à-vis the rather counterintuitive SDT), offer a powerful explanation for how behaviors are formed. The theory posits that the antecedents and consequences of an individual's behavior will modify the behavior. For example, if something desirable occurs following the behavior, the behavior is likely to be repeated under similar circumstances. On the other hand, if something undesirable occurs as a consequence of a behavior, it is likely that it will not be repeated (for a detailed outline of behavior modification, see for example Alberto & Troutman, 2012).

This principle can be applied to induce or inhibit certain behaviors. Rewards, or *reinforcement*, can be used to increase the frequency of a certain behavior, and punishment can be used to decrease frequency.[4] These principles should be easy to understand even for the layperson who has never heard of the term "operant conditioning," as they are a close analogue to how our labor and judicial systems work. However, it should be noted that in behaviorist theory and in practice, it is important to introduce reinforcement and/or punishment constantly and in a timely manner in order to ensure that the subject understands the contingency between the action and the consequence. In everyday life, reinforcements and punishments are not always introduced quickly enough, or they are not introduced consistently. In such cases, the intended behavior change does not occur effectively.

One example of a behavior modification technique is the token economy. Subjects participating in token economy programs are given "tokens" as rewards for predetermined desirable behaviors and have them confiscated as punishment for undesirable behaviors. These tokens, when accumulated, can be exchanged for other predetermined rewards, which can include anything from material gifts to services and privileges. Token economies were first introduced in the early 1960s in psychiatric settings, but rapidly spread to a wide range of applications (for a review, see Kazdin, 1982).

2.4 Limitations of Behavior Modification Approaches

While behavior modification techniques were widely used during the late 1960s and early 1970s, the scope has somewhat narrowed. A PsycInfo keyword search of the phrase "token economy" reveals that many studies were conducted during the 1970s, but the number has since decreased significantly: in the 1970s, there were 478 articles; in the 1980s, 187; in the 1990s, 70; and in the 2000s, 67 (in comparison, the number of SDT studies in the 2000s was 418). Although there have been studies on "normative" subjects, the focus of the approach has primarily been on people with difficulties. We could paraphrase in SDT terminology that these subjects are low in perceived competence. Of the recent studies on token economies in schools, a majority target children with behavioral difficulties (e.g., Maggin et al., 2011). Settings for other recent studies include closed mental wards (e.g., LePage et al., 2003), prisons with inmates who have serious mental health issues (e.g., Seegert, 2003), and patients receiving treatment for substance addiction (e.g., Garcia-Rodriguez et al., 2009). Although the reason that behavior modification approaches are not often used with "normative" subjects has not been well documented, we can speculate with some confidence that they did not catch on in settings in which they were not effective and continued in settings in which they were.

---

[4] While there are two theoretical views on punishment within behaviorism, one being that it is not as effective as rewards and the other that it is (Holth, 2005), the evidence seems to favor the former view that it is not effective (Kubanek et al., 2015). In practice, extinction (the withdrawal of reinforcement in response to problematic behavior) is encouraged over punishment. As aforementioned, punishment is viewed as detrimental in SDT.

One major criticism of behavior modification techniques including token economies is that the induced behavior change seems to be temporary and target behaviors disappear after the systematic administration of rewards is terminated (e.g., Kohn, 1993; Schwab, 2009). Even reviews by proponents of token economies concede that there is yet no evidence that the behavior change generalizes or is sustained (Kazdin, 1982; Kazdin & Bootzin, 1972). That token economies are not often used with "normative" subjects fits SDT's findings—compiled from studies with such subjects—that extrinsic rewards would decrease the subsequent amount of desired behavior in the lack of such rewards.

It is important to note that SDT posits that it is *not* the tangible rewards per se that would decrease subsequent behavior. In fact, SDT asserts that rewards will not decrease behavior if the rewards are *informational* in regard to conveying competence. That is, if rewards are administered in a manner that supports the need for competence, internalization will be facilitated and subsequent behavior will not be negatively affected. Contrarily, if rewards are administered in a *controlling* manner—that is, if they explicitly purport to control behavior and thus thwart the need for autonomy—while they may temporarily increase the desired behavior, internalization would not occur, and thus the behavior will decrease after the rewards are withdrawn (see Ryan, 1982 on the informational and controlling aspects of rewards).

2.5 *Implications from Successful Token Economy Programs*

As discussed in the previous section, behavior modification techniques including token economies are still widely used with subjects with behavioral difficulties. We can speculate that this is because they are effective in inducing behavior changes that would be difficult using other approaches. Nonetheless, whether such behavior change in token economies is sustainable is not clear: even some behavior modification workers assert that without further intervention, the positive effects cannot be maintained or generalized after reinforcement is terminated (e.g., Schwab, 2009). For the purpose of this thesis, which is to develop a theoretical framework for behavior change that is sustained for years after development aid projects end, it would be helpful to look at behavior modification studies that have tracked subjects for a number of years after program completion. However, while many studies do track the post-program maintenance of behavior change, most of them only report on outcomes in terms of weeks, rather than years, afterwards. (That said, many studies indicate that behavior changes are indeed maintained for those periods.) There are only 3 token economy papers searchable on PsycInfo that report on post-program behavior change for two or more years (Banzett et al., 1984; Heaton & Safer, 1982; Safer et al., 1981). Of these three, the two by Safer and colleagues are both follow-ups on the same program. Nevertheless, it could be said that both programs were successful to some degree in inducing sustained behavior change.

The reports by Safer and colleagues (Heaton & Safer, 1982; Safer et al., 1981) were regarding a token economy project for delinquent juveniles who had been suspended from school multiple times by the time they were in 7th grade. The study included a control group of comparable students from the same district who were not enrolled in the program. Key characteristics of the program were (a) it was conducted for 1 year when the students were in 7th grade; (b) participants were given a token for every 15 minutes they behaved appropriately in the classroom, and tokens could be exchanged for prizes or for privileges such as the right to leave school early; (c) the program was administered in a small class of 10–15 students; (d) the teachers in charge of the class were selected based on aptitude and were highly motivated; (e) counseling was provided to not just the students but also to their parents; and (f) the parents cooperated in administering tokens at home. Post-program follow-ups showed that program participants had significantly higher high school entrance rates and high school attendance rates, and that they had significantly fewer incidents of disruptive behavior in high school compared with the control group (Safer et al., 1981). Also, school dropout rates after 8th grade were significantly lower for participants for 3 years after the program, until 10th grade: however, there was no significant difference after 11th grade, and there was no difference in high school graduation rates (Heaton & Safer, 1982).

Banzett et al. (1984) followed up on former patients of a psychiatric ward 2–6 years after they left a token economy program, using a questionnaire mailed to the former patients' families. Key characteristics of this program were that (a) subjects were 58 former patients with diagnoses ranging from schizophrenia and autism to personality disorders and emotional disorders; (b) it was an intensive program that reinforced grooming, showering, housekeeping tasks, meal behaviors, leisure activities, and social skill training, and participants could exchange tokens for food, cigarettes, and privileges such as listening to music records and walking outdoors in the hospital premises; (c) the setting was a small 12-bed psychiatric ward with both inpatients and daycare patients participating; and (d) the staff included 15 nurses, a psychiatrist, social worker, psychologist, and rehabilitation therapist. Of the 58 families that responded to the questionnaire, 70% reported that the former patients were able to groom and shower themselves either voluntarily or with verbal cues, 64% were able to do housekeeping tasks and maintain tidy living spaces, and 45% actively participated in work or leisure for more than 60% of the time that they were awake. While this study did not have a control group, 80% of the respondents answered that the former patients had improved or at least maintained their levels of adaptive behavior since leaving the program, implying that the attained behavior change had been sustained for most subjects.

These studies indicate that behavior change is sustained for the long term at least in some programs. Although they represent a very limited sample, we can notice that the two successful programs had several aspects in common. Here, we will focus particularly on two aspects that seem to be key to sustainable behavior change. First, both programs provided intensive care, with relatively high staff-to-participant ratios. In the Safer and colleagues program, in addition to highly motivated and competent teachers, counselors and the participants' parents were also involved. In terms of SDT, it could be reasonably assumed that there was ample support for the need for relatedness. Second, as is common in behavior modification programs, the participants in both studies had difficulties in perceiving the effect of the target behaviors, which were basic skills that are necessary to lead an adaptive life in society. We can speculate that the tokens functioned as a tangible way to inform the participants of the effect of performing those skills. Additionally, as there were many staff members and, in the case of Safer and colleagues' project, parents, there would have been many opportunities for the participants to receive informative feedback on their performance in addition to the tokens, thus supporting their need for competence. Furthermore, while they initially may not have been able to appreciate the benefits of utilizing these skills, they could have gradually realized that adhering to them allowed for a more adaptive everyday life, making life much easier. This ultimate realization would lead the participants to continue the target behaviors even after the token economy program ended. For example, students who struggle academically in elementary school often feel helpless in secondary school, and thus find little reason to attend or sit still in a class that they cannot comprehend; they likely find more joy in drawing classmates' and teachers' attention by causing trouble. The tokens for sitting still in class may initially be extrinsic motivators, but with a competent teacher providing adequate support and instruction for the students to be able to learn, they would gradually be able to understand and realize the significance of the course material. Additionally, they would find that staying attentive in class would make life easier, as their relationships with their peers and teachers would improve. Therefore, these students would internalize the value of staying focused in class, and it is likely that they would continue to do so in the future.

To summarize, behavior modification techniques such as token economies are commonly used with people with behavioral difficulties, probably because they effectively induce behavior changes that would be hard to attain with other approaches. However, there are theoretical doubts, not just from SDT but also from behavior modification workers, on the sustainability of the behavior change. Although there are few reports on behavior changes that were maintained for years after the end of a program, the few programs that do provide such reports suggest that not just the reinforcement, but also supports for relatedness and competence are important. This is admittedly highly speculative and begs for evidence. However, as will be seen later with conditional cash transfers, this provides a plausible explanation as to why reward-induced behavior changes are maintained better in some cases than others.

2.6 A Modified SDT Framework

As we have seen, autonomy support does not seem to be effective in causing behavior change in subjects who have low perceived competence, whereas behavior modification approaches are. However, rewards alone are not sufficient in sustaining the behavior change.

To facilitate sustainable behavior change in such subjects, it seems key that, first and foremost, the subjects are able to perceive meaningful effects of their actions in order for the behavior to be enacted at all. This requires support for the need of competence, that is, *competence support*. Competence support would include the providing of informative feedback to aid the subject to be able to perceive the effect of his or her action, as was reported in the successful token economy programs discussed in the previous section. In some cases, it may be necessary to provide structure for the activity. This would consist of, for example, breaking down the target activity into small steps and then explaining at the beginning of each step what consequences or effects the subject can expect following the execution of the step. Through the providing of structure and informational feedback, subjects would be able to feel that they are dealing effectively with their task and thus be motivated to engage in the activity. Additionally, the activity should be of optimal difficulty: if it is too difficult, the subject would not be able to attain results and feel the effects of their engagement; if too easy, result may be attained, but the subject would not feel that they are meaningful.

An interaction is hypothesized between competence support and autonomy support, where autonomy support would not be as effective for subjects with low competence satisfaction.[5] Additionally, it seems that competence support and autonomy support need to be provided in a context that supports the need for relatedness, i.e., a three-way interaction is hypothesized between the three needs. *Relatedness support* is somewhat difficult to put in terms of specific acts, as the nature of a desirable relationship differs between people and between cultures. However, it should entail that the subject feels secure with the person(s) supervising the target activity, and feels able to rely upon the supervisor(s) when help is needed. This could be paraphrased as a kind of trust in the supervisor(s). This is important, as without this trust, informative feedback would not be taken at word value and thus not function as competence support. Furthermore, the underlying values of a task would be more readily accepted in such a trusting relationship. Environments such as those described in the aforementioned successful token economy programs, where supervisors were able to interact often with participants, are a necessary condition, but are not sufficient on their own; the quality of the interactions are probably important, too. Future research should focus on what kind of interactions support the need for relatedness.

Readers familiar with SDT may notice that some aspects of competence support and relatedness support described above overlap with what is currently considered autonomy support. For example, providing rationale is one method to provide autonomy support, but the current literature does not distinguish between types of rationale. Rationale could be an explanation of how certain knowledge is relevant to better understanding a topic, but it also could be on what results to expect from learning a certain technique: the latter case would better fit the description of

---

[5] Previous versions of this manuscript (Sayanagi, 2017a, 2017b) assumed a hierarchy in which competence support and relatedness support are prerequisites for autonomy support to facilitate behavior change. However, there has been no evidence that supports the hierarchy hypothesis. The studies cited in Sect. 2.2 of this chapter still indicate an interaction, so the hypothesis has been altered accordingly.

competence support. Accepting of feelings towards the task, currently an aspect of autonomy support, includes elements of relatedness support. One direction that may be useful in future studies would be to make a clearer distinction between specific methods of support and the needs they are relevant to. This would be especially important to detect the hypothesized interactions.

In sum, the modification to the SDT framework is mostly regarding the approach to facilitate internalization in subjects with low perceived competence. Autonomy support, the current "best practice" in SDT, may not be as effective for those who have low competence satisfaction. These supports must be provided in a relatedness-supporting context. To paraphrase in terms of causes and effects (see Fig. 6.1), relatedness support and competence support are moderators of the effects of autonomy support. Relatedness support would also moderate the effects of competence support. Admittedly, this argument is quite hypothetical. Sayanagi (2007) is the only study that reports an interaction between autonomy support and the support of other needs, and rigorous future empirical testing of this hypothesis—that there would be an interaction between autonomy support and competence support, as well as autonomy support and relatedness support—is warranted. However, as will be seen in the next section, it holds well at the anecdotal level.

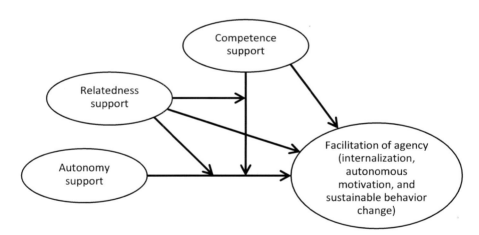

Fig. 6.1 Relatedness support and competence support as moderating variables of autonomy support. (This hypothesis has been modified from its original form in Sayanagi (2017a) to include direct paths from relatedness- and competence-support to the dependent variable. Note: Arrows between factors indicate cause and effect. Arrows pointing at other arrows indicate a moderating effect.)

3 Examination of Development Aid Approaches

In this section, we will look at selected approaches through the viewpoint of the modified SDT framework. As previously mentioned, the approaches chosen all explicitly aim to alter beneficiaries' behavior, are considered to be relatively successful, and are well-defined and administered in multiple projects.

3.1 Conditional Cash Transfers (CCTs)

CCTs are programs in which money is conditionally offered to poor families[6] raising children, the conditions usually being that they uptake certain public services such as sending their children regularly to school and seeking specific preventive health care measures for family members at health centers. To paraphrase in the parlance of behavior change, CCTs explicitly aim to alter the behavioral patterns of beneficiary families by making cash transfers contingent to the altered behavior, which is a very straightforward description of a typical behavior modification program. The alterations in behavior brought about by CCTs are supposed to promote behavioral habits that will help lift the beneficiaries out of poverty.

The first ever CCT program, Progresa, was launched in Mexico in 1997. The program was deemed a success, increasing secondary school enrollment in areas where the program was implemented from 67% to 75% for girls, and from 73% to 77% for boys, among other positive outcomes (Schultz, 2004). Subsequently, CCTs have become a tool of choice for reducing poverty around the world, spreading rapidly across Latin America and later to Africa and other regions.

One immediate worry from standpoint of SDT is that the contingent cash rewards might thwart the need for autonomy. While the cash transfers will probably increase the target behaviors in the short-term, there are doubts regarding the longer-term effects. School attendance obviously does not need to be extended beyond a child's age of schooling, but whether the beneficiaries internalize the value of education is a concern in terms of long-term development. If the parents do not embrace the merits of schooling, their attitudes towards school may be passed on to their children, who in turn may again need external nudging akin to CCTs when the time comes for their own children to attend school.

Indeed, Villatoro (2007: as cited in Pick & Sirkin, 2010) reports that one criticism of the Mexican CCT program Oportunidades, which succeeded the pioneering Progresa program, is that the structure of the program encouraged a dependency among beneficiaries on material rewards. Pick and Sirkin (2010) report narratives from Oportunidades beneficiaries that suggest that they do not whole-heartedly embrace the conditions put upon them (p. 78). These anecdotes suggest that the values promoted by CCTs, which intend to strengthen the beneficiaries' human

---

[6] The cash transfer is typically given to the mother.

capabilities but are presumably novel to them, indeed were not internalized. From non-CCT approaches that provide cash incentives, Sayanagi et al. (2016b) report cases where providing compensation seemed to cause an undermining effect (pp. 76–79, 93–94). This author has encountered multiple aid workers who report of would-be aid beneficiaries who refused to participate in aid projects unless they were paid in cash or in kind: these would-be beneficiaries had previously taken part in programs in which cash or material transfers were contingent to participation. Since reports on CCTs have not focused on the motivation and value internalization of the beneficiaries, we do not know yet how widespread of a problem the undermining effect and lack of internalization are. Hopefully, future studies on CCTs and other schemes that utilize cash incentives will focus on their subjective experiences in addition to the changes in their behavior and financial states.

Additionally, it is well known that children who grow up in impoverished families have fewer opportunities for education and also that they tend to be lower achievers than their more affluent peers, which is to a certain extent because their parents tend to have less education and their home environments have fewer educational stimuli. This would mean that even if these children were to go to school in exchange for cash transfers, many would be at a disadvantage for learning from the start. As anyone who has struggled in class would know, it is difficult to fully appreciate the importance of the educational content if one has difficulty understanding it. Consequently, it would be harder for such struggling children to internalize and embrace the underlying values of education. For these children to become able to embrace the values of school education, merely providing the opportunity (i.e., sending them to school) would not be enough: additional competence support from their relatedness-supporting teachers would also be necessary.

Surprisingly, at least from a psychologist's point of view, evaluations of CCTs do not always focus on rates of conditionality fulfillment. In one extreme example, cash transfers in Chile Solidario, the CCT program conducted by the Chilean government, were in practice given to everyone (Carneiro et al., 2009). Additionally, many CCT programs including Progresa and Oportunidades do not use actual fulfillment rate data but instead regional panel data as an indicator of changes in school enrollment and/or utilization of health care services. Panel data are not a good index of the targeted behavior change, as they are an indirect measure that leave room for alternative explanations: for example, it may have been the simple influx of cash into the region, rather than the contingencies, that caused the increase in school enrollment rates in areas where Progresa was introduced, and the rise may not be accounted for by only the beneficiaries' children. To accurately assess whether the program actually prompted participants to send their children to school, a direct measure of the beneficiaries' behavior is necessary.[7] Nonetheless, even from the data available from these reports, we can see that the degree of success in altering

---

[7] From the viewpoint of psychological research method, using regional panel data to assess the effectiveness of CCTs and calling them randomized controlled trials (RCTs) is inappropriate. While the trial and control groups may indeed be assigned randomly, the point of RCTs is to systematically rule out alternative explanations through controlling for crucial parameters such as

beneficiaries' behavior varies from region to region (see Cecchini & Madariaga, 2011, pp. 111–146 for a review).

Of the possible reasons that CCTs are ineffective in some cases, behaviorist theory would point to the timing of the cash transfer. If there is a substantial time lag between fulfillment and the cash transfer, for example due to a prolonged process to verify the fulfillment, behaviorist theory would predict that the contingency would be lost on the subject and consequently engagement in the target behavior would decrease. No studies have controlled for the timing of the cash transfer, so it is one factor that future studies should examine. The modified SDT framework would also predict that cash transfers would lose their informative value, if they were at all salient, if a substantial time lag existed.

Another factor that behaviorist theory would identify is the lack of contingency between the conditions and cash transfer. As Cecchini and Madariaga (2011) point out, CCTs vary in rigidness of conditionality (pp. 87–89), and indeed, some studies suggest that the strength of contingency was associated with indicators of fulfillment (De Brauw & Hoddinott, 2007; de Janvry & Sadoulet, 2006).

However, while such studies seemingly suggest that contingency of the conditions is the key, other findings suggest otherwise: it has been shown in projects from Malawi and Morocco that *un*conditional cash transfers (UCCTs) can have results similar to CCTs (Baird et al., 2009; Benhassine, Devoto, Duflo, Dupas, & Pouliquen, 2015). We may speculate that the rise in school attendance rates in UCCTs shows that the severely impoverished realize the value of education and health care in the first place (i.e., they already have autonomous motivation to send their children to school and receive health care), and that the unconditionally transferred cash allowed them to send their children to school rather than having them work to support the family. If the poor indeed were autonomously motivated towards these objectives, then making rewards contingent to them could potentially thwart the need for autonomy.

The aforementioned Chile Solidario did not make the cash transfers contingent on condition fulfillment, but nevertheless saw an increased uptake of subsidies and employee programs. One of the key characteristics of Chile Solidario was its provision of intense psychosocial support, called the Puente Program, which was implemented through local social workers who visited the beneficiaries at their homes (Carneiro et al., 2009). During these visits, the social workers worked with families to identify their main problems, work out the steps needed to resolve them, and introduce available social services. This can be considered a systematic provision of support for competence and relatedness. It is interesting that beneficiary families served by social workers with relatively lighter caseloads had higher rates of subsidy uptake (Chap. 10; Yanagihara, 2016). That is, the more support a social worker was able to provide per family, the more behavior change was observed. Taken together with the fact that the cash transfers were essentially not contingent to behavior change, it is

---

conditionality fulfillment: the so-called RCTs in CCTs, which in many cases do not control for such crucial parameters, leave much open for alternative interpretation.

implied that need support was more crucial than the cash transfers in inducing behavior change. That said, it is unknown whether the beneficiaries of Chile Solidario internalized the values regarding the target services, and this should be an issue that future studies address. Additionally, the degree to which the social workers were autonomy supportive would be predicted to be a factor that affected the degree of behavior change.

In any case, the evidence strongly suggests that the cash transfer itself is only one component in predicting the success of CCT programs, and perhaps there are other more important factors. Depending on the manner in which it is administered, the cash transfer may even be detrimental. From the standpoint of the modified SDT framework, one reasonable speculation is that successful CCT programs such as Chile Solidario provided sufficient competence support and relatedness support and were not controlling in administering the cash transfers. Future CCT studies should examine their beneficiaries' subjective attitudinal changes related to the contingent behaviors and degree of perceived need support as well as report more detailed fulfillment rates. In addition, it should be examined whether behaviors such as seeking preventive health care are sustained *after* the beneficiary has graduated from the CCT program.

3.2 The Life Improvement Approach (LIA)

The LIA originated in post-war Japan in the early 1950s. Its inception was led by the U.S. occupational government with the objective to improve the livelihoods of impoverished rural farmers in Japan. Under the slogan *kangaeru nomin*, or "thoughtful farmers," the program aimed to empower farmers, especially women, to be able to identify their own problems and work towards their solutions—which indeed can be paraphrased that LIA aimed to promote the agency, as defined in this chapter, of the farmers. LIA has been successful in Japan, and in some regions, there are still farmers actively participating in its activities. The approach has also been adopted in several developing countries, most notably in Central America and the Caribbean. Many of the recent LIA programs are overseen by Japan International Cooperation Agency (JICA). (For a review and update on recent developments of LIA, see Kozaki & Nakamura, 2017.)

A LIA program typically involves a field officer who organizes and trains groups of farmers on how to improve various aspects of their lives, whether it be housing, farming, or family management. Once a problem is identified, the field officer works with the farmers to find a solution. No cash or materials are distributed. If the problem is regarding farming technique, the officer, usually a specialist in agriculture, will provide training in person, or will connect the farmers to a specialist on the topic. If it is regarding housing, the officer will work to connect the farmers to financing and other resources: one successful initiative of the early Japanese LIA was the improvement of farmhouse kitchens, replacing floor-level open fire hearths with waist-high closed fire stoves, which ultimately were subsidized by the Japanese

3 Examination of Development Aid Approaches 111

government. Other initiatives, all based on problems identified by farmers, include the building of facilities to store and process excess crops, training on gender awareness, training on healthy cooking and eating, lectures on family planning, and simplifying ceremonies such as weddings and funerals that financially burdened the impoverished farmers. The essence of the LIA is that the participants, rather than the field officers take initiative in deciding what they need. The field officers' role is simply to moderate the farmers' discussion and to connect the farmers to appropriate resources.

As can be seen from this brief illustration, autonomy support and relatedness support are incorporated into the job description of a LIA field officer. Unlike CCTs, the target behavior differs from farmer group to farmer group, so in terms of researching the effects, a direct comparison across groups would be difficult. Furthermore, the long-term documentation on whether the intended behavior changes were sustained is not thorough, making evaluation somewhat difficult. However, based on the fact that many LIA groups in Japan remained active for years, and that some still are, we can reasonably assume that the changes in behavior were perceived as meaningful and also that they valued the activity, thus the farmers chose to continue the activity and to continue being active in LIA.

There has been some empirical research on successful Japanese LIA participants (Sayanagi & Aikawa, 2016) indicating that the motivation of the participants and field officers towards participating in the program is in most part autonomous. More research is warranted, particularly regarding the relationship between autonomous motivation to continue LIA activities and the sustaining of behavior changes. Also, the specific ways in which field officers provide autonomy and relatedness support would be of interest.

One aspect that is not salient in LIA field officers is competence support. It may be that the level of perceived competence of Japanese farmers was relatively high, and they did not require the support to continue. However, it also may be that the field officers subtly provided structure for the farmers. Future studies could look retrospectively on the details of Japanese field officers' work, or they could look at newer projects in Central America and the Caribbean to observe the initial levels of perceived competence in participants as well as the degree of need support provided and how they would predict a project's degree of success.

3.3 The Smallholder Horticulture Empowerment Project (SHEP) Approach

The SHEP approach was developed through a technical cooperation project in Kenya supported by JICA. Phase 1 of SHEP was launched in 2006 as a three-year project, and its successor SHEP UP was launched in 2011 (for an overview, see Aikawa, 2013). The project's third phase, SHEP PLUS, started in 2016. The approach trains farmers in a wide range of activities including not just farming techniques but also market research and gender sensitivity training. The initial SHEP project succeeded in increasing participants' average nominal income twofold. SHEP UP was expanded further in Kenya, and SHEP PLUS furthermore, and have attained results comparable with the first phase. The scheme has been so successful that the SHEP approach has been expanded to a total of 24 countries and 110,000 farmers as of 2019, and now JICA is aiming to spread the scheme to one million farmers by 2030 (Japan International Cooperation Agency, 2019).

SHEP is an agriculturally based approach which main goal is to help farmer groups profitably market their crops in a sustainable manner. It does not involve any transfer of cash or matter to the farmers. The approach is unique in that it does not start by training farmers to grow high-return crops, but with market research training. This is based on the observation that poor smallholder farmers usually do not grow to sell, and consequently are not able to sell their crops for much, if any, profit, making it difficult for them to escape poverty. Participant farmers are first trained to research their local markets on what crops will sell at what price at what time of the year. Once the farmers complete their survey, they decide which crops to grow at what timing to attain profit and find buyers before they actually plant their crops. The JICA-supported project headquarters provides a forum for the farmers and potential buyers. Once the farmers decide what crops to grow, the project headquarters provides training on the particular crop, as well as general training on farmland cultivation, using environmentally friendly pesticides and fertilizers, and irrigation. There is also an emphasis on gender sensitivity training.

The SHEP approach was designed to facilitate intrinsic motivation in the farmers (Aikawa, 2013). It is highly structured, with the crop-growing and marketing processes broken down into small steps. At each step, field officers provide intensive training to the groups on how to execute the step and what outcomes to expect, as well as detailed rationale to do so. Thus, there is ample support for competence and autonomy. Additionally, the field officers visit the groups every week, and the farmers are trained to work together. Thus, we can assume that the activities are conducted in the context of relatedness support, both from the field officers and within the farmer groups. From the viewpoint of the modified SDT framework of this chapter, the SHEP approach provides a highly need-supportive environment.

Sayanagi and Aikawa (2016) have found that the values underlying SHEP activities have indeed been internalized and that participants as well as field officers are autonomously motivated. Additionally, all interviewed participants and field officers stated that they intend to continue SHEP-related activities even after the program ends, and as an unexpected outcome, that participants are voluntarily teaching non-group neighbors the techniques that they learned in SHEP group activities (Sayanagi et al., 2016a). Field reports indicate that the participants indeed are continuing their SHEP-trained activities after program termination. It has been observed that the degree of internalization between groups differs (Sayanagi et al., 2016b), and future studies should examine whether this is predicted by the degree of perceived need support, and whether internalization predicts long-term engagement.

3.4 The Framework for Enabling Empowerment (FrEE)

The roots of the FrEE approach are Mexican psychologist Susan Pick's work in the early 1970s facilitating family planning practices in slums on the outskirts of Mexico City (Pick & Sirkin, 2010, p. ix). Pick later founded the non-governmental organization Mexican Institute of Family and Population Research (IMIFAP), where FrEE was ultimately developed. IMIFAP's first program in the early 1980s was a sex education program for impoverished youth in Mexico, which was based on their research that identified protective sexual behaviors among those adolescents. This program was successful and was used as a basis for Mexico's official ninth-grade curricula that was introduced in 1994 (p. 257), and subsequently has been adapted for other grade levels, too. The approach has been expanded and adapted for programs on the prevention domestic violence, health education, business development, parental development, and community development, among other objectives that are relevant for poor adolescents and adults to be able to escape from poverty.

FrEE is theoretically based upon the theory of planned behavior (TPB: Ajzen, 1991, 2002), a popular theory of motivation that is often referred to in help-seeking studies. TPB posits that an individual's *intention* to undertake a particular behavior is the key determinant of a behavioral outcome, and that intentions are an outcome of *subjective norms* and *attitudes* towards the behavior. Thus, interventions to modify behavior focus on fostering intention through changing perceptions of what is expected of the person (i.e., subjective norms) and facilitating positive attitudes and self-efficacy towards the action. The emphasis on the subjective experience of the agent is akin to that of aforementioned poverty-reduction studies and also the SDT framework of this chapter.

Because the existing "research behind [TPB] focused on a literate and educated population and on behavioral outcomes that were within the control of the participants," (Pick & Sirkin, 2010, p. 120), Pick and colleagues had to modify the theory in its application in the shantytowns of Mexico. As Pick (2007) points out, intentions can exist only if basic control exists, so FrEE interventions first focus on giving participants a sense of control over their own actions. Note that this theoretical adaptation also has parallels with the modification to SDT in this chapter, that existing studies were conducted in mostly high-income nations and for individuals to effectively exercise their sense of autonomy, they must be able to perceive competence regarding the action. FrEE is also influenced by Amartya Sen's conceptualization of agency (Sen, 1999), and draws from psychological concepts related to agency such as self-efficacy (Bandura, 1997, 2001), locus of control (Rotter, 1966), and autonomy[8] (Kagitcibasi, 2005).

Unlike LIA and SHEP, which are conducted in agricultural settings, FrEE was originally developed in classroom settings, and programs are usually conducted in the context of education. FrEE workshops aim to impart information (e.g., basic

---

[8] Note that this concept of autonomy slightly differs from the conceptualization of SDT.

information on biology, reproduction, and contraception in sex education), but rather than relying on rote memorization methods, workshops employ many participatory and analytical thinking exercises with the aim of having participants think of how they can actualize the information in their daily lives.

There is much documentation on the success of FrEE programs (see Pick & Sirkin, 2010 for an exhaustive list of references). As previously mentioned, the original sex education program was adapted as a part of Mexico's national curriculum. In addition to the increased likelihood of contraceptive use in participants, there were also non-targeted changes. The adolescents who participated later worked on other IMIFAP programs on violence prevention, drug abuse prevention, and employment, and young women showed increased participation in the community and local government, increased employment, and demanded better public services (Pick & Sirkin, 2010, p. 257). Many other FrEE programs also report non-targeted behavior change in which participants became more assertive in regard to taking control of aspects of their lives that they had been previously passive about. These unexpected changes are congruent with the definition of agency as defined in Chap. 3. Additionally, there are some follow-up studies that indicate that targeted behavior changes were maintained for at least over a year (Venguer et al., 2007)

Not much information is available on the specifics of how teachers and facilitators interact with their students and participants, so it is not possible to conduct an informed examination on how basic psychological needs are supported in FrEE, but the theoretical emphasis on voluntary intention and agency imply that workshops are held in an autonomy supporting, rather than controlling, manner. In order for students be able to feel a sense of control, there would have to be competence support. Also, in general terms, relatedness support would be vital for student participatory and action learning techniques to succeed. That adolescent participants worked in subsequent workshops suggests that there indeed was a sense of trust fostered through relatedness support.

While the literature indicates that FrEE is an efficient approach, it would be expected that the degree of success between programs would vary. The theoretical framework presented in this chapter would predict that the variance in need support would explain the variance in the degree of program success. Also, studies on the specific ways in which FrEE teachers and facilitators support psychological needs would provide information not just on how to improve FrEE workshops, but also how the project leaders of other approaches can support participants.

Although FrEE is based upon a psychological theory that differs from the SDT framework in this chapter, neither approach is exclusive of the other. As we have seen, they are similar and can be complementary. FrEE, which is based on TPB, focuses on the subjective perception of the agent, while SDT focuses on different aspects of subjective perception but also takes into account contextual and environmental conditions that are precursors to such perceptions. Additionally, since psychology is a discipline that inherently deals with intangible concepts, one theoretical viewpoint provides but a one-sided view of the psychology of the subject. The application of other psychological theories to the field of development aid should be welcomed.

4 Conclusion and Future Directions

People living in chronically impoverished conditions tend to form behavioral patterns that make it difficult for them to escape those very conditions. These behavioral patterns are prone not to change. Many development aid projects aim to change such behavioral patterns, with mixed results. This is apparently because of the lack of understanding on the subjective experiences and psychology of the poor. Surprisingly, very few psychological studies have focused on the beneficiaries of development aid, perhaps because there is no adequate theoretical framework.

This chapter proposes a modified SDT framework that accommodates for disadvantaged subjects. SDT purports that there are three fundamental psychological needs, and traditional SDT studies have asserted that supporting one need, autonomy, is the best practice to facilitate internalization. However, other studies indicate that for subjects with low perceived competence, autonomy support alone is not effective in bringing about behavior change. This chapter argues that for such subjects, competence support would make autonomy support more effective, and that it would have to be done in a relatedness supporting context for the behavior to be enacted and sustained.

Selected development aid schemes that aim to alter the behavior of beneficiaries were examined with this modified framework. Indeed, it seems that schemes that succeed in facilitating sustained behavior change, whether they are CCTs, the LIA, the SHEP approach, or the FrEE, provide support for all three needs. As we have seen especially in the discussion on CCTs, the degree of need support indeed does seem to make a difference in sustainable behavior change. The framework could also be applied to other aid paradigms, not just to analyze the degree of need support in a given approach, but also to identify deficits in need support and ways to improve.

It should be noted that it is not *what is done* per se, but *how the beneficiaries perceive* what is done that is important in supporting psychological needs. That is, the same method could be perceived differently depending on the context or culture, and even among people participating in the same project. Thus, the method for supporting a certain need may differ between contexts or cultures, but the three needs are universal, as are the perceptions of having the need supported. This underscores the importance of understanding the subjective experiences of project participants.

All of the analyses in this chapter have been post-hoc and anecdotal, and much empirical verification is warranted. One of the major assumptions of the framework—that autonomous motivation is moderated by perceived competence and perceived relatedness—requires validation. Development aid would be an ideal field to test this assumption, as there is large variance in perceived competence and the effects of autonomy supportive approaches could be examined while controlling for competence and relatedness support. The assumption could also be tested in an experimental setting, which would not necessarily have to be in a development aid setting, with the free-choice paradigm, using a task in which subjects vary in perceived competence. The assumption would be supported if autonomy support were more efficient for subjects with high perceived competence but not those with low perceived competence.

Psychological measures that would allow the assessment of autonomous motivation to participate in capacity development projects are necessary to conduct empirical research. As will be discussed in detail in Chap. 9, there are very few psychological measures that have been developed for impoverished populations, and the development of such measures will be necessary to test the assumptions and to verify the presented SDT framework.

In conclusion, some issues that were not addressed in detail but that are relevant to the thesis of this chapter will be discussed. First, it is apparent that field officers play a crucial role in providing need support in aid programs. Study of the ways in which effective field officers support the basic psychological needs of participants would be of both academic and practical interest. Additionally, as the job of the field officers is labor intensive and it would therefore be especially beneficial for their motivation to be autonomous, identifying the conditions that would promote their autonomous motivation would be informative. Finally, the modified SDT framework presented in this chapter suggests that labor intensive capacity development projects in which field officers and staff work together in the fields with the farmers is the optimal way to facilitate sustainable behavior change necessary to break the poverty trap. It is difficult to imagine any other way to provide competence and relatedness support. However, such hands-on approaches are falling out of favor, and common basket approaches where multiple donor nations chip in financial but not human resources are becoming popular. One can only wonder how such indirect approaches can succeed in inducing behaviors that would sustainably lift aid beneficiaries out of poverty. This chapter represents but one position on the psychology of aid beneficiaries, but hopefully it will lead to more diverse discussions on their psychology and how to effectively help them.

References

Aikawa, J. (2013). Initiatives of SHEP and SHEP UP: Capacity Development of Small-Scale Farmers for Increased Responsiveness to Market Needs. In JICA Research Institute (Ed.), *For Inclusive and Dynamic Development in Sub-Saharan Africa* (pp. 143–169). JICA Research Institute. Retrieved January 15, 2022, from https://www.jica.go.jp/jica-ri/publication/booksandreports/jrft3q00000029aw-att/For_Inclusive_and_Dynamic_Development_in_Sub-Saharan_Africa_JICA-RI.pdf

Ajzen, I. (1991). The Theory of Planned Behavior. *Organizational Behavior and Human Decision Processes, 50*, 179–211.

Ajzen, I. (2002). Perceived Behavioral Control, Self-Efficacy, Locus of Control, and the Theory of Planned Behavior. *Journal of Applied Social Psychology, 32*, 665–683.

Alberto, P. A., & Troutman, A. C. (2012). *Applied Behavior Analysis for Teachers* (9th ed.). Prentice Hall.

Alkire, S. (2005). Subjective Quantitative Studies of Human Agency. *Social Indicators Research, 74*, 217–260.

References

Alkire, S. (2007). Choosing Dimensions: The Capability Approach and Multidimensional Poverty. *Chronic Poverty Research Centre Working Paper No. 88*. Retrieved January 15, 2022, from http://papers.ssrn.com/sol3/papers.cfm?abstract_id=1646411

American Psychological Association. (2000). *Resolution on Poverty and Socioeconomic Status*. Retrieved January 15, 2022, from http://www.apa.org/about/policy/poverty-resolution.aspx

Ariely, D. (2008). *Predictably Irrational: The Hidden Forces that Shape Our Decisions*. Harper Collins.

Baird, S., McIntosh, C., & Ozler, B. (2009). Designing Cost Effective Cash Transfer Programs to Boost Schooling in Sub-Saharan Africa. *World Bank Policy Research Working Paper No. 5090*. Retrieved January 15, 2022, from http://elibrary.worldbank.org/doi/abs/10.1596/1813-9450-5090

Bandura, A. (1997). *Self-Efficacy: The Exercise of Control*. Worth Publishers.

Bandura, A. (2001). Social Cognitive Theory: An Agentic Perspective. *Annual Review of Psychology, 52*, 1–26.

Banerjee, A. V., & Duflo, E. (2011). *Poor Economics: A Radical Rethinking of the Way to Fight Global Poverty*. Public Affairs.

Banzett, L. K., Liberman, R. P., Moore, J. W., & Marshall, B. D. (1984). Long-Term Follow-Up of the Effects of Behavior Therapy. *Hospital and Community Psychiatry, 35*, 277–279.

Benhassine, N., Devoto, F., Duflo, E., Dupas, P., & Pouliquen, V. (2015). Turning a Shove into a Nudge? A "Labeled Cash Transfer" for Education. *American Economic Journal: Economic Policy, 7*, 86–125.

Bowlby, J. (1969). *Attachment and Loss, Vol. 1: Attachment*. Basic Books.

Brown, E. D., Ackerman, B. P., & Moore, C. A. (2013). Family Adversity and Inhibitory Control for Economically Disadvantaged Children: Preschool Relations and Associations with School Readiness. *Journal of Family Psychology, 27*, 443–452.

Carneiro, P., Galasso, E., & Ginja, R. (2009). *The Impact of Providing Psycho-Social Support to Indigent Families and Increasing Their Access to Social Services: Evaluating Chile Solidario*. http://www.ucl.ac.uk/~uctprcp/chile.pdf

Carr, S. C. (2013). *Anti-Poverty Psychology*. Springer.

Carr, S. C., McAuliffe, E., & MacLachlan, M. (1998). *Psychology of Aid*. Routledge.

Carr, S. C., & Sloan, T. S. (Eds.). (2003). *Poverty and Psychology: From Global Perspective to Local Practice*. Kluwer Academic/Plenum Publishers.

Cecchini, S., & Madariaga, A. (2011). *Conditional Cash Transfer Programmes: The Recent Experience in Latin America and the Caribbean*. Santiago, Chile: Economic Commission for Latin America and the Caribbean (ECLAC), United Nations Publication. Retrieved January 15, 2022, from https://repositorio.cepal.org/handle/11362/27855

Chirkov, V. (2014). The Universality of Psychological Autonomy Across Cultures: Arguments from Developmental and Social Psychology. In N. Weinstein (Ed.), *Human Motivation and Interpersonal Relationships: Theory, Research, and Applications* (pp. 27–51). Springer Science.

Davis, R. P., & Williams, W. R. (2020). Bringing Psychologists to the Fight Against Deep Poverty. *American Psychologist, 75*, 655–667.

De Brauw, A., & Hoddinott, J. (2007). *Must Conditional Cash Transfers Be Conditioned to Be Effective? The Impact of Conditioning Transfers on School Enrollment in Mexico*. IFPRI Discussion Paper, No. 00757, International Food Policy Research Institute, Washington, DC. Retrieved January 15, 2022, from http://www.ifpri.org/publication/must-conditional-cash-transfer-programs-be-conditioned-be-effective

de Charms, R. (1968). *Personal Causation: The Effect of Affective Determinants of Behavior*. Lawrence Erlbaum Associates.

De Janvry, A., & Sadoulet, E. (2006). Making Conditional Cash Transfers More Efficient: Designing for Maximum Effect of the Conditionality. *The World Bank Economic Review, 20*(1).

Dean, E. B., Schilibach, F., & Schofield, H. (2017). Poverty and Cognitive Function. In C. Barrett, M. Carter, & J. P. Chavas (Eds.), *The Economy of Poverty Traps* (pp. 57–118). NBER Books.

Deci, E. L. (1971). Effects of Externally Mediated Rewards on Intrinsic Motivation. *Journal of Personality and Social Psychology, 18*, 105–115.

Deci, E. L. (1975). *Intrinsic Motivation*. Plenum Publishing.

Deci, E. L., Eghrari, H., Patrick, B. C., & Leone, D. R. (1994). Facilitating Internalization: The Self-Determination Theory Perspective. *Journal of Personality, 62*, 119–142.

Deci, E. L., Koestner, R., & Ryan, R. M. (1999). A Meta-Analytic Review of Experiments Examining the Effects of Extrinsic Rewards on Intrinsic Motivation. *Psychological Bulletin, 125*, 627–668.

Deci, E. L., & Ryan, R. M. (1985). *Intrinsic Motivation and Self-Determination in Human Behavior*. Plenum Press.

Deci, E. L., & Ryan, R. M. (2000). The "What" and "Why" of Goal Pursuits: Human Needs and the Self-Determination of Behavior. *Psychological Inquiry, 11*, 227–268.

Deci, E. L., & Ryan, R. M. (2008). Facilitating Optimal Motivation and Psychological Well-Being Across Life's Domains. *Canadian Psychology, 49*, 14–23.

Garcia-Rodriguez, O., Secades-Villa, R., Higgins, S. T., Fernandez-Hermida, J. R., Carballo, J. L., Perez, J. M. E., & Diaz, S. A. (2009). Effects of Voucher-Based Intervention on Abstinence and Retention in an Outpatient Treatment for Cocaine Addiction: A Randomized Controlled Trial. *Experimental and Clinical Psychopharmacology, 17*, 131–138.

Goode, J. (2010). How Urban Ethnography Counters Myths About the Poor. In G. Gmelch & W. Zenner (Eds.), *Urban Life: Readings in the Anthropology of the City* (5th ed., pp. 185–201). Waveland Press.

Grolnick, W. S. & Ryan, R. M. (1989). Parent Styles Associated with Children's Self-Regulation and Competence in School. *Journal of Educational Psychology, 81*, 143–154.

Grolnick, W. S., Deci, E. L., & Ryan, R. M. (1997). Parent Styles Associated with Children's Self-Regulation and Competence in School. In J. E. Grusec & L. Kuczynski (Eds.), *Parenting and Children's Internalization of Values: A Handbook of Contemporary Theory* (pp. 135–161). Wiley.

Haushofer, J., & Fehr, E. (2014). On the Psychology of Poverty. *Science, 344*, 862–867.

Heaton, R. C., & Safer, D. J. (1982). Secondary School Outcome Following a Junior High School Behavioral Program. *Behavior Therapy, 13*, 226–231.

Holth, P. (2005). Two Definitions of Punishment. *The Behavior Analyst Today, 6*, 43–47.

Japan International Cooperation Agency. (2019). *Joint Declaration for Achieving Better Lives of One Million Small Scale Farmers Through SHEP Approach*. TICAD VII SHEP Approach Side Event press release, August 29. https://www.jica.go.jp/english/our_work/thematic_issues/agricultural/shep/c8h0vm0000bm5c1m-att/declaration_en.pdf

Joussemet, M., Koestner, R., Lekes, N., & Houlfort, N. (2005). Introducing Uninteresting Tasks to Children: A Comparison of the Effects of Rewards and Autonomy Support. *Journal of Personality, 72*, 139–166.

Kagitcibasi, C. (2005). Autonomy and Relatedness in Cultural Context: Implications for Self and Family. *Journal of Cross-Cultural Psychology, 36*, 403–422.

Kazdin, A. E. (1982). The Token Economy: A Decade Later. *Journal of Applied Behavior Analysis, 15*, 431–445.

Kazdin, A. E., & Bootzin, R. R. (1972). The Token Economy: An Evaluative Review. *Journal of Applied Behavior Analysis, 5*, 343–372.

Keiffer, M. J. (2008). Catching Up or Falling Behind? Initial English Proficiency, Concentrated Poverty, and the Reading Growth of Language Minority Learners in the United States. *Journal of Educational Psychology, 100*, 851–868.

Kohn, A. (1993). *Punished by Rewards: The Trouble with Gold Stars, Incentive Plans, A's, Praise, and Other Bribes*. Houghton Muffin.

Kosmala-Anderson, J. P., Wallace, L. M., & Turner, A. (2010). Confidence Matters: A Self-Determination Theory Study of Factors Determining Engagement in Self-Management Support Practices of UK Clinicians. *Psychology, Health & Medicine, 15*, 478–491.

References

Kozaki, T., & Nakamura, Y. (2017). The Evolving Life Improvement Approach: From Home Taylorism to JICA Tsukuba, and Beyond. *JICA Research Institute Working Paper No. 146*. https://www.jica.go.jp/jica-ri/ja/publication/workingpaper/wp_146.html

Kubanek, J., Snyder, L. H., & Abrams, R. A. (2015). Reward and Punishment Act as Distinct Factors in Guiding Behavior. *Cognition, 139*, 154–167.

Kukita, J. (1996). Kaihatsu enjo to shinrigaku [Development Aid and Psychology]. In K. Sato (ed.), *Enjo kenkyu nyumon: Enjo gensho e no gakusai-teki approach* [*Introduction to Aid Studies: An Interdisciplinary Approach to Aid Phenomena*] (pp. 281–320). Chiba: Institute of Developing Economies, Japan External Trade Organization.

LePage, J. P., DelBen, K., Pollard, S., McGhee, M., VanHorn, L., Murphy, J., Lewis, P., Aboraya, A., & Mogge, N. (2003). Reducing Assaults on an Acute Psychiatric Unit Using a Token Economy: A Two-Year Follow-Up. *Behavioral Interventions, 18*, 179–190.

Levy, S. (2008). *Good Intentions, Bad Outcomes: Social Policy, Informality, and Economic Growth in Mexico*. Brookings Institution Press.

Lewis, O. (1966/2010). The Culture of Poverty. In G. Gmelch & W. Zenner (Eds.), *Urban Life: Readings in the Anthropology of the City* (5th ed., pp. 175–184). Waveland Press.

Lott, B. (2002). Cognitive and Behavioral Distancing from the Poor. *American Psychologist, 57*, 100–110.

Maggin, D. M., Chafouleas, S. M., Goddard, K. M., & Johnson, A. H. (2011). A Systematic Evaluation of Token Economies as a Classroom Management Tool for Students with Challenging Behavior. *Journal of School Psychology, 49*, 529–554.

McWayne, C. M., Melzi, G., Limlingan, M. C., & Schick, A. (2016). Ecocultural Patterns of Family Engagement Among Low-Income Latino Families of Preschool Children. *Developmental Psychology, 52*, 1088–1102.

Neuman, S. B., & Celano, C. C. (2012). *Giving Our Children a Fighting Chance: Poverty, Literacy, and the Development of Information Capital*. Teachers College Press.

Núñez, J. L., & León, J. (2015). Autonomy Support in the Classroom: A Review from Self-Determination Theory. *European Psychologist, 20*, 275–283.

Pick, S. (2007). Extension of Theory of Reasoned Action: Principles for Health Promotion Programs with Marginalized Populations in Latin America. In I. Ajzen, D. Albarracin, & R. Hornik (Eds.), *Prediction and Change of Health Behavior: Applying the Reasoned Action Approach* (pp. 223–241). Lawrence Erlbaum Associates.

Pick, S., & Sirkin, J. T. (2010). *Breaking the Poverty Cycle: The Human Basis for Sustainable Development*. Oxford University Press.

Reynolds, A. J., Ou, S., Mondi, C. F., & Giovanelli, A. (2019). Reducing Poverty and Inequality Through Preschool-to-Third-Grade Prevention Services. *American Psychologist, 74*, 653–672.

Ross, L. (1977). The Intuitive Psychologist and His Shortcomings: Distortions in the Attribution Process. In Berkowitz, L. (Ed.), *Advances in Experimental Social Psychology* (Vol. 10, pp. 173–220). Academic Press.

Rotter, J. B. (1966). Generalized Expectancies for Internal Versus External Control of Reinforcement. *Psychological Monographs, 80*, 1–28.

Ryan, R. M. (1982). Control and Information in the Intrapersonal Sphere: An Extension of Cognitive Evaluation Theory. *Journal of Personality and Social Psychology, 43*, 450–461.

Ryan, R. M. (1995). Psychological Needs and the Facilitation of Integrative Processes. *Journal of Personality, 63*, 397–427.

Ryan, R. M., & Deci, E. L. (2000). Self-Determination Theory and the Facilitation of Intrinsic Motivation, Social Development, and Well-Being. *American Psychologist, 55*, 68–78.

Ryan, R. M., & Deci, E. L. (2002). Overview of Self-Determination Theory: An Organismic Dialectical Perspective. In E. L. Deci & R. M. Ryan (Eds.), *Handbook of Self-Determination Research* (pp. 3–33). University of Rochester Press.

Ryan, R. M., & Deci, E. L. (2006). Self-Regulation and the Problem of Human Autonomy: Does Psychology Need Choice, Self-Determination, and Will? *Journal of Personality, 74*, 1557–1586.

Ryan, R. M., & Deci, E. L. (2011). A Self-Determination Theory Perspective on Social, Institutional, Cultural, and Economic Supports for Autonomy and Their Importance for Well-Being. In V. I. Chirkov, R. M. Ryan, & K. M. Sheldon (Eds.), *Human Autonomy in Cross-Cultural Context: Perspectives on the Psychology of Agency, Freedom, and Well-Being* (pp. 44–63). Springer Science + Business Media.

Ryan, R. M., & Deci, E. L. (2017). *Self-Determination Theory: Basic Psychological Needs in Motivation, Development, and Wellness*. The Guilford Press.

Sachs, J. (2005). *The End of Poverty: Economic Possibilities for Our Time*. Penguin Books.

Safer, D. J., Heaton, R. C., & Parker, F. C. (1981). A Behavioral Program for Disruptive Junior High School Students: Results and Follow-Up. *Journal of Abnormal Child Psychology, 9*, 483–494.

Sayanagi, N. (2007). *Competence as a Facilitating and Moderating Factor of Autonomy and Behavior Enactment: An Empirical Study on Schoolchildren's Behavior and Motivation in Studying*. Unpublished doctoral dissertation, International Christian University, Mitaka, Japan.

Sayanagi, N. R. (2017a). Breaking the Poverty Trap: Facilitating Autonomous Motivation for Sustainable Behavior Change in Developmental Aid Recipients. *JICA Research Institute Working Paper, 151*. https://www.jica.go.jp/jica-ri/ja/publication/workingpaper/wp_151.html

Sayanagi, N. R. (2017b). Hinkon no wana wo uchiyaburu: Enjo puroguramu hiekisha no jiritsuteki dokizuke to jizoku kano na kodo henyo no sokushin ni kansuru shinrigakuteki riron kasetsu [Breaking the Poverty Trap: Facilitating Autonomous Motivation for Sustainable Behavior Change in Developmental Aid Recipients]. *Journal of International Development Studies, 26*, 25–50.

Sayanagi, N. R., & Aikawa, J. (2016). The Motivation of Participants in Successful Development Aid Projects: A Self-Determination Theory Analysis of Reasons for Participating. *JICA Research Institute Working Paper No. 121*. https://www.jica.go.jp/jica-ri/publication/working-paper/wp_121.html

Sayanagi, N. R., Aikawa, J., & Asaoka, M. (2016a). *The Relationship Between Motivation and Outcomes in Development Aid Projects: Implications from an SDT-Based Approach in Kenya*. Paper presented at The 6th International Conference on Self-Determination Theory, Victoria, BC.

Sayanagi, N. R., Aikawa, J., Shuto, K., & Asaoka, M. (2016b). *Introduction to the Psychology of International Cooperation: Seventeen Motivation Case Studies Collected from the Field*. Japan International Cooperation Agency. Retrieved January 15, 2022, from http://libopac.jica.go.jp/images/report/12092193.pdf

Schultz, P. (2004). School Subsidies for the Poor: Evaluating the Mexican Progresa Poverty Program. *Journal of Development Economics, 74*, 199–250.

Schwab, A. M. (2009). Does Graduation from a Token Economy Predict Long-Term Outcomes of a Residential Treatment Program? *Dissertation Abstracts International: Section B: The Sciences and Engineering, 69*, 6435.

Seegert, C. R. (2003). Token Economies and Incentive Programs: Behavioral Improvement in Mental Health Inmates Housed in State Prisons. *The Behavior Therapist, 26*, 210–211.

Sen, A. (1999). *Development as Freedom*. Anchor Books.

Su, Y. L., & Reeve, J. (2011). A Meta-Analysis of the Effectiveness of Intervention Programs Designed to Support Autonomy. *Educational Psychology Review, 23*, 159–188.

Tanaka, S. (2011). *Kurashi no kakumei: Sengo noson no seikatsu kaizen jigyo to shin-seikatsu undo*. [Revolution of Life: Life Improvement Projects and the New Living Movement in Post-War Agricultural Villages]. Tokyo: Rural Culture Association.

Tuason, M. T. (2002). Culture of Poverty: Lessons from Two Case Studies of Poverty in the Philippines; One Became Rich, the Other Stayed Poor. *Online Readings in Psychology and Culture, 8*. https://doi.org/10.9707/2307-0919.1069

Tuason, M. T. (2010). The Poor in the Philippines: Some Insights from Psychological Research. *Psychology and Developing Societies, 22*, 299–330.

Tuason, M. T. G. (2013). Those Who Were Born Poor: A Qualitative Study of Philippine Poverty. *Qualitative Psychology, 1*, 95–115.

United Nations Innovation Network. (2021). *United Nations Behavioural Science Report*. United Nations Innovation Network.

Vasquez, A. C., Patall, E. A., Fong, C. J., Corrigan, A. S., & Pine, L. (2016). Parental Autonomy Support, Academic Achievement, and Psychosocial Functioning: A Meta-Analysis of Research. *Educational Psychology Review, 28*, 605–644.

Venguer, T., Pick, S., & Fishbein, M. (2007). Health Education and Agency: A Comprehensive Program for Young Women in the Mixteca Region of Mexico. *Psychology, Health & Medicine, 12*, 389–406.

Villatoro, P. (2007). *Las transferencias condicionadas en América Latina: Luces y sombras [The Conditional Transfers in Latin America: Lights and Shadows]*. Paper presented at the CEPAL Conference "Evolución y desafos de los programas de transferencias condicionadas [Evolution and Challenges of Conditional Transfer Programs]. Brasilia, Brazil. (As cited in S. Pick & J. T. Sirkin (2010). *Breaking the Poverty Cycle: The Human Basis for Sustainable Development*. New York: Oxford University Press.)

Weinstein, N., & Ryan, R. M. (2012). Parental Autonomy Support and Discrepancies Between Implicit and Explicit Sexual Identities: Dynamics of Self-Acceptance and Defense. *Journal of Personality and Social Psychology, 102*, 815–832.

White, R. W. (1959). Motivation Reconsidered: The Concept of Competence. *Psychological Review, 66*, 297–333.

Williams, G. C., McGregor, H. A., Sharp, D., Levesque, C., Koutides, R. W., Ryan, R. M., & Deci, E. L. (2006). Testing a Self-Determination Theory Intervention for Motivating Tobacco Cessation: Supporting Autonomy and Competence in a Clinical Trial. *Health Psychology, 25*, 91–101.

Wilson, A. J., Liu, Y., Keith, S. E., Wilson, A. H., Kermer, L. E., Zumbo, B. D., & Beauchamp, M. R. (2012). Transformational Teaching and Child Psychological Needs Satisfaction, Motivation, and Engagement in Elementary School Physical Education. *Sport Exercise and Performance Psychology, 4*, 215–230.

World Bank. (2013). Jim Youn Kim Says World Can End Extreme Poverty and Increase Shared Prosperity. Retrieved January 15, 2022, from http://www.worldbank.org/en/news/video/2013/04/02/jim-kim-world-can-end-extreme-poverty

World Bank. (2015). *World Development Report 2015: Mind, Society, and Behavior*. World Bank.

World Bank & International Monetary Fund. (2012). *Global Monitoring Report: Food Prices, Nutrition, and the Millennium Development Goals*. Retrieved January 15, 2022, from https://openknowledge.worldbank.org/handle/10986/6017

Yanagihara, T. (2016). User-Centered Approach to Service Quality and Outcome: Rationales, Accomplishments, and Challenges. *JICA Research Institute Working Paper No. 123*. Retrieved January 15, 2022, from https://www.jica.go.jp/jica-ri/publication/workingpaper/wp_123.html

Yoshikawa, H., Aber, J. L., & Beardslee, W. R. (2012). The Effects of Poverty on the Mental, Emotional, and Behavioral Health of Children and Youth. *American Psychologist, 67*, 272–284.

Chapter 7
User-Centered Approaches to Service Transactions and Agency of Service Users

1 Introduction: Question and Focus

Recent emphasis on the "User-Centered Approach (UCA)" to service provision is one context in which "agency" on the part of service users is importantly featured. This chapter addresses the rationales, accomplishments, and limitations of UCA proposed and practiced as a solution to the problem of poor quality and insufficient outcome of services observed in impact evaluations, *Monitoring Report 2011 (GMR2011)* among others.

GMR2011 provides a useful review and analysis of an apparent "disconnect between spending and outcomes" as observed in impact evaluations in health and education in developing countries (World Bank, 2011). It states that while increased spending for improving access to services have met with some success, it has been much more difficult to improve the quality of services and to achieve positive changes in human development outcomes. This recognition calls for a thorough review of the links in the service provision and uptake chain and possibly a search for nonconventional approaches to service provision. This is a matter of general significance, insofar as all development efforts are conducted ultimately for the realization of well-being outcomes.

The present chapter is organized as follows: Sect. 2 gives a summary of messages of *GMR2011* as well as an overview of the main contents of this chapter.

Section 3 provides conceptual and analytical approaches to the question of service transaction and utilization. First, an analytical framework on supply-uptake-utilization links will be presented, followed by conceptual articulation and classification of the nature of services based on degrees of discretion and transaction-intensity, as well as conjectures on two types of failures. Next, in discussing the effectiveness of the UCA models (co-production and self-management), the definition and articulation of two key terms, agency and motivation, will be presented, followed by typologies of user-provider relations and of user agency in service transaction and utilization.

Section 4 reviews and highlights some of the important proposals and experiences of UCA. Proposals and experiences are summarized in the form of general propositions on co-production in public services, people-centered primary care and chronic illness care, and in a summarized case study of a salient program in social work, i.e., Nurse Family Partnership (NFP).

Section 5 addresses the activation and augmentation of user agency for effective partnership in co-production and for self-management. Following a general conceptual examination of "empowerment," important cases of intervention for agency activation and agency augmentation will be discussed with a view to drawing generalizable implications.

Brief discussion on the rationales, accomplishments and limitations of the UCA concludes the chapter.

2 Public Service Failures in Developing Countries and the UCA as Possible Remedy

GMR2011 points to wide-ranging phenomena and sources of the problem of poor quality of services and limited outcomes and reports on evaluations of effectiveness of attempted remedies. It cites the results of impact evaluations on some of the standard measures based on conventional wisdom and concludes as follows with reference to schooling:

> Attempting to fill narrowly defined resource gaps in schooling by increasing the provision of traditional inputs has not been very successful for improving learning outcomes. Traditional inputs that have been tested on this dimension include textbooks, school meals, blackboards and other visual aids (like flip charts), teacher training, and even smaller class sizes. (p. 83)

With regard to CCTs, the Report's summary statement reads as follows:

> CCTs help increase the uptake of services, but their impact on health and learning outcomes is mixed. (p. 84)

As stated in the quotations above, neither input-related measures on the provider side nor financial incentives on the user side seem to be effective in bringing about improvements in service outcomes. Inconclusive as they may, these findings may suggest the significance of desire and capacity on the user side as determinant of service utilization and outcome.

GMR2011 makes a cursory mention of the role of service users when it states that it is important to ensure that "potential clients have the ability and desire to use services efficiently and hold service providers accountable for quality" (p. 72). It places, however, particular emphasis on the latter role of service users, or incentive and accountability issues associated with the lack of effective governance mechanisms on the behavior of front-line service providers, making reference to the analytical framework presented in *World Development Report 2004 (WDR2004)*, while virtually disregarding the former (i.e., "ability and desire to use services efficiently" on the part of potential users) (World Bank, 2003).

Conspicuously absent from the review and discussion of service provision in developing countries in *GMR2011*, and *WDR2004* for that matter, is attention to attempts to increase the role of service users in the process of production of services and thus change supply side-dominated nature of service provision. Such attempts represent a non-conventional approach, commonly called "User-Centered Approach (UCA)," for the improvement of the quality and well-being outcomes of services.[1]

With this overall assessment of the service quality and outcome question as a backdrop, this chapter has a narrowly limited purpose of examining some of the proposals and experiences in "User-Centered Approach (UCA)" to service provision. Specifically, we will take up two models of UCA in which service users make significant contributions in the process of production of services:[2]

- The first model of UCA, "service co-production", involves users in the process of service production. In this model, service users are viewed as active participant and partner in the production of services. JICA's promotion of Child-Centered Approach (CCA) in education and WHO's advocacy of People-Centered Primary Care (PCPC) in public health are important examples of this model in developing countries. It is also the central philosophical pillar of the on-going reform of public services in the United Kingdom;
- The second model emphasizes self-management as a stronger case of UCA. Its application is most prominent in the domains of the care of chronic diseases, such as The Improving Chronic Illness Care (ICIC) Program, and of social work, such as the Nurse-Family Partnership (NFP) program and the *Chile Solidario* (CHS) program.[3]

In this chapter we will address the question of the quality and well-being outcomes of services paying particular attention to the principles and experiences of the two models of UCA with a view to identifying their rationales, accomplishments and limitations. The co-production model deals with communications and collaborations in the process of service transactions. By contrast, the self-management model, taken singly, focuses on the service user as central provider of the service; in reality, however, in most cases self-management is prompted, guided and supported by professional service providers like doctors and nurses, thus constituting a component of the co-production model broadly defined.

---

[1] One model of UCA works at the upstream, or design and decision-making stages, of supply of services and tries to have user demands and desires reflected therein. Community-Driven Development (CDD) and Community-Based Management of Schools (CBMS) are examples of this model. This model is relatively well-documented and covered in the review and evaluation of *GMR2011* and *WDR2004*.

[2] *WDR2004* does refer to service users as "co-producers," but only in the role of monitoring actions of service providers.

[3] We will provide a case study of Nurse-Family Partnership (NFP) later in this chapter. The experience of the *Chile Solidario* (CHS) program will be presented and examined in Chap. 10.

As philosophy and principle, both of the UCA models discussed in this chapter, with potentials of being humanistic and efficacious at the same time, have a lot to be recommended. In the policy domain, co-production of public services constitutes one of the central pillars of the reform of public sector in some European countries, most notably the United Kingdom.

On the academic front, there was an important call from Elinor Ostrom on the crucial role of co-production in service provision in developing countries:

> [C]oproduction of many goods and services normally considered to be public goods by government agencies and citizens organized into polycentric systems is crucial for achieving higher levels of welfare in developing countries, particularly for those who are poor. Prior efforts directed at improving the training and capacity of public officials have frequently had disappointing results. Efforts directed at increasing citizen "participation" in petitioning others to provide goods for them have also proved disappointing. Efforts directed at increasing the potential complementarities between official and citizen production or problem-solving activities may require more time at the initial stage of a process, but promise a much higher, long-term return. (Ostrom, 1996, p. 1083)

Ostrom documents the case of low-cost waterborne sanitation systems in Brazil as a case of effective co-production of public services.[4]

Increased attention to the role of service users entails better understanding of the user-side conditions impinging on the production and utilization of services and resultant effects on activities of daily life. Eligibility to and availability of services are conditions set by the supply side and do not, in and of themselves, guarantee the accessibility to and uptake/utilization of services by (potential) users. User-side conditions are multifaceted ranging from physical to psychological, from technical to behavioral, and from individual to relational. We will address this question in the latter part of the chapter with focus on the psychological, behavioral and relational aspects of activities of daily life of service users.

Discussion of the co-production model centers on interactions between service users and providers. There are two contexts in which user-provider interactions are involved. One is of general relevance referring to increased and indispensable role of users in service transaction processes. The second consists of psychosocial support for the enhancement of psychological, behavioral and relational (pre)conditions for effective participation of users in service transactions and utilization of services. The process and activity in this second context is commonly referred to as "empowerment" of service users. When empowerment is attempted, there are two different settings: in the first case, empowerment is effected simultaneously within the context of service transactions; in the second case, empowerment is conducted as a separate stage prior to the initiation of the service transaction. In terms of agency on the service user's part, the first case may be conceived as activation of the existing stock of agency, while the second as augmentation of the stock of agency.

---

[4] In the present chapter our main attention will be paid to types of services where direct interactions between providers and users are involved in service transactions. Cases of infrastructural services will not be covered. Incidentally, Ostrom's case of sanitation service co-production incorporates self-management on the part of service users as one component.

In the first case, the provision of psycho-social support is of short-term, catalytic nature. In the second case, by contrast, psycho-social support is of long-term, transformative nature.

The discussion on empowerment above is equally relevant to the self-management model. The only distinction might be found in the following point: while the directly relevant type of empowerment for the co-production model is "relational empowerment," the most important type for the self-management model is "personal empowerment," as discussed in Sect. 5.

It is to be noted that psycho-social support is an extremely transaction-intensive type of service with heavy characteristics of counseling. Thus, to be effective, psycho-social support itself may also need to be conducted in a co-productive manner.

3 Analytical Framework, Conceptual Articulation, and Conjectures

In this section, we will first present an analytical framework for service transactions, followed by articulation and elaboration of key concepts employed to classify services into four distinct types. Particular attention will be paid to "practice"-type services, and conjectures will be put forth regarding possible failures in the provision of that type of services. Secondly, we will propose another set of conceptual-analytical schemes for the understanding of the place and role of agency on the part of service users in the transaction and utilization of services.

3.1 Analytical Framework on Supply-Uptake Links

GMR2011 proposes an analytical framework to be applied to the question of the disconnect between spending and outcomes. It argues that the causal chain that links public spending to changes in outcomes needs to be understood with focus on behaviors of agents involved, most importantly front-line service providers and recipients, and on variables influencing them such as capacity, resources, information, incentives and accountability, as informed by insights of the New Institutional Economics and highlighted in World Bank (2003, 2011). Let us summarize the main features of the analytical framework presented therein.

The links between public expenditure and outcomes (in terms of increased well-being) are stylized as follows:

1) Public financial, physical and human resources → 2) Generation of goods and services → 3) Uptake of goods and services → 4) Well-being outcomes

The first link (i.e., components 1 and 2 as well as the arrow connecting them) represents supply-side factors and processes, including policy decisions and administrative realities of organizations involved. Availability of resources, resource allocation and deployment decisions, and governance of administrative behavior are important elements on the supply side.

The second link (components 2 and 3 and the arrow connecting them) incorporates behaviors of, and interactions between, front-line service providers and users in specific contexts of service transaction. Here, capacities, constraints, attitudes and motivations on the part of providers and users, as well as incentives faced by them, are important determining factors of how services are delivered and received.

The third and final link (components 3 and 4 and the arrow connecting them) represents user-side factors and processes and is importantly affected by conditions, attitudes and behaviors of service users in the context of their daily life. This link has traditionally received much less attention than the first two. We will pay much attention to the second and third links, highlighting the importance of user-side factors and conditions for effective uptake and utilization of services.

The present chapter will address some of the important factors impinging on service delivery and uptake from micro and system analytic angles, building on foundational contributions by Lant Pritchett and Michael Woolcock: first, conceptual articulation based on a two-way classification of types of services according to degrees of discretion and transaction-intensity (Pritchett & Woolcock, 2004); and secondly, hypotheses for mechanisms of systemic and persistent implementation failures (Pritcheet et al., 2010).

3.2 *Conceptual Articulation and Classification of Services*

Services may be classified into four types based on a two-by-two framework according to degrees of discretion and transaction-intensity. Labels and characteristics of those four types are as follows (Table 7.1) (Pritchett & Woolcock, 2004, pp. 194–195). Illustrations from education and health fields of the four types of services are also provided (Table 7.2).

"Transaction intensity" refers to the extent to which the delivery of a service (or an element of a service) requires purposive actions on the part of service providers, oftentimes involving some face-to-face contact. Services are "discretionary" to the extent that their delivery requires decisions by providers to be made on the basis of information that is inherently imperfectly specified and incomplete, thereby rendering them unable to be standardized. As such, these decisions usually entail

Table 7.1 Classification of natures of service

	Discretionary	Non-discretionary
Transaction-intensive	"Practice"	"Program"
Non-transaction-intensive	"Policy"	"Rule/Procedure"

Source: Pritchett and Woolcock (2004, pp. 194–195)

3 Analytical Framework, Conceptual Articulation, and Conjectures

Table 7.2 Illustration of the four types of services

Type\Sector	Education	Health
"Policy"	Criteria for teacher certification	Criteria for drug certification
"Program"	Standardized examination	Vaccination
"Practice"	Classroom teaching	Clinical consultation
"Rule/Procedure"	Class registration	Clinical registration

Source: Author

professional (gained via training and/or experience) or informal context-specific knowledge. Discretionary decisions are taken in the process of service delivery; the right decision depends on conditions that are difficult to assess (*ex ante* or *ex post*), and hence it is very difficult to monitor and determine whether or not the right decision was taken.

It is important to distinguish clearly these different modes of services and understand their distinctive characteristics and challenges for effective delivery: "policies" are primarily technocratic; "programs" are primarily bureaucratic; and "practices" are primarily idiosyncratic. The primary challenges for "programs" are technical (finding an effective and least-cost solution) and logistical (carrying out the mandated actions reliably). In contrast, the provision of those elements of services which are discretionary and transaction-intensive—"practices"—poses inherent difficulties for public administration, because they are intrinsically incompatible with the logic and mechanism of large-scale, routinized, administrative control. Large organizations, by nature and design, are essentially constrained to operate exclusively in terms of policies and/or programs, and not apt to manage practices.

We accept and adopt the definition and characterization of the distinctive natures of the four types of services proposed by Pritchett and Woolcock (P-W). We find it necessary to apply a number of comments for further articulation of their definition and characterization, however. Our comments relate to both "transaction intensity" and "discretion":

(P-W) Transaction intensity refers to the extent to which the delivery of a service requires interactive transactions, nearly always involving some face-to-face contact.

Comment #1:

There are distinct differences in required degrees of interaction in service transactions between "practice" and "program."

Comment #2:

Interactive transactions entail ability and willingness to engage on the part of both providers and users of services.

(P-W) Discretionary decisions are taken in the process of service delivery and uptake; the right decision depends on conditions that are difficult to observe or assess (*ex ante* or *ex post*), and hence it is very difficult to monitor and determine whether or not the right decision was taken."

Comment #3:

There is room for front-line service providers to reduce "interactive transactions" by standardizing and routinizing transactions (i.e., turning "practice" into "program") in an attempt to minimize transaction intensity (and thus levels of time/psychic costs entailed).

Comment #4:

There is room for service users to reduce "transaction intensity" in the interactive process of service transactions. Users also could use discretion in utilization of services proffered (as in failure to adhere to instructions and prescriptions).

3.3 Conjectures on Two Types of Failures in Service Provision

Discretionary and transaction-intensive services have the character of being interactive, collaborative and co-productive, and these features apply not only to service providers but to users as well; not only teachers (clinicians) but also students (patients) need to be meaningfully engaged in the transactions for the quality of services, and well-being outcomes, to be achieved. There are two types of failures related to the generation and uptake of discretionary and transaction-intensive services:

Type1: opportunistic behaviors on the part of front-line service providers and service users toward minimization of transaction-intensity

Type2: idealistic pursuit of the maximization of transaction-intensity on the part of policymakers/aid agencies

Failure Type1 in "practices" takes the form of the minimization of transaction intensity. Front-line service providers (teachers and clinicians) may not be able (or willing) to achieve the stipulated modes and levels of transaction-intensity, with consequent deterioration in the quality of service, as discretionary nature of the engagement may allow them to disregard required standards. This is observed in education as in monotonous lecturing, and in health as in routinized diagnosis and prescription. Similarly, service users may not be able (or willing) to achieve the stipulated modes and levels of transaction-intensity; they may not be sufficiently attentive or responsive in classrooms or clinics.

Failure Type2 in "practices" may possibly arise from idealistic pursuits of the maximization of transaction-intensity. Trying to realize stipulated engagement from the users, may excessively heighten the demand for transaction-intensity on the part of service providers, resulting in persistent implementation failures. This concern seems to be particularly pertinent in the assessment of feasibility and effectiveness of the user-centered approach.

In parallel with the above-stated failures in service transactions, there may also be failure (on the part of service users) in self-management in the utilization of services proffered, as mentioned in Comment #4 above.

3.4 Definition and Articulation of Agency and Motivation

In discussing the effectiveness of the UCA models (co-production and self-management), it will be essential that one has systematic understanding of the subjective and objective conditions of the (potential) users of services. Among the subjective conditions are importantly included agency and motivation of the user with regard to the transaction and utilization of services.

Here we propose the working definitions of two terms, agency and motivation, their conceptual clarification and articulation, and an analytical framework for the understanding of the relationship between them.

As in Chap. 4, "agency" is defined as "disposition and capacity for self-determination and self-management of one's own actions and activities." It is postulated as a latent potentiality and something generic with possibilities of application in a wide range of contexts and activities. In contrast, "motivation is defined to be "a factor or process by which agency is activated in a specific context or activity."

As stated in Chap. 4, It is important to distinguish between "agency in existence (AE)" and "agency activated (AA)." We postulate that AE, which is latent, is activated and realized up to the level of AA to the extent that the individual is "motivated" to direct and exert AE to carry out a specific activity. The level of AA exhibited in a certain activity thus is a function of the level of AE and the intensity of motivation for the activity in question. The level of AE at any point in time, on the other hand, may be stipulated to be determined by the following three factors: the initial level of AE, the level of AA over time, and external influences affecting the level of AE.

3.5 Typology of User-Provider Relations and User Agency in Service Transaction and Utilization

In the context of service transaction and utilization, both the level of the existing stock of agency and the intensity of motivation for its activation in the specific context or activity of the service in question are relevant. For the immediate action what matters is the intensity of motivation as the level of the existing stock of agency is given and unalterable at a point in time. Over time, however, the level of the stock of agency can be augmented.

In discussing the role of agency in service transaction and utilization, an additional scheme of classification of services will be in order. Unlike the previous classification scheme, this one places direct focus on different modes of interactions between the user and provider of service, with particular attention to the subjective condition of the service user (Table 7.3). We propose a four-way classification of the user-provider relationship: "(user-driven) service delivery", "consulting" service, "counseling" service, and "pre-counseling" service.

Table 7.3 Typology of user-provider relationship in service transactions

Type 1 "(User-driven) service delivery"
User side Desire and sufficient ability to self-determine "solutions" and express them as wants
Provider side Supply of services to meet user's wants on demand
Type 2 "Consulting service"
User side Desire but insufficient ability to self-determine "solutions" or express them as wants
Provider side Consultation and supply of ideas for "solutions" to user's desire
Type 3 "Counseling service"
User side Vague desire and lack of ability to identify "solutions" or express them as wants
Provider side Counseling and clarification of recipient's desire (through interactive process of communication)
Type 4 "Pre-Counseling service—Outreach"
User side Lack of desire and/or willingness to engage in communication or activity
Provider side Proactive attempts at establishing communication with and providing support to potential users

Source: Author

In some cases, the user clearly identifies what service she wants and is capable of conveying it to the provider as demand. The provider responds to the demand and deliver. These cases may be classified as "(user-driven) service delivery." In some other cases, the user has broad idea as to what she wants but will need to consult with the provider as to appropriate specification of the service to be provided to meet the user's desire. In such cases provision of service will contain elements of "(technical) consulting" in the process of reaching an "informed decision." In yet other cases, the user may desire to change the situation but may not be clear as to what service they want. In such cases, the service will take on the nature of "(psychosocial) counseling", consisting of clarifying the situation, identifying possible solutions, accompanying in the process of mental and behavioral changes, and providing moral support throughout the process. In all cases above, the service user has ability and willingness to engage in service transactions. In some cases, that might not be the case and the provider side might operate proactive "outreach" activities so that potential users of the service be contacted and brought into service transactions, oftentimes of the counseling type.

It is to be recalled that user-provider relations are characterized not only by differing levels of transaction intensity but also by varied degrees of discretion on both sides. Transaction intensity entails sustained attention, judgment and communication, all of which demand exercise of cognitive resources. Discretionary services allow room for reducing transaction intensity. Discretion refers to the condition of service transaction and/or utilization in which effort level realized is left to the person in question. When services are discretionary, there is room for reduced intensity in transaction and/or self-management, thus undermining the quality and outcome of the service. Focusing our attention on the user side, the ability and willingness on the part of (potential) users to engage in service transactions are determined by the activated level of agency. In the short term, with the level of potential agency given, it is a matter of motivation; in the long term, however, it is a matter of agency development, or a change in the level of potential agency. The same considerations on potential and activated agency apply to self-management in the utilization of services on the part of the service user.

These different types of user-provider relations are associated with varying degrees of transaction intensity and discretion on the part of both front-line service providers and service users (Table 7.4).

In the case of "(user-driven) service delivery" interactions between service users and providers tend to be highly standardized and pre-programed involving low levels of transaction intensity and discretion.

Both "consulting" and "counseling" services constitute instances of service co-production insofar as they involve the user and the provider in close communication and collaboration. As well, they also have aspects of self-management on the part of the service user to the extent co-produced services need to be implemented and internalized into the user's routine activities. There seems, however, to be a difference in degree between "consulting" and "counseling" in the levels of transaction intensity and discretion on the part of both service user and provider.

While in "consulting service" the nature of communication and decision is technical and functional, in "counseling service" it is psycho-social and involves personal relationship between the service user (client) and provider (counselor) as essential constituent of interactions between them; as such, "counseling service" almost inevitably involves emotions and subconscious factors. That, it is presumed, makes "counseling service" more transaction-intensive and discretionary than "counseling service." Discretion on the part of the client seems to be of particular significance for "counseling services"; in some extreme cases, the client may not show up for an appointment and when she does she may not engage in conversation with the counselor.

In fact, such is precisely the condition that characterizes the attitude and behavior of potential service users in the state of "self-exclusion" from communication and activity. In such cases, for counseling processes to be initiated, the provider side needs to engage in outreach in a proactive mode. It would typically involve

Table 7.4 Types of user-provider relations and degrees of transaction intensity and discretion

Type 1 "(User-driven) Service delivery"
Λ
Type 2 "Consulting service"
Λ
Type 3 "Counseling service"
Λ(?)
Type 4 "Pre-Counseling service—Outreach"

Source: Author
Note: The sign Λ indicates presumed ascending degrees of transaction intensity and discretion between the four types of user-provider relations

sustained attempts at contact and communication on the part of the front-line service providers like social workers or health workers. To that extent and in that manner the "pre-counseling outreach" will be transaction-intensive on the part of the provider, if not on the potential user's part. It might also be discretionary when and as there is no meaningful feedback from the potential user.

From the perspective of user agency (UA), the following characterization for each type of user-provider relations will be in order (Table 7.5): in "(user-driven) service delivery" UA is manifested as desire for solutions and self-determination of services to be demanded for delivery; in "consulting service" UA is less complete and takes the form of desire for solutions and informed consent to proposals worked out by the consultant; in "counseling service" UA is even less complete and takes on fuzzier tones as expressed as vague desire for the resolution of a problematic situation coupled with willingness, more or less, to engage with the counselor. In "pre-counseling outreach" UA takes on a negative appearance and manifest itself in the act of "self-exclusion" from communication and activity.

The UCA models entail certain level of activated agency on the part of service users in the context of service transactions. Activation of agency is mediated by motivation for the engagement in question. In some cases, this prerequisite for the UCA model may not be met in a short term and there might be need for preceding, preparatory process of agency development.

4 Proposals and Experiences of User-Centered Approach (UCA) to Service Provision

Two models of User-Centered Approach (UCA) to service provision—co-production and self-management—have been proposed and practiced in the recent decades. Co-production and self-management both point to the desirability of increased role of service users in the processes of transaction-intensive services with a view to achieving higher quality, outcome, and satisfaction. Here we will review in a summarized fashion some of the representative initiatives and practices of these two models of UCA, with particular attention to the need of and support for empowerment.

Co-production and self-management are conceptually distinct models, but in practice they are often applied in combined manners. We will see various modes of

Table 7.5 Typology of services and User Agency (UA) ... and implicit stages of Agency Development

Type 1	"(User-driven) service delivery"	UA as "Desire and self-determination"
Type 2	"Consulting service"	UA as "Desire and informed consent"
Type 3	"Counseling service"	UA as "Desire and willingness to engage"
Type 4	"Pre-Counseling service—Outreach"	UA as "Self-exclusion"

Source: Author

such combinations in our review of some general propositions and of important cases of social work.

4.1 General Propositions

Here we will review some general propositions in the form of proposals for and summaries of experiences in User-Centered Approach to service provision.

4.1.1 Co-Production in Public Services (UK Government)

Unlike goods, which can be pre-fabricated, services are generated and received simultaneously in the process of transactions. Therefore, there are bound to be elements of co-production in the realization of service transactions. Going beyond this generality, proponents of co-production emphasize the importance of expanding and legitimizing the role of service users and thus establishing collaborative partnership between the equals.

The central question here is whether providers and users of the service are able and willing to engage actively in the process of service transactions as expected in the co-production model. It is precisely for that reason that provider re-training and user empowerment is proposed in the context of the co-production model.

To date, the most comprehensive advocacy of the co-production model, and User-Centered Approach (UCA) for that matter, is found in a report to the UK government on co-production in public services (Horne & Shirley, 2009). In this report, co-production of services is defined as "a partnership between citizens and public services to achieve a valued outcome." It is argued that "partnerships empower citizens to contribute more of their own resources and have greater control over service decisions and resources" (p. 3). With regard to the importance of co-production, the report states that "co-production should be central to the Government's agenda for improving public services because of emerging evidence of its impact on outcomes and value of [sic] money, its potential economic and social value and its popularity," proposing that co-production in public services be accelerated through such approaches and measures as "more control passed down to individual users and front-line professionals, support for civic society and mutual help, and professional training and culture," among others. (p. 3) At the same time, the report duly acknowledges the scope of its appropriate application when it states that the greatest potential benefits are in 'relational' services such as early years' education, long-term health conditions, adult social care and mental health, rather than in episodic services. (p. 5)

In the co-production model, service users are viewed as being able, and are expected, to contribute their own resources in the form of:

Knowledge, understanding, skill and expertise;
Time, energy and effort;
Will power and personal agency;
Motivations and aspirations; and
Social relationships within families and communities. (pp. 3–9)

Already in the 1980s, Warren et al. (as cited in Pestoff, 2006, p. 507), among others, claimed that co-production can lead to expanded opportunities for citizens to participate, higher service quality and cost reductions, thus opening an avenue for enhanced quantity and quality of public services. Catherine Needham, a noted British scholar on public sector management, identified three advantages of co-production over traditional bureau-professional models of service provision (Woodham, 2008): first, co-production emphasizes the importance of frontline interactions; second, it can transform citizen attitudes in ways that improve service quality, with the emphasis on user agency and empowerment facilitating the creation of more involved, responsible users; and third, with user inputs into the productive process, frontline providers and their managers can become more sensitive to user needs and preferences and better tailor services to them, improving relevance, effectiveness and efficiency of service provision.[5]

There are challenges as well. Co-production demands mutual readjustment on both providers and users of services. We will return to this issue in what follows in some specific contexts.

4.1.2 People-Centered Primary Care (WHO)

World Health Organization (WHO, 2008) called for a switch to "people-centered primary care" in its flagship publication *World Health Report 2008 (WHR2008)* featuring on primary health care. People-centered primary care was characterized in contrast with conventional medical care as "focused on health needs" (as against on illness and cure), "continuous personal relationship" (as against episodic encounter), and "partnership in health management" (as against subjugation and passivity) (Table 3.1, p. 43).

According to *WHR 2008*, in conventional medical care, clinicians rarely address their patients' concerns, beliefs and understanding of illness, and seldom share problem management options with them. They limit themselves to simple technical prescriptions, ignoring the complex human dimensions that are critical to the appropriateness and effectiveness of the care they provide. Thus, technical advice on

---

[5] Durose et al., while stating that there is some evidence that co-production may lead to better quality service provision, caution that there are inherent difficulties in applying standard evaluation methodology based on outcome indicators to co-production practices. There are emotional and reflexive elements involved in service transactions. Co-production is described as a process through which the emotional knowledge of users, such as the experience of having a particular disease, is taken into account. It is relational aspects of care that patients prioritize (respect, dignity, being treated as an individual) and these intangibles are hard to pin down in quality indicators.

lifestyle, treatment schedule or referral all too often neglects not only the constraints of the environment in which people live, but also their potential for self-help in dealing with a host of health problems (p. 46).

There has been progress in recent years, more notably in high-income countries. Confrontation with chronic disease, mental health problems, multi-morbidity and the social dimension of disease has focused attention on the need for more comprehensive and user-centered approaches and continuity of care. This resulted not only from client pressure, but also from professionals who realized the critical importance of such features of care in achieving better outcomes for their patients (pp. 45–46). A considerable body of research evidence has shown that people-centered primary care measurably improved the quality of care, the success of treatment and the quality of life of those benefiting from such care (Table 3.2, p. 47).

There remain challenges, however. Few health providers have been trained for user-centered care. Lack of proper preparation is compounded by cross-cultural conflicts, social stratification, discrimination and stigma. As a consequence, the considerable potential of people to contribute to their own health through lifestyle, behavior and self-care, and by adapting professional advice optimally to their life circumstances is underutilized. There are numerous, albeit often missed, opportunities to empower people to participate in decisions that affect their own health and that of their families (Box 3.4, p. 48).

4.1.3 Improving Chronic Illness Care Program (Robert Wood Johnson Foundation)[6]

The Improving Chronic Illness Care (ICIC) Program was initiated in 1998 by the Robert Wood Johnson Foundation (RWJF), a US philanthropy with strong interest in the improvement of health care practice, with a view to addressing the problem of treatment of patients with ongoing, incurable illness. The ICIC Program endorsed and helped propagate the Chronic Care Model (CCM) proposed by Dr. Edward Wagner. The Chronic Care Model (CCM) is designed to help facilities improve patient health outcomes by changing the routine delivery of ambulatory care through six interrelated system changes meant to make patient-centered, evidence-based care easier to accomplish. The aim of the CCM is to transform the daily care for patients with chronic illnesses from being acute, reactive and episodic to planned, proactive and population-based. It is designed to accomplish these goals through a combination of the following measures: effective team care and planned interactions; self-management support bolstered by more effective use of community resources; decision support integrating medical and psycho-social considerations; and patient registries and other supportive information technology. These elements

---

[6] This section draws on information provided on the homepage of the Robert Wood Johnson Foundation (RWJF). http://www.rwjf.org/en/our-work.html.

are designed to work together to strengthen the provider-patient relationship and improve health outcomes (Coleman et al., 2009).

A Rand Corporation study examined fifty-one organizations, posing the following two questions: first, can practices implement the CCM? and secondly, if they can, will their patients benefit? (Cretin et al., 2004) The study's summary propositions read as follows: On the first question, intervention practices were able to implement the CCM, making an average of forty-eight practice changes across all six CCM elements. Three-fourths of practices sustained these changes one year later, and about the same proportion spread the CCM to new sites or conditions. On the second question, patients of intervention practices received improved care compared to patients in control practices as reflected in knowledge level, increased uptake of recommended therapies, fewer days in the hospital, fewer visits to the emergency department, and improved quality of life.

The real-world implementation and sustenance of the CCM in busy practices is not without challenges. The typical primary care situation in the United States as of early 1990s was described by Dr. Edward Wagner as follows (Wielawski, 2006).

- The typical primary care office is set up to respond to acute illness rather than to anticipate and respond proactively to patients' needs, as is adequate to meet the needs of chronically ill patients in order to avoid acute episodes of illness and debilitating complications.
- Chronically ill patients are not sufficiently informed about their conditions, nor are they supported in self-care beyond the doctor's office.
- Physicians are too busy to educate and support chronically ill patients to the degree necessary to keep them healthy.

This might well be the typical condition in many developing counties at present.

In the process of introducing the CCM in the United States, there were many obstacles for individuals and organizations to change long-standing ways of practicing medicine. Physicians were not immediately comfortable with transferring clinical responsibilities to colleagues traditionally viewed as subordinates; the chronic care model's emphasis on clinical teamwork challenges medicine's traditional hierarchy, forcing recognition of other health care professionals as equal or superior to physicians in certain patient care tasks. Patients did not necessarily jump at the chance to become collaborators and self-managers after years of following doctors' orders (Wielawski, 2006).

4.2 Case Study

4.2.1 Nurse-Family Partnership[7]

The Nurse-Family Partnership (NFP) program constitutes an important case of co-production and self-management. The program was developed in the United States, where it has been rigorously tested over the course of 35 years

In NFP, trained nurses visit first-time young mothers 64 times over a 30-month period covering six months of pregnancy before the birth of a child and the first two years of the child's life. The program focuses on low-income, first-time mothers—a vulnerable population segment that sometimes has limited access to good parenting information or role-models. When a young woman becomes pregnant before she is ready to take care of a child, the risk factors for the entire family escalate—often resulting in dysfunctional family life. The transition to motherhood can be particularly challenging for many low-income, first-time mothers. Many are socially isolated or are experiencing severe adversity. An early intervention during pregnancy will allow for any critical behavioral changes needed to improve the health and welfare of the mother and child.

The NFP program is informed by the following four philosophical standpoints:

Client-Centered: the nurse is constantly adapting to ensure the visit and materials are relevant and valued by the parent. The goals and aspirations of the nurse and family are aligned and a sense of responsibility is established in the client with clear structure and understanding of what the program entails.

Relational: the relationship between the nurse and the client is the fundamental basis for learning and growth in each family served, with intimacy and continuity building trust. The nurse provides care and guidance for mothers and family members to deal with stress and anxiety.

Strengths-Based: the intervention is based on an adult learning and behavior change theory. Adults and adolescents make changes most successfully when they are building on their own knowledge, strengths and successes. Building on the person's strengths and previous successes leads to improved self-efficacy.

Multi-Dimensional: the life of each program participant is viewed holistically, and what the program offers is tied to multiple aspects of personal and family functioning: personal and environmental health, parenting, life course development, relationships with family and friends, and community connections.

In accordance with the above-mentioned philosophical perspectives, the NFP model is expressed in 18 elements of principles and operational guidelines. Among them the following are of particular interest (underlines added):

- Client participates voluntarily in the Nurse-Family Partnership program (Element 1).

---

[7] This section draws on information provided on the homepage of the Nurse-Family Partnership (NFP). http://www.nursefamilypartnership.org/.

- Client is visited one-to-one, one nurse home visitor to one first-time mother or family (Element 5).
- Client is visited in her home (Element 6).
- Nurse home visitors, using professional knowledge, judgment, and skill, apply the Nurse-Family Partnership visit guidelines, individualizing them to the strengths and challenges of each family and apportioning time across defined program domains (Element 10).
- Nurse home visitors apply the theoretical framework that underpins the program, emphasizing self-efficacy, human ecology, and attachment theories, through current clinical methods (Element 11).
- A full-time nurse home visitor carries a caseload of no more than 25 active clients (Element 12).
- A full-time nurse supervisor provides supervision to no more than eight individual nurse home visitors (Element 13).
- Nurse supervisors provide nurse home visitors clinical supervision with reflection, demonstrate integration of the theories, and facilitate professional development essential to the nurse home visitor role through specific supervisory activities including one-to-one clinical supervision, case conferences, team meetings, and field supervision (Element 14).

NFP is designed to achieve the following three goals by means of home-visitor nurses offering a combination of technical advice and practical support (on breastfeeding, child development and childhood illnesses), coaching in life skills, and addressing psychological issues:

– Improve pregnancy outcomes by helping mothers engage in good preventive health and prenatal practices, including getting appropriate prenatal care from healthcare providers, improving their diet, and reducing their use of cigarettes, alcohol, and illegal substances. Nurses also help the mother prepare emotionally for the arrival of the baby by educating her on the birth process and the immediate challenges of the first few weeks after delivery (e.g., breastfeeding and potential postpartum depression).
– Improve child health and development by providing individualized parent education and coaching aimed at increasing awareness of specific child development milestones and behaviors, and encouraging parents to use praise and other nonviolent techniques.
– Improve the economic self-sufficiency of the family through life coaching, i.e., helping parents develop a vision for their own future, plan future pregnancies, continue their education, and find work

Effectiveness of the NFP interventions is rigorously demonstrated.[8] Three well-conducted randomized controlled trials were carried out, each in a different popula-

---

[8] The Top Tier Initiative's Expert Panel has identified NFP intervention as *Top Tier*, meeting the Congressional Top Tier Evidence standard, defined as: *Interventions shown in well-designed and implemented randomized controlled trials, preferably conducted in typical community settings, to*

tion and setting. The specific effects that were replicated, with no countervailing findings, in two or more of the trials—and thus are the most likely to be reproducible in a program replication—are: (i) reduction in measures of child abuse and neglect (including injuries and accidents); (ii) reduction in mothers' subsequent births during their late teens and early twenties; (iii) reduction in prenatal smoking among mothers who smoked at the start of the study; and (iv) improvement in cognitive and/or academic outcomes for children born to mothers with low psychological resources (i.e., intelligence, mental health, self-confidence). It is important to recall that the three trials all found the program to produce sizable, sustained effects on important mother and child outcomes, which provides confidence that this program would be effective if faithfully replicated in other, similar populations and settings.

5 Empowerment of (Potential) Service Users for Partnership and Self-Management

The term "empowerment" has broader and narrower acceptations; in some cases, it could focus on legal stipulation and institutional arrangement; in some other cases, it may refer to the process of enhancement of technical capacities to conduct certain tasks; in yet others, it may relate to internal change on the part of an individual touching on the psychological and attitudinal state of the person. In what follows we will discuss most relevant and important aspects and dimensions of empowerment in the context of this chapter.

Psycho-social support for (potential) service users constitutes a central component in "counseling" service aimed for their effective participation in service transactions and for self-management. Alongside it, there might also be "consulting" service aimed at providing information and helping with a decision for the service user.

5.1 General Propositions

One important question in the application of UCA is whether (potential) service users are able and willing to engage actively and positively in the process of service transactions as expected in the co-production model and/or conduct their daily lives as expected in the self-management model. It is precisely for that reason that user empowerment is proposed in the context of UCA. As "empowerment" has various

---

produce sizable, sustained benefits to participants and/or society. See Coalition for Evidence Based Policy homepage. http://toptierevidence.org/programs-reviewed/interventions-for-children-age-0-6/nurse-family-partnership.

aspects and dimensions, it will be useful to clarify the usage of the term in this chapter. We will rely on Rowlands (1997) as base camp for our exploration.

Classification schemes on forms of "power" and for dimensions of "empowerment" proposed by Rowlands (1997) have been widely accepted and referred to. The scheme on power comprises the following four forms of power and corresponding understandings of empowerment (p. 13):

- **power over:** controlling power
- **power to:** generative or productive power which creates new possibilities and actions
- **power with:** a sense of the whole being greater than the sum of the individuals, especially when a group tackles problems together
- **power from within:** the spiritual strength and uniqueness that resides in each one of us and makes us truly human. Its basis is self-acceptance and self-respect.

For the purpose of this chapter the most relevant and important form of power is "power from within," which, we presume, essentially coincides with our notion of human agency as disposition and capacity for self-determination and self-management.

Rowlands (1997, p. 15) proposes a three-way classification scheme on dimensions of "empowerment":

- **personal:** developing a sense of self and individual confidence and capacity, and undoing the effects of internalized oppression
- **relational:** developing the ability to negotiate and influence the nature of a relationship and decisions made within it
- **collective:** where individuals work together to achieve a more extensive impact than each could have had alone

For the purpose of this chapter the first two dimensions of "empowerment" are more relevant than the third. In particular, we will focus on the process of empowerment on the "personal" dimension as an aspect of goal of human development, as a necessary condition for effective partnership in co-production and self-management, and as a necessary basis for empowerment on the other dimensions. In relation to our conceptual configuration, personal empowerment will be viewed either "activation of (existing) agency" or "development of agency" depending on the nature and duration of the process of change. Empowerment on the "relational" dimension will be of particular significance in the context of engagement of service users in service transactions.

It is widely recognized that knowledge dissemination alone rarely generates behavioral changes including those related to uptake and utilization of services. The act of uptake and utilization of services entails a certain degree of activation of agency. The knowledge of eligibility to and availability of services does not automatically translate into such action; accessibility of services for specific individuals and manageability of the action of uptake and utilization may pose high hurdles to clear before potential users convert themselves into actual users of services, even when they are desired. More fundamentally, services may not be desired to start with due to weak agency (i.e., insufficiency in disposition and capacity for self-determination and self-management).

In the next section, where we review specific cases of interventions for empowerment of (potential) service users, we will discuss the nature, intensity and duration of intervention for activation or development of agency as key factor in personal and relational empowerment. Interventions vary in nature, intensity and duration depending on the goals they seek to achieve. For instance, counseling service may be of short-term or long-term nature: it may aim to increase motivation and thus raise the level of activated agency through a small number of brief interventions; or it may be directed toward a heightened level of potential agency through continuous accompaniment to a gradual, cumulative process of internal change of the client.

5.2 Cases of Interventions for Agency Activation and Agency Development

Intervention for empowerment consists of "consulting" (technical support through education and advice) and/or "counseling" (psycho-social support through accompaniment and encouragement). In some cases, intervention is carried out over a short period of time, with relatively more emphasis on consulting, to increase motivation for certain action. In other cases, by contrast, intervention continues over a long period of time, with relatively more emphasis on counseling. The former typically aims at motivation and activation of agency, while the latter at development of agency. Interventions of both types need to be tailored to the conditions of the person being attended, but such considerations will be of higher significance in the case of agency development, as it involves more fundamental changes in strengthening self-esteem, self-control and self-efficacy and enhancing expectations for positive change in life.

5.2.1 Interventions for Agency Activation

Here we take up two important examples of intervention for agency activation. The first, a patient education program developed at Stanford University called Chronic Disease Self-Management Program (CDSMP), is essentially in the nature of consulting, offering information and providing technical training for self-management for people with chronic diseases. The second, Motivational Interviewing (MI), is in the nature of counseling, providing psychological support for increased motivation for change.

Chronic Disease Self-Management Program[9]

The Chronic Disease Self-Management Program (CDSMP) is a short-term consulting cum counseling program offered for two and a half hours, once a week, for six weeks. People with different chronic health problems attend together in community settings such as senior and community centers, churches, libraries, senior housing, retirement communities and physician offices. The workshops are facilitated by two trained leaders; one or both have a chronic condition. The six-week workshop covers techniques to deal with problems such as: frustration, fatigue, pain and isolation; appropriate exercise for maintaining and improving strength, flexibility and endurance; appropriate use of medications; communicating effectively with family, friends and health professionals; nutrition; and how to evaluate new treatments.

The details of the six-week workshop curriculum are as follows:

Session One:
- Principles of self-management
- Problems caused by chronic illness
- Difference between chronic disease and acute disease
- Common elements of various chronic health problems
- Causes of symptoms
- Introduction of self-management techniques
- Overview of "distraction skill"
- Introduction of action plans as a key self-management tool

Session Two:
- Problem-solving techniques
- Discussion and management of anger, fear and frustration
- Benefits of exercise; different types of exercise; choosing an appropriate fitness program
- Action planning

Session Three:
- Causes of shortness of breath
- Practice in better breathing techniques
- Introduction to progressive muscle relaxation
- Introduction to causes of pain and fatigue
- Introduction to pain and fatigue management techniques
- Development and monitoring of an endurance exercise program
- Action planning

Session Four:
- Overview of good nutrition and rationale for eating better
- Ways to change eating practices and make healthier eating choices

---

[9] This section draws on information on the homepage of the Chronic Disease Self-Management Program (CDSMP) http://patienteducation.stanford.edu/programs/cdsmp.html.

5 Empowerment of (Potential) Service Users for Partnership and Self-Management 145

- Future plans for health care
- Techniques for improving communication
- Practice of problem-solving: helping self and others
- Action planning

Session Five:
- Medication management
- Differences between drug allergy and side effects
- Strategies to reduce side effects
- Overview of depression symptoms and means of managing minor depression
- Strategies to change negative thinking to positive thinking
- Action planning

Session Six:
- Communication skills useful for talking with physicians
- Participant identification of patient's role in care of chronic condition
- Making a plan to deal with future health problems

It is the process in which the CDSMP is taught that makes it effective. Sessions are highly participative, and mutual support and success build participants' confidence in their ability to manage their health and maintain active and fulfilling lives.

The CDSMP was designed on the basis of research at Stanford University, whose purpose was to develop and evaluate, through a randomized controlled trial, a community-based self-management program that assists people with chronic illness. The CDSMP process design was based on the experience of the investigators working on self-efficacy, people's confidence that they can master a new skill or affect their own health.

The content of the workshop was the result of focus groups in which people with chronic health problems discussed which content areas were the most important for them.

There are a number of assumptions that underlie the CDSMP:

- People with chronic conditions have similar concerns and problems.
- People with chronic conditions must deal not only with their disease(s), but also with the impact these have on their lives and emotions.
- Lay people with chronic conditions, when given a detailed leaders' manual, can teach the CDSMP as effectively, if not more effectively, as health professionals.
- The process or way the CDSMP is taught is as important, if not more important, as the workshop's subject matter.

About 1000 people with heart disease, lung disease, stroke or arthritis participated in a randomized, controlled test of the program and were subsequently followed for up to three years. Changes were recorded in many areas: health status (disability, pain and physical discomfort, energy/fatigue, shortness of breath, health distress, self-rated general health, social/role limitations, depression, and psychological well-being/distress); health care utilization (visits to physicians, visits to emergency department, and hospital stays); self-efficacy (confidence to perform self-management behaviors, manage disease in general and achieve outcomes); and self-management behaviors (exercise, cognitive symptom management, mental stress management/relaxation, use of community resources, communication with physician and advance directives).

CDSMP has undergone extensive evaluation in several countries. The program has been proven effective across socioeconomic and education levels and the health benefits persist over a two-year period even when disability worsens. CDSMP's health and utilization effects, compiled by The Centers for Disease Control and Prevention in partnership with the National Council on Aging, are summarized as follows:

There is strong evidence that CDSMP has a beneficial effect on physical and emotional outcomes and health-related quality of life. When participant outcomes were evaluated at four months, six months, one year and two years, program participants, when compared to non-participants, demonstrated significant improvements in exercise, cognitive symptom management, communication with physicians, self-reported general health, health distress, fatigue, disability and social/role activities limitations. All outcomes reported have statistical significance.

From the perspective of this chapter, it is interesting to note that improvement in communication with physicians is included in the positive outcomes of the program, presumably reflecting the effects of components such as "techniques for improving communication" in Session 4 and "Communication skills useful for talking with physicians" in Session 6 in the six-week workshop curriculum. Judging from the listing of the items in the curriculum, this program seems to be essentially of consulting nature, offering knowledge and technical skills, with few, if any, elements of psychological support.

Motivational Interviewing[10]

Motivational Interviewing (MI) is a method of counseling that aims to enhance a person's motivation to change problematic behavior by exploring and resolving his ambivalence about change. MI is a relatively brief intervention, typically delivered within one to four sessions each lasting 20 to 60 minutes. It can be delivered as a free-standing intervention or as part of other treatments, such as cognitive-behavioral therapies. It has been used extensively to treat substance use and other problems. This is an important instance of the application of Carl Rogers' client-centered approach to counseling. Its central purpose is efficacious self-management of problematic behavioral tendencies.

MI assumes a collaborative partnership between the client and the practitioner. MI addresses a situation in which client behavior change is needed, thus having a more specific goal than the client-centered method, which is a broad approach to

---

[10] This section draws on Soederlund (2010) and information on the homepage of Motivational Interviewing (MI). http://www.motivationalinterview.org/ (accessed 14/09/20).

counseling. MI involves an active collaborative conversation and joint decision-making process between the practitioner and the client. MI practitioners seek to activate clients' own motivation and resources for change instead of just giving them what they might lack, for example, medication or information. This involves connecting behavior change with a client's values and concerns. This requires an understanding of the client's own perspective and, for that purpose, evoking the client's own arguments and reasons for change (Rollnick et al., 2008).

MI was first developed in the 1980s by William R. Miller, an American psychologist, in response to concerns about the traditional confrontational approach used in addiction treatment, typically involving overt, aggressive confrontation and challenging people with the threat of strongest negative effects of their current situation. In MI it is assumed that clients have "intrinsic motivation" to change and MI's goal is to facilitate movement towards, and consolidate commitment to, change. MI enhances motivation for behavior change by expressing empathy and support, exploring the discrepancies between present behavior and current or future values and goals, eliciting "change talk", "rolling with resistance" rather than arguing for change, supporting self-efficacy and affirming the client's choice and autonomy (Miller & Rollnick, 2002).

MI emphasizes helping a client to make their own decision to change, rather than the client being pressured from external sources. Clients must bear the responsibility of deciding for themselves whether or not to change and how best to go about it. The intention is to transfer the responsibility for arguing for change to the client by eliciting "change talk", that is, overt declarations by the client that demonstrate recognition of the need for change, concern for their current position, intention to change, and the belief that change is possible (Miller & Rollnick, 2002). The counselor's role in the process is to help clients clarify their motivations for change; provide information and support; and offer alternative perspectives on the present problem behaviors and potential methods for changing these behaviors (Miller & Rollnick, 2002).

There are typically two phases of MI sessions. The client is often ambivalent about change in the first phase and may be insufficiently motivated to accomplish change. Hence, the aim of this phase is to resolve the client's ambivalence and facilitate increased intrinsic motivation to change. The second phase commences when the client shows signs of readiness to change. This may be manifested by talk or questions about change and descriptions that suggest that the client is envisioning a future when the desired changes have been made. The focus in the second phase shifts to strengthening the commitment to change and supporting the client to develop and implement a plan to achieve the changes.

The effectiveness of MI in achieving behavioral changes has been examined in a large number of randomized controlled trials (RCTs) on behavioral changes since the late 1990s. These studies have been conducted in various settings and for a number of health-related behaviors, including alcohol, drugs, diet, exercise, and smoking. The largest body of literature concerns the use of MI in addressing alcohol abuse and dependence. According to the most comprehensive review so far, MI is significantly more effective than no treatment and generally at least equal to other treatments for problems such as substance abuse (alcohol, marijuana, tobacco and other drugs) for reducing risky behaviors and increasing client engagement in treatment (Lundahl & Burke, 2009).

5.2.2 Intervention for Agency Development

Here we take up an important case of intervention for agency development introduced in Sect. 3.2, investigate the nature of long-term intervention carried out, and offer tentative judgment as to the necessary conditions for the realization of the development of agency.

Nurse-Family Partnership (NFP)

First of all, it is important to recall that the Nurse-Family Partnership (NFP) program is designed to have sufficient intensity and duration (64 visits over a 30-month period) for a trustful, committed relationship to be formed between the nurse and the mother. Another important consideration is the level of workload for nurses (no more than 25 active clients) and for supervisors (no more than eight individual nurse home visitors). These stipulations help secure sufficient intensity of interactions between the nurse and the mother and between the supervisor and the nurse.

It is interesting to note that the impact of the program was more pronounced among children born to mothers with limited psychological resources to manage well the care of their children while living in concentrated social disadvantage (limited psychological resources manifest themselves in higher levels of depression, anxiety, and lower levels of intellectual functioning and sense of mastery over their lives). This was demonstrated in lower incidence of injuries and in higher school readiness (i.e., better language development and ability to control impulses) compared with their control-group counterparts. In contrast, there were no benefits of the program for these types of outcomes among children born to mothers with relatively high psychological resources (those with greater wherewithal to manage caring for their children while living in poverty). This contrast seems to imply the existence of a certain threshold level in the mother's psychological resources needed to attain sufficient level of agency and to exercise self-control and provide adequate care to their children.

To achieve the third goal of the program, i.e., to improve the economic self-sufficiency of the family, nurses offer life coaching, helping mothers develop a vision for their own future, plan future pregnancies, continue their education, and find work. While working with their nurse home visitor, many of the young mothers in the Nurse-Family Partnership program set goals for themselves for the very first time. Research shows that NFP does, indeed, improve maternal life course. Apparently, nurses help the mother to feel empowered to make sound choices about education, workplace participation, partner relationships, and the timing of subsequent pregnancies that enable her to take better care of herself and her child.

Based on these pieces of evidence, it may be reasonable to conclude that the NFP program has succeeded in the augmentation of agency among participating young mothers with particularly significant impacts on those of them with less favorable initial conditions. As stated as Element 1 in Sect. 4.2, the NFP program works with mothers who voluntarily participate. To that extent it presupposes clients' agency to engage. The nature of user-provider relations is a combination of consulting and counseling, initially relatively more in the nature of counseling and subsequently and gradually relative importance of consulting increasing over the course of the program. This represents a cumulative process of activation and development of agency on the part of the client, with disposition and capacity for self-determination and self-management strengthened through repeated actions and continued support.

6 Concluding Remarks

The User-Centered Approach (UCA) has humanistic as well as practical appeals. There are certain goals and target populations that could be only reached and served through the UCA. There are cases of notable successes of the UCA achieving more active roles of service users, with agency activation as in CDSMP and MI, and with agency development as in the Nurse-Family Partnership (NFP) and other similar social work programs. These examples do highlight the rationales and accomplishments of the UCA. At the same time, however, they seem to point to rather demanding conditions needed for its successful implementation.

We started this chapter with reference to poor quality and insufficient outcome of services in developing countries as documented in impact evaluations as in *Global Monitoring Report 2011 (GMR2011)*. The effectiveness and scalability of the UCA in developing countries needs to be examined against the realities of public services at question, from the viewpoints of transaction intensity and discretion on the parts of both providers and users of services, and also with the conjectures on service system failures in mind. So far, the evidence base for the experiences of UCA models is limited and there is little empirical basis to indicate their effectiveness in the context of dire situations of public service failures in developing countries.

There are ideational and theoretical rationales for the UCA as presented in the advocacy and proposals of its application. It needs to be subjected to a reality check for its feasibility and effectiveness. The UCA entails higher intensities of transactions thus demand more psychic and cognitive resources from both sides of service transactions. Especially for service users, it involves a qualitatively different role of taking charge of their own affairs in partnership with service providers and through self-management. To discharge such a role, they have to pay active attention, interact with others, and make decisions and act on them, all demanding individual efforts in the utilization of psychic and cognitive resources, or activation of agency, and causing psychic costs. As a matter of human nature, transaction intensity tends to bring about discretionary response toward averting such costs and thus avoiding the activation of agency. And, more often than not, there are existing competing demands on the use of these resources. This is and will likely remain a fundamental constraint on the scalability of UCA models.

References

Coleman, K., Austin, B. T., Brach, C., & Wagner, E. H. (2009). Evidence on the Chronic Care Model in the New Millennium. *Health Affairs, 28*(1), 75–85.

Cretin, S., Shortell, S. M., & Keeler, E. B. (2004). An Evaluation of Collaborative Interventions to Improve Chronic Illness Care: Framework and Study Design. *Evaluation Review, 28*(1), 28–51.

Horne, M., & Shirley, T. (2009). *Co-Production in Public Services: A New Partnership with Citizens.* Cabinet Office.

Lundahl, B., & Burke, B. L. (2009). The Effectiveness and Applicability of Motivational Interviewing: A Practice-Friendly Review of Four Meta-Analyses. *Journal of Clinical Psychology, 65*(11), 1232–1245.

Miller, W. R., & Rollnick, S. (2002). *Motivational Interviewing – Preparing People for Change.* .

Ostrom, E. (1996). Crossing the Great Divide: Coproduction, Synergy, and Development. *World Development, 24*(6), 1073–1087.

Pestoff, V. (2006). Citizens and Co-Production of Welfare Services: Childcare in EIGHt European Countries. *Public Management Review, 8*(4), 503–519.

Pritchett, L., & Woolcock, M. (2004). Solutions When the Solution Is the Problem: Arraying the Disarray in Development. *World Development, 32*(2), 191–212.

Pritchett, L., Woolcock, M., & Andrews, M. (2010). *Capability Traps? The Mechanisms of Persistent Implementation Failure.* Center for Global Development Working Paper, (234).

Rollnick, S., Miller, W. R., & Butler, C. (2008). *Motivational Interviewing in Health Care: Helping Patients Change Behavior.* Guilford Press.

Rowlands, J. (1997). *Questioning Empowerment: Working with Women in Honduras.* Oxfam.

Soederlund, L. L. (2010). *Motivational Interviewing in Theory and Practice.* Linkoeping University Medical Dissertations 1198. http://www.diva-portal.org/smash/get/ diva2:356212/FULLTEXT01.pdf

Wielawski, I. M. (2006). *Improving Chronic Illness Care.* HSMC, University of Birmingham and NHS Institute for Innovation and Improvement.

Woodham, C. (2008). Realising the Potential of Co-production: Negotiating Improvements in Public Services. *Social Policy and Society, 7*(02), 221–231.

World Bank. (2003). *World Development Report (WDR) 2004: Making Services Work for Poor People.* https://doi.org/10.1596/0-8213-5468-X

World Bank. (2011). *Global Monitoring Report (GMR) 2011: Improving the Odds of Achieving the MDGs.* http://hdl.handle.net/10986/2293

World Health Organization. (2008). *The World Health Report 2008: Primary Health Care Now More Than Ever.* https://www.paho.org/hq/dmdocuments/2010/PHC_The_World_Health_Report-2008_overview.pdf

Part III
Visualizing and Measuring Agency

Chapter 8
Writing, Telling, Expressing Self in Association with Others: Revisiting and Examining Life Record Movement as an Origin of Story-Based Methods in Japan

1 Introduction: Power of Telling Stories

Having been given countless opportunities to visit people and listen to their life stories as an anthropologist, when recalling those interviews, the author often remembers not only the contents themselves but also the "side utilities" of those interviews. The interviewees, usually women living in suburban and rural communities, either in developing or developed countries, often appreciated how their narratives were listened to closely and transformed into "meaningful" stories. Some have even said that they felt their life was approved and recognized to be meaningful for the first time in their lives. The author often feels that telling and listening to life stories themselves generates spaces for interviewees (and perhaps for interviewers as well) to recognize their value and foster a sense of self-respect.

Another example that taught the author power of telling a story was sociodrama. While managing adolescent reproductive health programs in Nicaragua in the early 2000s, the author launched a socio drama project with a local art non-profit organization. Some adolescents participated in the project, which allowed them to act in a drama and make the drama itself with professionals, reflecting their voices and experiences. It was quite impressive to observe how they improved their postures and vocalization in a short period, which also seemed to influence their personalities and levels of "self-esteem" positively.

Telling stories to others itself can also be powerful. In the preceding chapter, the author introduced and examined the case study of a Methodology of Motivation and Organization (MMO) in Nicaragua. In each MMO session, either local facilitators or participants read stories related to the session themes aloud. Although they have not necessarily made the stories themselves, they seemed to enjoy narrating stories, sometimes inserting their episodes or slightly modifying the story plots to remake them anew, reflecting a few of their own episodes.

The last example is *Haiku*, a form of Japanese short poetry. Some rules exist to compose *Haiku*, such as using *Kigo* (it should include a season word in each *Haiku*) and limiting the number of syllables (17 syllables are used in general) and what is read is a seasonal relevant phenomenon, with a slight dash of reflections of one's stories and feelings somewhat metaphorically. The author joins a *Kukai* (Haiku Circle) and makes *Haiku* and read other members' *Haiku* to make comments monthly in a *Kukai*. The author always appreciates the power of *Haiku* that gives an enormous sense of peacefulness and vitality. Recently, a Haiku poet named Rin Kobayashi published a couple of Haiku Poetry Collections which have been selling very well. Kobayashi, having been born prematurely, his classmates bullied him for being skinny and tiny. So he decided not to go to junior high school and chose to homeschool, kept making *Haiku*, and published a couple of books, some of which became bestsellers. In addition, he made it possible to connect himself with others through *Haiku* (Kobayashi, 2018).

Listening, reading, interpreting, making, and remaking stories is thus fundamental and indispensable for human wellbeing. Story-based methods and narrative approaches are also utilized in psychological counseling and social work (Yamada, 2008). In International Development, some story-based methods such as sociodrama and digital storytelling (DST) have also been applied in many projects.

In some Japanese academic articles, such as Ogawa (2018), we learn that one of the crucial origins of Japanese story-based methods is the postwar Life Record Movement (LRM) *Seikatsu Kiroku Undo* in Japanese. According to Kazuko Tsurumi (1958, pp. 439–440), a life record is a text written by adults regarding their daily life experiences and feelings concretely, using their own words to convey their feelings and thoughts to other people. Tsuji (2015, p. 3) explains that such attempts were continuous and called a "movement."

In the fields of History, Sociology, and Pedagogy, proceeding studies regarding LRM have accumulated since the 1950s. According to the list by Tsuji (2015, pp. 13–19), there are 125 books and articles about LRM from 1952 till 2014. Significant research has been done by scholars such as Tsurumi (1970), Ogushi (1981), and Okado (2012). One of the major research topics is the "self-formation" of participants (such as Nishikawa, 2009 and Tsuji, 2015), who were often teenage girls and young women from rural villages working in textile factories in cities. As similar situations are observed in currently developing countries, the author feels motivated to learn the contents in detail to extract meaningful lessons. However, in International Development Studies, LRM has not been researched, and there are few publications regarding LRM in English in any field of study.

Based upon the above contexts and backgrounds, in this chapter, the author traces historical elaborations of LRM in the post-war context to find meaningful suggestions to current social and international projects that incorporate agency development or empowerment aspects. As an Anthropologist, the author focuses more on participants' realities reflected in primary sources and the subjective changes felt by them.

The author sets the following three inquiries to understand LRM from the aspect of agency development that are to be discussed and contested:

(a) What could be facilitating factors and inhibitors of LRM activities to commence, develop, and endure?
(b) How can subtle transformation, which could be understood as agency development, be observed in members' texts and narratives and those of the supporters?
(c) What can be plausible mechanisms of agency development interpreted from the case study?

Research methods are a literature review (both primary and secondary data, but all available as printed media) and its analysis. No interviews were conducted because of research restrictions under COVID-19 situations.

In the following sections, first, the author traces the roots and development of LRM in postwar Japan, explicating its history, emergence, mechanisms, and logic of "agency development" explained by researchers. Subsequently, a case of a writing circle and its members' compositions is introduced. Thirdly, their reflections on their compositions and experiences are to be shared. Fourthly, the author analyses the case according to the above three questions related to agency development. Finally, implications for current social and international development projects, including empowerment components, will be extracted and discussed.

2 Roots and Development of Life Record Movement in the Postwar Japan

This section introduces and explores LRM in the postwar context. The author overviews its historical trajectory and its facts and logic of agency development explained by intellectuals though not expressed.

2.1 Historical Trajectory from the Edo Era

According to the seminar record by Sociologist Kazuko Tsurumi at Kochi Citizen's College in 1957 (Tsurumi in Ukai, 2012), one of the origins of LRM at the grassroot level can be traced back to *Terakoya*, which are small private schools for children often run at temples in the Edo era. At *Terakoya*, reading, copying, and writing letters by hand are important educational methods to understand how to express and explain one's feelings and experiences to others. However, in the Meiji Era, such education was abandoned under government control because of the educational reforms. In the Taisho Era, a children's literature journal *Red Bird* was published, where children were taught to express their experiences and feelings as they were. In the early Showa era (in the 1930s, schoolteachers introduced "Life Composition" in their classes not only to express children's lives but also to share experiences and critically reflect upon them for persuading individual changes and social transformation, which was called the Life Composition Movement (LCM), *Seikatsu*

Tsuzurikata Undo in Japanese. However, during World War II, approximately 300 schoolteachers, including those who led LCM, were arrested (ibid.).

According to Tsurumi (1970), many ordinary adult people, especially women, kept diaries secretly as their mental safety valves to console their feelings in oppressive societies but did not have opportunities to share the contents and learn from their own experiences with others. However, after the war ended, LCM again became activated, and two books were published. One was *"Atarashii Tsuzurikata Kyoshitsu* (New Composition Class)" by Ichitaro Kokubun (1951), who was a schoolteacher in Yamagata Prefecture. The other was *"Yamabiko Gakko* (Echo from a mountain school)," which was a student composition anthology edited by Seikyo Muchaku (1952), who was also a schoolteacher/monk in Yamagata Prefecture. The latter became a best seller and an inspiration for many educators and scholars dealing with adult learning (Tsurumi in Ukai, 2012).

2.2 Facts of Life Record Movement

In the 1950s, inspired by LCM and related publications, many life record circles were established among farmers, female factory workers, and housewives. Thus, ordinary adult people started making writing circles to write their experiences and discuss the contents critically from the 1950s. Such a boom could be facilitated because of the radical social transformation from Militarism to Democracy (Tsurumi, 1970).

Unlike diaries kept secretly as soliloquies, in LRM, members wrote their diaries to be read and shared with other members to discuss and change their situations. (Tsurumi in Ukai, 2012). In 1965, 6000 booklets from 1500 writing circles were legally deposited by the National Diet Library (Tsurumi, 1970). The movement was active in the 1950s but gradually lost its momentum under the post-war rapid economic development (Tsurumi in Ukai, 2012).

Tsurumi (1970) explains circles' processes as below: (1) write individual experiences otherwise never expressed, (2) share compositions in a small group of people who were usually from similar social settings and in the same communities or factories, (3) discuss the contents critically, and (4) reflect such learning upon consciousness or take actions though they are subtle or not shown in actions (ibid.).

Saruyama (2011), through analysis of the notebooks taken by writing circle members in Tokyo, analyses that each writing circle consisted of around ten people of the same interests, and they also discussed how to run the circles and how to self-study their compositions to take necessary actions. They also formed other circles to record war experiences, study social science, and join in singing activities. Those groups had monthly gatherings to share their experiences and discuss common topics for reflection.

2.3 Logics of Agency Development Explained by Researchers and Intellectuals

According to Saruyama (2014), Tsurumi was inspired by John Dewey's Philosophy of communication and democracy, which made her take initiatives to incorporate into LRM. She thought ordinary women did not have opportunities to share their feelings with other women and could not feel free to discuss matters with their "superiors (men, seniors, and those in higher positions)," which made their voices unexpressed/unheard and social conditioning oppressed. Therefore, she thought democratization of communication and human relationships was essential (ibid.). In other words, for Tsurumi, LRM was a sort of "social tool" to realize post-war democracy in daily life.

Tsurumi in Ukai (2012) describes the process of LRM as "emancipating and expanding oneself" or "becoming a new woman emancipated from conventional family systems" through situating one's experience into the society to recognize it not as being personal but as social.

In her Ph.D. dissertation, Tsurumi (1970) interviewed the LRM members in Mie and witnessed that they were more "emancipated" from the following observations: becoming members of labor unions and demanding raises, joining and leading strikes against exploitive work situations, achieving higher productivity than non-members and winning reemployment after the termination of their contracts.

Recently, some researchers have revisited LRM as adult education methods for "self-formation" or "self-education." For example, Saruyama (2011) reevaluates LRM circles consisting of housewives in Tokyo and concludes that Tsurumi pursued developing a new approach for adult female education based on dialogues to conquer dis-communication and achieve self-formation. Tsurumi asked the members to write their life events as they are but with "fictions" so that wider audiences would read their experiences beyond the circle to connect them with larger societies (ibid.). Tsuji (2015, pp. 290–291) extensively researched the case of a circle consisting of young female factory workers in Mie and concluded that LRM influenced self-formation of "marriage age" women's life decisions through understanding their mothers' realities and discussing how differently they would/could live. Tsuji (ibid., p. 414) also points out that LRM was to identify concrete themes and issues to encourage efforts and accept conflicts, contradictions, and discrepancies between theories/ideals and practice/realities affirmatively.

All literature points out that reading, writing, speaking, and listening are integrated into the learning process indivisibly and emphasize the importance of mutual understandings with conflicts and differences for deepening learning processes. Although no literature uses the term agency development, they use emancipation, self-formation, and democratization of communication, which should be strongly connected with agency and its development.

3 Case Study: Recording Life Circle in Mie Prefecture

3.1 Overview of the Case

There were two popular LRM circles in the 1950s: Recording Life Circle (*Seikatsu wo Kirokusuru Kai*) in the Mie Prefecture led by Yoshiro Sawai and Describing Life Circle (*Seikatsu wo Tsuzuru kai*) led by Kazuko Tsurumi in Tokyo. This article will describe and analyze the former case because the contexts surrounding the case are much closer to those of contemporary rural communities in many developing countries.

Mr. Sawai joined a textile factory in Yokkaichi city in Mie Prefecture in 1945. During that period, General Headquarters (GHQ) guided Japanese companies to organize labor unions, and Sawai was assigned to promote cultural matters, and he organized drama, singing, and writing circles in 1949 (Sawai, 2012, pp. 13–17). According to Tsuji (2010, pp. 26–27), most young women who participated in the writing circle led by the labor union had just graduated from junior high schools and worked at the factory to send money back home, living in the factory's dormitory. As they could not go to high schools and wanted to keep studying, the writing circle substituted higher education opportunities. The company had also opened a vocational school, but it had become unpopular as it was mainly for bride training (ibid.).

However, all the circles did not go well at first. In the drama circle, the members did not get along with each other at all. A schoolteacher instructed a chorus group in the singing circle, but it was difficult for newcomers to join. The members made two anthologies in the writing circle, but they were lowly rated as cooky-cutters (Sawai 2012, pp. 132–140). Mr. Sawai struggled and found a songbook and music records for young people, and they started enjoying singing along with handclapping (ibid.). In 1951, *Yamabiko Gakko*, an anthology of life compositions by junior high school students in a village in the Yamagata prefecture, was published. The members read it and felt quite moved and decided to write about the reality of their lives back home (ibid., pp. 140–147).

According to Sawai (2012, pp. 22–24), when they brought their compositions about their home for the first time, nobody was willing to read them aloud, as it was a sort of taboo to report their realities. However, through sharing their compositions, they understood that their situations were quite similar. As a result, twenty-two compositions were collected, and an anthology titled *My Home (Watashi no Ie* in Japanese) was printed as a mimeograph and distributed in 1952, which got many positive reactions.

During that period, the number of dormitory residents doubled compared to 1950, and the residents experienced many troubles because of deteriorating living conditions. The writing circle members wrote about their situations in detail, which was taken seriously by union leaders and facilitated the realization of dormitory extensions. This event made the writing circle popular, and the number of people increased to 134 in total, including ten men (Tsuji, 2010, p. 35). They kept writing collective diaries to share issues and write and discuss compositions. In 1953, they

3 Case Study: Recording Life Circle in Mie Prefecture

published two mimeograph anthologies: *My Mother* (*Watashi no Okasan* in Japanese) and *Mother's History* (*Haha no Rekishi* in Japanese). They also developed methods to self-study their compositions for analyzing their situations and dealing with identified problems. (Sawai, 1954, pp. 148–156).

However, harassment for the circle gradually intensified by the company, and new members left the circle. The members were considered communists, and their parents were instructed to persuade their daughters to quit the circle, but they never gave up writing compositions (Tsuji, 2015, pp. 156–159). In 1954, a book called *Mother's History* (*Hahano Rekishi* in Japanese) was commercially published, which consisted of selected compositions from four anthologies. The company became alerted and dismissed Sawai unfairly in 1954, which resulted in a trial. After his dismissal, the members kept writing compositions and published some mimeograph anthologies.

In 1958, the company started reducing operations as well as temporarily laying off female factory workers. Often, these women were never allowed to return to work. The company also promoted marriage retirements with monetary incentives, and the members gradually left the company, marrying full-time farmers back home and starting busy lives (Sawai, 2012, pp. 249–250). However, from 1965 until recently, the members have held reunions every five years, and around twenty members have kept gathering. Mr. Sawai has paid continuous efforts for printing, copying, and sending correspondences to them (Tsuji, 2015, Chap. 4 and 5). Unfortunately, he passed away in 2015.

3.2 Their Compositions

According to Tsuji (2010), there were some key topics written in their compositions; (1) their back home realities, especially their mothers' life situations, (2) their dormitory situations, and (3) love and marriage. As the members were from rural and low-income families, the first topic was the most common. Thus, in this section, the author focuses on the compositions dealing with the first theme. Their written narratives are quite polished with verbal narratives from "*Voices of the Poor*," a research report conducted for the World Development Report 2000/2001, using participatory methods to collect voices of the marginalized living in the developing countries (Narayan et al., 2000).

The following narratives are extracted from *Haha no Rekishi* (Mothers' History), edited by Dramatist Junji Kinoshita and Sociologist Kazuko Tsurumi (Kinoshita & Tsurumi, 1954). According to Tsuji (2015, p. 221), Sociologist Tsurumi practically selected the compositions and designed the book's structure.

The publication consists of selected compositions of four mimeograph anthologies, *Watashi no Ie* (*My Home(1952)*), *Watashi no Okasan* (*My Mother (1953)*), *Haha no Rekishi* (*Mothers' History(1953)*), and *Atarashii Aijo* (*New Affection, 1953*). As the most written is the first topic and one of the focused themes of this book is alleviating poverty and development of agency of the marginalized, the author selects the narratives representing the first topic from the first three anthologies. The book also includes editor's notes of each anthology and a chapter explaining how the book was elaborated. Finally, the author summarizes their compositions in their voices because they are too long to be directly quoted.

3.2.1 *My Home* (Seikatsu wo Kirokusurukai 1952)

Though my house is situated at the foot of a mountain, no water comes, no river is nearby. Thus, no rice can be cultivated, only millets we produce. I used to feel hesitant to ask my parents to give me money for school trip expenditures (*My home*, Hisako Suzuki, pp. 13–16).

My grandfather became indebted, and all the good fields were sold. The family could not live only with farming. So, I am working at this factory instead of going to high school. I send money to my parents so that my younger sister can go to a high school (*My family*, Michiko Tanaka, pp. 17–21).

Though we work all year round without resting, income is not enough because of tax deductions and expenditures for fertilizers. My family is indebted because my father bought new farming machines. I often could not bring money to the school when it was being collected, lying that I just forgot it (*My village and my home*, Ayako Kobayashi, pp. 22–26).

My grandfather lived a fast life and borrowed against his family's property, and we are very poor. My elder sister and I work at factories, live by ourselves, and send money to our parents. Even so, our family's life situation has not improved at all (*About my home*, Motoe Yoneyama, pp. 27–24).

From a distance, our house is like a hut resided in by native people of the South Pacific as our thatched roof is semi-broken. My dad was killed during World War II, and the family became poorer, so I started working in the factory, giving up going to a high school. I always send money to my mother, but it is never enough (*My home*, Harumi Shiga, pp. 35–43).

3.2.2 *My Mother* (Seikatsu wo Kirokusurukai 1953a)

I do not want to marry as marriage is just to have a very hard life. My mother gets up very early to prepare breakfast as well as taking care of livestock. Then, she goes to the field to work without any rest. Before noon, she goes back home to prepare lunch. While my father rests after eating lunch, she must do housework. Then, she works in the field until it gets dark and goes back home to prepare supper. After eating, she still has plenty of housework to do (*Mother*, Tsuneko Tonouchi, pp. 47–54).

My mother must work all day long as well as taking care of my sick uncle, who complains all day long. She does not even have time to browse newspapers. She is always busy, without being able to tell us how she feels about her life (*My Mother*, Nobuko Tabata, pp. 55–58).

3 Case Study: Recording Life Circle in Mie Prefecture

My mother got ill because of my elder brother's death in the war, and fatigue accumulated over the years. Only a small mortuary tablet was sent back home without any bones for his death (*My Mother*, Hisako Sakamaki, pp. 61–65).

Not only my mother, my grandmother, and all my paternal aunts were fabric factory workers. When my mother talks about her experiences in the factory, she never complains. I think this is because it was "normal" for them to work all day long and to be sent back home when they became ill without being given any treatment (Harumi Shiga, pp. 65–79).

My mother went to work in a factory only after finishing elementary school married my father by arrangement, so she has many kids. As my father is at his mother's beck and call, my mothers' opinions are not heard by him at all. My mother injured her legs when she was forced to work by her mother-in-law three days after delivering her baby. She always walks with a limp but works even on New Years' Day. I never want to live such a life. I want to live a decent life when I become a mother (*My Mother*, Hisako Suzuki, pp. 79–82).

3.2.3 Mothers' History (Seikatsu wo Kirokusurukai 1953b)

Though it has been twenty years, my mother has never been able to make a new kimono, and she cannot address this with my father. I do not want such an unhappy marriage. I am working in the residents' association and being involved in the circle activities to be able to express my own opinions (*My mother's life*, Michiko Tanaka, pp. 88–92).

My maternal grandfather passed away when my mother was in the third grade of her elementary school. So, she was sent into service and taking care of babies as well as going to school half the day. After she started the fourth grade, she was asked to work in sericulture and could go to school only a week each month. After graduating from elementary school, she was sent to work at a factory and then married my father by arrangement (*My mother's history*, Hisako Suzuki, pp. 93–98).

My mother died of TB, and my father was called up for military service. It was my grandmother who raised me as well as my brothers and sisters. My father returned from the war and remarried, but I do not get along with my stepmother (*Three Mothers*, Tsuneko Tonouchi, pp. 102–103).

3.3 Editor's Note of Each Anthology

They also write editor's notes for each anthology, in which they express how the anthologies were elaborated and what they wanted to do with them. The following are summaries of the notes:

3.3.1 *My Home* (1952) (Titled as *Starting from "My Home,"* Written in the Labor Literature Circle, Dated 30th of August 1952)

This anthology was completed on the 22nd of June, Sunday. We sent it to our junior high schools and Seikyo Muchaku (the editor of Yamabiko Gakko) and Ikutaro Shimizu (Critics). This is the third anthology. In this anthology, we wrote our realities as they were, which we learned was most important from other anthologies such as Yamabiko Gakko. While making this anthology, we discussed a lot about whether and why we (have to) send money to our parents monthly. We concluded that we needed to know the living conditions of our villages in detail. Through making this anthology, we found so many problems of rural villages but could not find relevant solutions, feeling overwhelmed. We also want to appreciate those who sent us letters to give opinions and encouragement (pp. 10–13).

3.3.2 *My Mother* (1953) (No Title Notes Written by Yaeko Furukawa Before and After the Anthology)

I asked male colleagues to write about their mothers, although most of them did not. I asked them a couple of times to write, as I wanted to know what they wanted their own wives to be like through narrating their mothers' life histories (p. 46).

I was just so happy when this anthology was finally printed. In this anthology, we identified a variety of problems. It is getting warmer, and we want to try hard to discuss what kind of mothers we want to become (p. 83).

3.3.3 *Mother's History* (1953) (No Title, Written as Women Division of the Labor Union and Life Record Circle, pp. 109–110)

Reading letters from our mothers, we always feel their opinions are so different from ours, a wide gap between us. Maybe this is what we call "history." Our mothers were just graduated from elementary schools, always educated to be obedient, giving up everything that they wanted. In the near future, when we become mothers and have daughters to write letters, we want to write that we will discuss how to solve problems together, instead of nothing to be done. We know our activities should continue for a long period. We also want to involve men in our practice.

Most important is to read the compositions carefully. However, just reading them, we cannot really make them our own. Thus, taking notes for analyzing the contents is very important, that can be done in the following process:

(1) Extracting problems and issues from compositions and write them in your notebook, think by yourself, or discuss with others and write down possible solutions.
(2) If comfortable with the first step, try to make a short summary of a composition so that you can grasp the contents.

4 How the Members and Supporters Look Back at the Experiences and Transformations   163

(3) If you feel that you can handle the second step, try to make outlines. Make several inquiries such as why we must write compositions, whether our mothers are happy, why they keep working all day long, why we are poor and whether we can eradicate it, what can be the ideal lives for mothers. Then, identify summaries of compositions as references of each inquiry and try to find and write answers to the inquiries with your own words through discussions with others.

4 How the Members and Supporters Look Back at their Experiences and Transformations

In this sub-section, the author overviews how the members look back on their experiences in the circle and how they think their experiences have had specific influences on their daily lives. The author also extracts how the supporters, such as Sawai and Tsurumi, observe and express changes of the members.

4.1 How They Look Back on Their Experiences in the Circle

In 2006, a lengthy interview was conducted at a community center in Iida city of Nagano Prefecture, where five circle members gathered (Takeuchi et al., 2008). The following is an extract of what they learned from the circle experiences when they were working at the factory. As their original narratives are pretty long, the author summarizes the contents. In addition, the author also underlines key phrases that seem to be related to agency development.

Some superiors of the company kindly gave us advice to encourage us <u>not to accept our situations as fate and to challenge them with our will to change our situations</u>. This experience and learning became the foundation of my life until this day. Through the experience, <u>my life had begun to form for the first time</u> (Tsuneko Ito, p. 61).

Through writing and sharing compositions, <u>our solidarity became stronger and social ties among the workers' unions also became tighter</u>. This taught me the <u>importance of speaking up and negotiating instead of keeping silent</u>. My parents had to be very surprised that their obedient daughters had changed a lot, demanding their company to raise their salaries. I also <u>wrote to my parents to speak up and express their needs to change their daily situations</u> (Tsuneko Ito, p. 62).

Recruiters were those who introduced us to the company as well as delivered our salaries to our parents. They were agents of the company and reported about us to our parents. The company also held annual meetings with our parents. As the company gave small gifts to them and they were very poor, most of them participated in the meeting. If we were members of the circles, our parents were told to persuade us to quit as the activities were "read" in front of others. <u>My parents were very</u>

stunned and wrote to us to quit the circle, but we loved the circle and our collogues. Thus, instead of quitting it, we wrote about the event immediately, which had to be troublesome for the company (laughter) (Hisako Takeuchi, p. 64).

We became able to talk with male co-workers easily because of the circle. Other girls were envious of us and joined the circle! (Hisako Takeuchi, p. 65).

When we went camping, all of us sang on the bus so lively and felt very encouraged. It was Sawai who organized them. He organized the singing and drama circles too, and such activities made our ties stronger. For making and performing a drama, we had to collaborate a lot, and the process was quite complicated. After the two circles, we finally encountered "Yamabiko Gakko," and the LRM circle was smoothly organized (Hisako Takeuchi, p. 65).

It was OK for me to criticize the company through writing. Even if we wrote about the company badly, we could not write about our friends negatively, which was quite good (for making our ties stronger). There were always things to write in the factory, and we decided to have monthly meetings to discuss issues and organize matters to print compositions. We rented a room in a labor union building once a month, usually on a Sunday morning, although our discussions were not active. When nobody spoke up,

Mr. Sawai commented on our reluctant attitudes at the closures of our meetings (Masako Hayashi, p. 66).

As the members lived in the same dormitory, we did everything together. Meals were provided three times a day, and when we were off from work, we had plenty of free time. So, we could always get together, writing, discussing, and editing compositions (Hisako Takeuchi, p. 66).

From the above narratives, we can understand that they became able to negotiate with others, speak up, and keep writing despite the company's harassment. Some of them even became able to persuade their parents to change their passive attitudes.

4.2 *How the Members Evaluate Influences of the Circle Activities on Their Daily Life After Marriage*

The following is also a summary of their narratives about their daily life after they married full-time farmers.

Mr. Sawai has kept sending us correspondences regularly. So, we roughly know who does what till today. We have also organized reunions every five years. In our reunions, we have always talked that we should write as we used to. Our association has kept more than forty or forty-five years (Masako Hayashi, p. 75).

I feel ashamed that I have not been able to spare time for writing. I have tried to keep memos while working, but for some reason, it is not possible to write compositions (Masako Hayashi, p. 73).

Although I wrote not to become like my mother and we did many activities there, after the marriage, I have perhaps lived like my mother, like a Meiji-era-born woman (Tsuneko Ito, pp. 73–74).

What we have learned through the circle activities, I think, is to have critical perspectives. Not only writing but always keep thinking and raising inquiries (Hisako Takeuchi, p. 77).

I think that becoming a local leader is incredible, but it is not fundamental. Getting along with neighbors and becoming able to discuss daily matters such as for whom we vote. We think such daily matters are our activities (Hisako Takeuchi, p. 78).

Young wife associations were organized by community halls. I organized a book club as its activity, and we also invited a schoolteacher to the club. Usually, such a club is boring, just reading books. But, I kept raising questions to the participants to develop discussions, connecting the contents of books with our own experiences and feelings. I am sure my experience in the circle helps a lot (Hisako Takeuchi, p. 76).

I have kept dealing with kids' activities even after my own children had grown up. Once, I printed mimeograph communications for school kids, and schoolteachers were quite impressed and asked me to come over for storytelling activities for kids. Then, I was involved with organizing a private small kid's library as well as organized a kid's theatre through collaborating with nursery schools. I also printed mimeograph communications with my colleagues. I feel that my circle experiences made me capable of doing such things (Masako Hayashi, p. 76).

When the district council organizes senior clubs, I am asked to teach them singing. I can easily lead them to sing along with songs that I sang when I was in the factory. I can do such a thing without hesitation. So, I feel that what I did in the circle at that time really helped me a lot today (Tsuneko Ito, p. 77).

I often go to Nagoya and Osaka for gatherings of mothers. I continue going to attend public lectures till today. I have always been curious to learn something new (Masako Hayashi, p. 63).

I kept working so hard as a breadwinner. My husband and family did not understand what I wanted to do at all. So, I did all the housework perfectly and went out to local study groups at night. I kept trying not to lose what I had done when I was young, always trying not to live like my mother (Masako Hayashi, p. 76).

I decided to go out instead of just keep working at home. I think that because of my experience at the circle, I do what I want, and my husband does not complain, though I am extremely busy. Though I must do all the work before going out, I just say to myself, "it's OK. Let's do what I want" (Hisako Takeuchi, p. 78).

The narratives can be categorized into four: (1) they cannot write as they did, (2) but they have become able to be reflective and critical in daily life, (3) they have kept involved with organizing local activities, and (4) they have kept learning through being active. Thus, it can probably be concluded that all the interviewed members feel that their experiences in the circle have fostered their agency and enabled them to live "not like their mothers," although their life might not be the one they had dreamed of or idealized.

4.3 How the Supporters Observe Their Changes Through Circle Activities

There are not many essays or interviews regarding how the members changed or grew through the circle activities by supporters. However, Sawai (who led the circle) and Tsurumi (who advised the circle) share some comments.

Sawai (1954, pp. 159–162) writes that the circle members (to whom he expresses as friends) would feel confused when asked how they have changed through writing compositions. However, at least, they became able to eradicate the feelings of inferiority as textile factory workers. They also became not hesitant to take action and learn from their experiences instead of keeping silent. He applauds that although they are slow, their way of thinking is consistent, and when taking action, they do their very best for others. In 2012, Sawai published an autobiography and told that only recently, he and the members have become able to conclude with absolute certainty that their activities in the circle have been meaningful for their lives (Sawai, 2012, pp. 250–251).

Tsurumi (1954, pp. 179–194) raises four points that she learned from the circle. First, the members could develop a strong rapport through singing and acting in dramas that helped them feel open to sharing their experiences. They also became able to lead chorus groups when necessary. Second, they never gave up organizing circle activities and writing compositions despite all the pressure and harassment from the company. Tsurumi analyzes that their persistence is attributed to the rural poverty of their birthplaces from which they deserved emancipation. Third, they are slow but persistent in making the efforts necessary to change their situations in the factory and their home villages. Their circle activities are not based on ideologies but practices, through which they became able to think about how to change their rural societies. Fourth, their compositions reflect the outstanding development of their thoughts. In order to not live like their own mothers, in the beginning, they dreamed and tried to marry male colleagues at the factory so they would not have to go back home. Nevertheless, gradually, they understood that it was unrealistic, and they decided to become "proud mothers" of rural villages, who could change and improve their daily lives through writing and analyzing their own mothers' realities. Tsurumi (1970) also reported that they achieved higher productivity than non-members.

Thus, both Sawai and Tsurumi feel that they changed and are stronger and "empowered," especially appraising that they have become confident of themselves and consistent to make efforts even though they could not always achieve positive results and reactions. However, both point out that it is not easy to verbalize and visualize "radical changes" and design such changes mechanically by external supporters.

5 Analysis of the Case

The case can be understood as an outstanding record of "women empowerment/agency development" for nearly half a century. In this section, the author shares an analysis to understand enabling factors/inhibitors, subjectively felt changes, plausible mechanisms of agency development through answering the following three inquiries:

(a) What could be facilitating factors and inhibitors of LRM activities to be commenced, developed, and lasting?
(b) How can subtle transformation, which could be understood as agency development, be observed in members' texts and narratives and those of the supporters?
(c) What can be plausible mechanisms of agency development interpreted from the case study?

The author analyses the factors divided into social, human, and methodological and points out some inhibitors.

As for social factors, first, the literacy rate was relatively high in Japan. According to Saito (2012), the illiteracy rate in 1948 was just 3.7% in total, and among those who were between 15–19 years old, it was only 0.3%. Second, postwar democracy and radical social transformation should be a fundamental premise. As explained above, under GHQ initiatives, factories should establish labor unions and organize cultural activities. Thus, there was a sort of democratic environment to protect workers' rights. Additionally, the Life Composition Movement (LCM) came back into practice for children, and *Yamabiko Gakko* became a bestseller, influencing adult life education.

Although post-war Japanese society was being reconstructed, the girls working at the factory were from rural villages, where poverty was severe, and women were still oppressed in feudal family systems and societies. Thus, the girls lived in two very different worlds, and such dynamism perhaps enabled them to observe and write about their home village situations comparatively and reflectively. Third, some local factors can be influential. For example, Ina Valley in Nagano Prefecture, where the girls were from, has historical uniqueness. Many peasant families migrated to Manchuria from the valley before and during wartime, and when people came back, they also reclaimed the land. Thus, there might also be a nontraditional atmosphere in the villages. Additionally, where the factory and its dormitory were built in Mie Prefecture was suburban, and it was difficult for workers to seek entertainment outside the area, which might have facilitated cultural activities inside the factory.

First, Mr. Sawai's "soft and persistent leadership" should be the key regarding human aspects. He kept making efforts to organize singing, drama, and writing circles even though they were not initially successful. Mr. Sawai kept leading the writing circle and singing and drama activities, guiding the members until he was dismissed from the company. However, he never put his name as the first author of any anthologies and books and kept supporting the members as a "facilitator." Even after being dismissed from the factory, he kept sending correspondences to the members, which helped them keep their connectedness as "members" for such a long period. Second, rapport had already been built among the circle members through singing and making dramas prior to writing and sharing compositions organized by Sawai. Thus, they knew one another and perhaps felt a sort of friendship. Third, the members' motivation for learning was relatively high. After graduating from junior high school, they were sent to work at a textile factory and lived in the factory dormitory. As they could not go to high schools for economic reasons, they wanted to keep studying. The writing circle was, for them, a substitute for higher education. They also had plenty of time to commit to activities as they lived in the dormitory. They were also serious about understanding and changing their home situations as they had to go back there, which further boosted their motivation to learn. Fourth, the members were from similar social settings. All of them were from poor small farmers' families and from the same area. Thus, it was easy for them to share their feelings and experiences with empathy and compassion, strengthening their bonds.

People within and outside the factory also supported the circle activities. For instance, at the workplace, some male superiors encouraged the members directly or indirectly through union journals, sometimes using pen names. Beyond the factory, known scholars and cultural figures such as Sociologist Kazuko Tsurumi and Dramatist Junji Kinoshita had kept encouraging them. They also supported Sawai's trial.

5.1 *Methodological Factors: Communication Tools and Step-by-Step Approaches*

Regarding communication "tools," first, they enjoyed singing and making dramas together before writing and sharing compositions, which functioned as strong communication tools to build rapport. Those activities also helped them to boost morale while the writing circle activities were criticized. Second, before LRM, LCM of children had already become popular, and some publications, especially *Yamabiko Gakko*, were a good reference for the circle members to write about their home village's poverty situations. Third, was the diaries that they kept individually and collectively, which were seeds for their compositions. Fourth, compositions themselves were handy tools for the members to read again and visually monitor their achievements, such as how the length and wording of compositions changed.

As for methodology, they loosely adapted step-by-step approaches. First, to write compositions, the members kept diaries, and they informally discussed possible composition themes and plots among their close friends. Then, they wrote compositions and formally discussed the contents at the regular meetings to seeking solutions to change their living conditions. Thus, they perhaps did not feel so pressured to write compositions. Besides, the process of writing compositions consisted of four types of learning, writing, reading, discussing, and listening, and should also be cognitively effective. Second, the publication of their works was also in stages. Initially, their compositions were selected for mimeograph anthologies. Then, compositions in the anthologies were further selected for commercial publications. This system perhaps motivated them to write better compositions and rewrite and edit their compositions a couple of times for different occasions. Third, they had a gradual approach for recruiting new members. They first invited new female employees for singing and dramas and then to the writing circle because they probably knew this was the best way to build rapport and foster friendship.

5.2 Inhibitors

First were internalized oppressions that made them hesitant to talk about their own families and situations. If *Yamabiko Gakko* had not been published, they probably would not have felt "forgiven" for writing about their realities. The second was pressure and harassment from the company. Their activities became gradually criticized to be communistic by the company, while their voices were heard, and their compositions were commercially published. Mr. Sawai was also dismissed by the company unfairly. Third, although not being witnessed by the members, peer pressure might be intense among the members, and there could be hidden codes of conduct that made them exclude certain topics from being written. Fourth, most of them left the company for marriage, returning home to work as full-time farmers. Subsequently, they were not able to spare time for writing long compositions due to being busy.

However, overall, it can be said that there were far more facilitating factors than inhibitors for this case.

(a) How can subtle transformation, which could be understood as agency development, be observed in members' texts and narratives and those of the supporters?

Comparing the compositions, In *My Home (1952)*, the members mainly write in detail about their realities, especially how poor their families are. In *My Mother (1953)*, they write more on their mothers' lives at home, which are full of calamities, and seriously think how otherwise they could live as mothers-to-be in their near future. In *Mother's History (1953)*, they narrate and analyze how their mothers/grandmothers grew up and why they behave as they do and try to imagine what kind of villages be made where everybody can live with human dignity. Comparing the three anthologies, the length of their compositions is getting slightly longer. Besides, their sentences have become more analytical than descriptive and comparison targets, and the time axis is also expanding.

As for editors' notes, we can observe pronounced changes. In *My Home* (1952), they explain the process of elaborating the anthology and their mixed feelings in writing about their realities and difficulties to solve the identified problems. In *My Mother* (1953), they asked male colleagues to write about their mothers to understand men's views of women/wives. They also write that they would continue their discussions on what kind of mothers they want to become. In *Mother's History* (1953), they analyze letters from their mothers to understand how and why their opinions differ from mothers'. They also write that when they become mothers, they would write letters of encouragement to their daughters to discuss how to solve problems together, instead of writing nothing to be done. They also write that their activities would take quite a long term to make influences. They also share a sort of manual on how to self-study their compositions in a step-by-step manner. Thus, their ability to reflect upon their compositions deepened, and their time axis and activity targets grew. Their future perspectives accordingly have become longer in time scale and more detailed in contents.

From the interview records, we can understand that they have become able to (1) feel solidarity among the members through writing compositions, (2) understand and analyze their problems and try to deal with them, (3) raise voices instead of keeping silent as well as persuade others including their parents to break the silence, and (4) easily have discussions with male co-workers beyond gender norms, while they were working at the factory. Moreover, after they went back home for marriage, although they have not been able to write, they have been able to keep (1) having critical perspectives as life habits, (2) involving with community organizations and activities, and (3) having the curiosity to learn new things through attending forums and seminars even away from home.

Thus, they feel that their circle experiences have deeply fostered their "agency": self-reflectivity, critical perspectives, and ability to take actions. Sawada and Tsurumi also appreciated the members' mental growth and felt that they have become confident in themselves and consistent in changing their situations by themselves.

(b) What can be plausible mechanisms of agency development interpreted from the case study?

Table 8.1 explains four types of power in empowerment. In the previous section, the author referred to the same table.

Examining the four types of power, the first two are related with "stock (potential abilities to evaluate oneself and make associations with others)," and the last two are associated with "flow (actual/practical capabilities to make things happen)."

In the case study, we obviously can observe that "power with" is the core, which also has extended to manifestations of "power to" and "power over." They have not focused on "power from within" at all, but from their narratives, we can see that "power within" has also been cultivated recursively to work in groups.

Although not expressed in the definitions of the table, the author wants to assert that cognitive abilities to reflect one's experiences, situations, and feelings critically developed through writing and discussing compositions in groups foster not only power with itself but also function as fundamental sources to develop power from within.

Table 8.1 Types of power

Type of power	Rowlands (1997)	Ibrahim and Alkire (2007)
Power from within	The spiritual strength and uniqueness that resides in each one of us and makes us truly human. Its basis is self-acceptance and self-respect, which extend, in turn, to respect for and acceptance of others as equals.	Enhancing self-respect and self-acceptance
Power with	A sense of the whole being greater than the sum of the individuals, especially when a group tackles a problem together	Acting in group
Power to	Generative or productive power (sometimes incorporating or manifesting as forms of resistance or manipulation) creates new possibilities and actions without domination	Creating new possibility
Power over	Controlling power, which may be responded to with compliance, resistance (which weakens processes of victimization), or manipulation	Ability to resist manipulation

Elaborated by the author based on Rowlands (1997); Ibrahim and Alkire (2007, p. 11)

6 Concluding Remarks: Implications for International Development and Social Projects Including Empowerment and Self-reliance of the Marginalized

In this article, the author dealt with a detailed case study of LRM to extract meaningful implications for current International Development, especially for projects including "empowerment" and "self-reliance" activities and aspects. The following are possible lessons that we can learn from the case study, which are about power, media and self-reflectiveness, and visualizing impacts.

First, regarding power, the case teaches us the importance of developing "power with" through group activities that would foster other types of power recursively or as spillover effects. "Power from within," which is related to self-acceptance and self-respect, is fostered recursively through group activities. The members could feel connectedness through the circle activities and realize their growth through writing and discussing compositions. Besides, their activities and compositions enabled them to negotiate with those beyond their social classes and gender norms, resulting in fostering "power to" and "power over" as spillover effects. Thus, the case tells us the importance of focusing on "power with."

However, it is not necessarily easy to promote group activities among women in currently developing countries because of socio-cultural and local contexts. For instance, many women do not have daily contact with non-family members for their religions or simply living in remote areas. Thus, what preconditions are necessary for facilitating group activities should be further examined, such as frequency of meetings, contents of activities, and appropriate communication tools, including the internet and social networking services (SNS).

Second, self-reflection is critical to foster "power from within," and writing is a good tool for communication and developing individual cognitive abilities. Through circle activities, the members express their experiences, which are recorded in their text. Their activities encompass four types of learning (writing, reading, discussing, and listening), stimulating various cognitive abilities effectively. Additionally, compositions are "handy" as they can be easily read back and compare the contents and length at hand.

In many developing countries, however, literacy rates are still not high enough so that women can write compositions by their own hands. However, although they cannot write, they can enjoy singing together and acting out dramas, which should be great for icebreaking and building relationships. Otherwise, they can make short sentences to use SNS even in remote areas, and they can perhaps share their life stories through such media. For instance, digital storytelling (DST) and sociodramas are getting more popular even in developing countries and utilized in development and social projects in practice. However, it still has not been examined what kind of cognitive skills such media can develop and how people can foster not only "power from within" but "power to" and "power over" through activities, which should be further studied.

Finally, as for impacts, the case tells us that changes and transformations can be observed within a couple of years when conditions are met. Subjective changes can also be felt and realized continuously, although it may take a while to be verbalized clearly with confidence. The case is an outstanding example to show that transformations could be observed in a short period and last over half a century.

In many social projects both in developed and developing countries, project periods are only for a couple of years. Thus, it is widely believed that no changes in agency development can be observed in such a short period. However, this case challenges such a discourse. If applying different types of evaluation schemes such as Most Significant Changes and Appreciative Inquiries, changes may be more easily observed.

Additionally, the case witnesses that agency development can be continuous for an extended period. Currently, ex-post development evaluations are usually applied after five years from the termination of the projects. However, profound project impacts can be found after a couple of decades, like in this case, which can be taken more seriously.

In this article, the author introduced, described, and analyzed the case of LRM in post-war Japan to understand plausible mechanisms and extract lessons for current practices, especially in developing countries. Unfortunately, there are still few articles discussing LRM in English, and there were no articles on LRM from the perspective of International Development Studies. Therefore, the author truly hopes that this article will become a meaningful reference to the front-line workers and policymakers who are making daily efforts to develop the agency of the marginalized population.

References

Ibrahim, S., & Alkire, S. (2007). Agency and Empowerment: A Proposal for Internationally Comparable Indicators. *Oxford Development Studies, 35*(4), 379–403.
Kinoshita, J., & Tsurumi, K. (Eds.). (1954). *Mothers' History (Hahano Rekishi)*. Kawade Shobo.
Kobayashi, R. (2018). *Randoseru Haijin Karano Sotsugyo*. Bookman Publication.
Kokubun, I. (1951). *Atarashii Tsurujikata Kyoshitu*. Nihon Hyoronsha.
Muchaku, S. (1952). *Yamabiko Gakko*. Seidosha.
Narayan, D., Chambers, R., Shah, M. K., & Petesch, P. (2000). *Voices of the Poor: Crying Out for Change*. Oxford University Press.
Nishikawa, Y. (2009). *Sengo no Seikatsukiroku ni Manabu: Tsurumi Kazuko Bunko tono Taiwa, Mirai heno Tsushin*. Japan Library Center.
Ogawa, A. (2018). Bundan no Jidai Ni Okeru Naratibu to Sutooriteringu Kyoiku: Kyodogata Dejitaru Sutoriteringu jissen nojirei. *Gengo Bunka Kyoiku Kenkyu, 16*, 45–54.
Ogushi, T. (1981). Seikatsukiroku Undo: Senzen to Sengo, Oboegaki. *The Journal of Social Sciences and Humanities, 150*, 141–158.
Okado, M. (2012). Seikatsu, Inochi, Seizon wo Meguru Undo. In T. Yasuda (Ed.), *Shirizu Sengonihonshakai no Rekishi (3) Shakai wo Tou Hitobito: Undo no naka no Ko to Kyodosei*. Iwanami Publication.
Rowlands, J. (1997). *Questioning Empowerment: Working with Women in Honduras*. Oxfam.
Saito, Y. (2012). Shikijinouryoku Shikijiritsuno Rekishiteki Suii: Nihon no Keiken. *Kokusai Kyoiku Kyouryokuronshu, 15*(1), 51–62.
Saruyama, T. (2011). Tsurumi Kazuko no Seikatsu Kiroku Undo ni Okeru Gakushusosiki no Tenkai: Seikatsu wo Tsuzurukai ni Okeru Hanashiaino Kirokunoto no Bunseki kara. *Kyotodaigakudaihakuin Kyoikugakukenkyukakiyou, 57*, 559–572.
Saruyama, T. (2014). Trurumi Kazuko no Seikatsukirokuundo ni okeru comunikaishon to kiroku: SeikatuwoTsuzurukai no Gakushusosiki no Keisei wo Megutte. *Shakaikyoikukenkyu, 50*(2), 11–20.
Sawai, Y. (1954). Noronoroto Ayundekita Nakamatachi. In J. Kinoshita & K. Tsurumi (Eds.), *Mothers' History (Hahano Rekishi)*. Kawade Shobo.
Sawai, Y. (2012). *Garikirino Ki: Seikatsukiroku Undo to Yotsukaichi Kogai*. Kageshobo.
Seikatsu wo Kirokusurukai. (1952). Watashino Ie. In J. Kinoshita & K. Tsurumi (Eds.), *Mothers' History (Hahano Rekishi)*. Kawade Shobo.
Seikatsu wo Kirokusurukai. (1953a). Watashi no Okasan. In J. Kinoshita & K. Tsurumi (Eds.), *Mothers' History (Hahano Rekishi)*. Kawade Shobo.
Seikatsu wo Kirkusurukai. (1953b). Haha no Rekishi. In J. Kinoshita & K. Tsurumi (Eds.), *Mothers' History (Hahano Rekishi)*. Kawade Shobo.
Takeuchi, H., et al. (2008). Seikatsukirokuundo wo Furikaette: Chosakiroku. *ShakaikyoikuKenkyu, 26*, 56–78.
Tsuji, T. (2010). Bosekijohiroudosha no Seikatsukiroku Undo. *Quadrante, 17*(19), 23–44.
Tsuji, T. (2015). *Senijoseiroudousha no Seikatsukiroku Undo: 1950nendai sakuru undo to Wakamoto Tachi no Jikokeisei*. Hokkaido University Publication.
Tsurumi, K. (1970). *Social Change and the Individual: Japan Before and After Defeat in World War II*. Princeton University Press.
Tsurumi Kasuko. (1958). Seikatsukioku. In Nihonsakubunnokai, ed (Ed.), *Seikatsutsuzurikata Jiten* (pp. 439–440). Meiji Publication.
Tsurumi, K. (1954). Hahano Rekushi wo Tsukutta Hitotachi. In J. Kinoshita & K. Tsurumi (Eds.), *Mothers' History (Hahano Rekishi)*. Kawade Shobo.
Ukai, M. (2012). Koenkiroku: Tsurui Kazuko Kendaishiso to Keikatsukirokuundo. *Ningengakukenkyu, 13*, 1–29.
Yamada, Y. (2008). *Jinsei to Yamai no Katari*. Tokyo University Publication.

Chapter 9
The Psychological Measurement of Agency: Recent Developments and Challenges of Psychometrics in Poverty Contexts

1 Introduction

This chapter will review the psychological literature on the measurement of agency with a special focus on the challenges of such psychometrics in poverty contexts, where difficulties in taking initiatives are often observed. The definition of agency proposed in Chap. 3 was *the ability and capacity to self-determinedly act towards the goal(s) of improving the environment and/or circumstances*, and the chapters on psychology in this volume take the position that autonomous motivation as proposed by self-determination theory (SDT) is the central mechanism of agency. As was the case in Chap. 3, we shall begin with a primer on the basic assumptions behind psychometrics for readers who do not specialize in the field of psychology.

1.1 Psychometrics

The term *psychometrics* refers to the measurement of psychological concepts, or *constructs*. As discussed in Chap. 3, the main purpose of psychometrics is to detect individual differences. Since constructs do not necessarily have substance or entity but are merely assumed to exist, there is great emphasis on the *validity* and *reliability* of measures. Psychometrics usually refer to measurement in quantitative studies, but the principles are also important in qualitative studies.

1.1.1 Validity

Validity is a concept that pertains to the degree that a measurement accurately reflects the definition of the construct that it is purported to measure. Unlike physical measurements such as length and mass which can be directly measured, constructs often do not have any substance or entity, and accordingly, these psychological states and processes can only be inferred indirectly. Thus, ensuring and assessing validity is a somewhat intricate exercise.

Since validity is judged based upon the definition of the construct being measured, it is crucial that the construct is well-defined. There usually two levels of definitions, the *theoretical definition* and *operational definition*.

Theoretical definitions are typically abstract and describe the psychological state and/or process and their functions, which usually cannot be directly observed. For example, one well-known definition of intelligence posits that it "is not only the ability to learn, to abstract, to profit from experience, but also to adjust and to achieve (Wechsler, 1950)."[1] As can be seen in this theoretical definition, the ability itself is not something that can be observed, while its results (i.e., learning, abstracting, profiting from experience, etc.) can.

The way operational definitions are provided differ between research methods, but they generally are presented as an inventory of such observable actions or states. Note that operational definitions are often not explicitly stated.

Psychometric tests such as IQ tests usually involve an array of tasks which performance are assumed to reflect the construct: for intelligence this would for example include abilities in abstract thinking, comprehension, reasoning, and processing speed, all which are supposedly components of intelligence (e.g., Wechsler, 2008). As a rule of thumb, measures that take on the title of "test" usually are rigorously tested with data of sample sizes in their thousands. While there may be disagreement on the definition of constructs between theories (hence different IQ tests), each test is developed upon thorough consideration of whether the task accurately reflects the operational definition of the concept according to the theoretical viewpoint that it is based upon. Established psychometric tests can be considered to have a high level of validity, albeit limited to the populations that they were developed in (see Chap. 3 of this volume). Furthermore, there are very few psychometric measures that have been standardized and can be called a "test." The self-reported scales to be discussed in the next paragraph are seldom standardized and cannot be considered as "tests" in this sense.

Perhaps the most used psychometric method is in self-reported Likert scales, in which respondents rate their agreement to an assortment of statements that are deemed to reflect various aspects of the target construct. For example, the widely cited Rosenberg self-esteem scale includes 10 statements, or *items*, that are assumed to be associated with self-esteem such as "On the whole, I am satisfied with myself"

---

[1] There are several definitions of intelligence within psychology that differ between theoretical stances. This cited paper argues against different definitions, and also discusses the validity of existing measurement methods.

1 Introduction

which respondents rate their agreement on a scale of 1 to 4 (Rosenberg, 1979). Self-reported Likert scales can tap directly into the subjective perception of respondents and are very efficient and convenient compared to other psychometric methods (hence their popularity). However, this is still an indirect measure of the target construct, which is inferred through the pattern of responses to the items. Additionally, because of their convenience, there are multitudes of scales and new scales are constantly being developed. Consequently, many of these scales are of poor quality. Even established scales such as the Rosenberg self-esteem scale have been criticized that they do not accurately reflect the concept that they are purported to (e.g., Deci & Ryan, 1995). There are several aspects of validity that should be considered when developing new psychometric scales and when selecting existing scales to use, which shall be discussed below.

Content validity concerns whether the items accurately reflect the definition of the construct. Also important in content validity is whether the items cover the full breadth of the construct. Scale items are usually scrutinized when scales are developed, and also when being published in peer-reviewed journals, but there are no objective criteria regarding the standards that should be met, and as a result, the scrutiny does not necessarily guarantee content validity.

Criterion-related validity is often examined post-hoc statistically by assessing the degree that the scale score is associated with other related concepts or outcomes. For example, scores for a scale that supposedly measures depression should be positively correlated with tests that screen for other mental illnesses, as depression is a key symptom in most of them. Depression scale scores should also be positively correlated with physicians' diagnoses of depression. This type of criterion-related validity is sometimes called *convergent validity*. Contrarily, if a depression scale had relatively lower correlations with a scale for social anxiety, it would be considered to have a degree of *divergent validity*, as it seems to be able to discriminate between depression and anxiety, which are related but distinct constructs. Another form of criterion-related validity is *predictive validity*, which would be assessed as the degree of correlation between the scale score and another score or behavior that the construct is expected to predict. For example, the score from a scale for self-efficacy (see Chap. 3) towards schoolwork would be expected to predict academic achievement test scores.

Factor validity, or *structural validity* is sometimes considered for constructs that have multiple dimensions or facets, such as personality. The examination of factor validity is also conducted post-hoc using the factor analysis statistical procedure. If items that are considered to measure different dimensions load on different factors and those considered the measure the same dimension load on the same factor, it would be one piece of evidence that supports the validity of the scale. If the factor structure is stable across samples and time, that too would be evidence that supports validity.

All these forms of validity are considered to fall within the concept of *construct validity* (for a more technical discussion, see Messick, 1995),[2] but this is not an exhaustive list. Many scale development papers claim that their "validity has been confirmed," but in most cases, they have but examined a few of the many aspects of validity. Even if multiple aspects have been corroborated, it is impossible to "confirm" the validity of a scale through just a handful of studies, and in any case, adapting a scale to a population that differs from the sample that it was developed for warrants further examination of validity. In more practical terms, confirming the validity of a scale is time- and labor-consuming, and few research projects have the resources to fully validate a scale before conducting their studies. It would be more realistic to acknowledge the limitations in measurement and interpret results accordingly.

Validity is also relevant to experimental research. Experimental studies that employ psychological scales as their dependent variables obviously are relevant, but other experiments observe differences in certain reactions or behaviors that are deemed to reflect the degree of a construct. For example, experiments on intrinsic motivation often use the amount of time spent on an interesting task in the absence of any external prods as an indicator of intrinsic motivation (e.g., Deci, 1971; Lepper et al., 1973). The free-time experimental paradigm utilized in these experiments where subjects are stealthily observed to record the time that they engage in the task when left alone is generally accepted as a valid indicator of intrinsic motivation, but some other paradigms such as game theory experiments, which recently have crossed over into psychology from economics, have been somewhat controversial. For example, results of the ultimatum game are supposedly an indicator of fairness, and the dictator game of altruism, but whether the results of these games reflect real-world social preferences and behaviors has been called into question (e.g., Levitt & List, 2007). While there are some studies that suggest the validity of these methods (e.g., Fischbacher et al., 2012; Franzen & Pointner, 2013), there are still very few studies that provide evidence of their validity. Additionally, most experiments are conducted with university students, and whether the results and their interpretation can be generalized to other populations is questionable (Levitt & List, 2007). However, the validity of game theory experiments is seldom questioned, yet they have been widely used to inform policymaking in development contexts (e.g., Dinar et al., 2008).

Although there is much less discussion on the topic, validity is also relevant to qualitative studies. While qualitative research may not produce numeric scores, many studies interpret that their results reflect certain constructs—which can be considered a form of measurement. Due to the bottom-up, or data-driven, nature of qualitative studies, it may not always be appropriate to assume and rigidly define a target construct a priori, but interpretations of data as manifestations of certain constructs calls for scrutiny of whether the phenomenon is indeed so as claimed. As discussed in Chap. 3, there have been some recent studies on the facilitation of

---

[2] In view of the anticipated audience of this chapter, the types of validity described in this chapter focus on more practical aspects of construct validity and do not reflect those listed in Messick (1995) word for word.

1 Introduction

agency in underprivileged populations, but it is difficult to evaluate these claims as they do not provide definitions for the construct of agency.

1.1.2 Reliability

Reliability is also an important aspect of the measurement of psychological constructs. Reliability pertains to the stability and consistency of a measure. For physical measurements, tools are generally stable and consistent: length measured using the same ruler will probably be the same no matter who measures a particular object, and a scale for measuring weight would probably display the same value no matter how many times a person steps on it. Matters are not so simple for psychological measures, but methods have been devised to infer the degree of reliability.

For psychometric Likert scales, the most common procedure is to compute coefficients such as Chronbach's alpha and McDonald's omega, which represent the degree of inter-correlation, or *internal consistency*, among the scale items. The higher the correlation between item responses, i.e., the more consistent responses are between different items, the higher the reliability is considered to be.

The relationship between reliability (as internal consistency in psychometric scales) and validity can be expressed as Fig. 9.1. The figure likens measurement using psychometric scales with shooting a target for practice. The smaller circle at the center of the target is an analogy of the construct, and the dots are where the shots struck. Ideally, the shots would hit the center of the target *and* cover most of the area of the smaller circle as the left figure. This is analogous to a scale with high internal consistency and high validity. However, high internal consistency alone is not sufficient, as can be seen in the central figure. Reliability does not guarantee validity, and scales with high internal consistency can be low in validity. Finally, as can be seen in the right figure, low reliability would be considered a sign of low validity.

Another index of reliability is *test-retest reliability*, which concerns the stability of measurement of a psychometric scale. The same scale is administered twice to the same group of respondents, usually a couple of months apart, and a coefficient

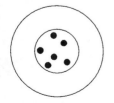
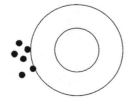
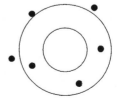

High internal consistency and high validity   High internal consistency but low validity   Low internal consistency and low validity

Fig. 9.1 Relationship between reliability and validity in psychometric scales (figure adapted from Toshima & Seiwa, 1993)

that reflects the degree of within-person score change is computed. The less the change, the higher the reliability, i.e., the more the scale is considered to be stable. Test-retest reliability is not used as commonly as internal consistency indices, one reason being that it requires longitudinal data which is harder to collect. Another reason is that stability is only relevant for constructs that are assumed to be stable such as personality and intelligence, and less so for constructs such as motivation that are expected to fluctuate according to the situation.

Reliability is also relevant to qualitative research. Qualitative data such as observational videos and interview transcripts are often coded by the researchers who judge whether certain behaviors or responses are manifestations of certain constructs. To evaluate the reliability of the coding, multiple coders will independently judge an array of behaviors or responses and later compute the degree of inter-coder agreement (e.g., Sayanagi & Aikawa, 2016).

1.2 Issues Regarding the Measurement of Constructs in Poverty Contexts

As has been discussed, the objective of psychometrics is to assess the individual differences of the degree of the construct in question. The validity and reliability of any given measure is usually examined and improved within the context that it has been developed. However, there have been very few psychological studies that have been conducted in the context of poverty (Davis & Williams, 2020; Henrich et al., 2010; Sayanagi, Chapter 6 of this volume), and as Sayanagi et al. (2021) and Sayanagi and van Egmond (in press) assert, almost all studies that utilize psychological measures that are translated from scales that were developed in high-income contexts. Thus, it can be said that the validity of the measurement in these studies is questionable.

A study by Laajaj et al. (2019) illustrates a case in which the validity of translated scales is low. Their study examined Big Five Index data across 23 low- and middle-income countries and found that the factor structure was incongruent (i.e., the factor validity is poor) and internal consistency was low for the five personality traits in most cases. This calls into question the conclusions drawn from studies that use the Big Five Index in developing countries, many from the field of development economics.

The fact that there are very few psychological scales that have had their validity examined to any degree in poverty contexts presents a big challenge to any psychological research that endeavors to study such populations, as there are no scales that can be used to examine the convergent validity of the new scale.

There are also several practical difficulties involved in poverty-context psychometrics. As Sayanagi et al. (2021) point out, rates of literacy are low in regions where extreme poverty is prominent, making paper-and-pencil and web-form questionnaires unviable. Indeed, Sayanagi et al. (2021) and many of the data sets in

Laajaj et al. (2019) were obtained through oral interviews, which is exponentially more time-consuming than the administering of self-report questionnaires. Accessing such poor populations would also be a challenge due to logistic and security reasons (Sayanagi & van Egmond, in press).

2 The Measurement of Agency

As stated in Chap. 3, agency is a term that is commonly used in psychology, but the construct has seldom been rigorously operationalized, much less in poverty contexts. One notable exception is a study by Pick et al. (2007) which developed a scale in Spanish for the measurement of personal agency and empowerment for marginalized populations in Mexico. For non-poverty contexts, there are scales of self-efficacy for which there is much evidence to support their validity (see Bandura, 1997 for a review), but there are no scales of agency per se as defined in Chap. 3 that validity has been widely scrutinized.

This section will first review the measurement of (autonomous) motivation in SDT that has been conducted in high-income countries. As discussed in Chap. 3 of this volume, autonomous motivation as defined by SDT is posited to be the main mechanism behind agency. The (limited) attempts to measure motivation in SDT studies in poverty contexts will also be reviewed, and the issues of measuring agency in such contexts—where the facilitating of initiative-taking is most needed—will be discussed.

2.1 The Qualitative Measurement of (autonomous) Motivation

The *why questions* approach first developed by Chandler and Connell (1987) provides a template for assessing the quality of motivation for any given task. The method is simple: it is an interview that repeatedly asks why the respondent thinks they are engaging in a task until they can think of no more reasons. The verbatim records of the reasons stated are later coded and classified into motivation types as specified by SDT that can be placed on a continuum based on the degree of autonomy (see Ryan & Deci, 2017, pp. 192-193, for the SDT taxonomy of motivation).

Sayanagi and Aikawa (2016) used the why questions approach to assess the motivation of rural farmers in Japan and Kenya: the latter group consisted of mostly impoverished respondents. Inter-coder agreement of the reasons for participating in farmer training programs was high, with a weighted kappa of .96. Another study by Sayanagi (2019) also used the why questions approach with impoverished farmers from Kenya (including a different sample from the previous study) and Madagascar, and again the inter-coder agreement was high, with weighted kappas of .90-1.00. It thus can be said that this method of qualitative measurement has some degree of reliability. Additionally, since the coding was conducted using a manual based on the definition of the different types of motivation, the measurement can also be considered to have some degree of validity.

2.2 The Quantitative Measurement of (autonomous) Motivation

The *self-regulation questionnaire* (SRQ) psychometric approach, first developed by Ryan & Connell (1989), is widely utilized in SDT studies. The SRQ is an extension of the above why questions approach. An SRQ measure involves asking why the respondent engages in a particular behavior or class of behaviors and having the respondent self-report their agreement to a set of possible reasons to do so. For example, the lead question for an SRQ on exercise would ask "Why do you exercise?" and respondents would report their degree of agreement to statements such as "Because it's fun," "Because I want to stay healthy," and "Because someone will not think well of me if I don't" using a Likert scale.

The SRQ has been used for research in diverse fields, including education, psychotherapy, health care, sports and physical activity, work, and video gaming (see Ryan & Deci, 2017 for an exhaustive review of the domains in which research has been conducted), and the approach's validity and reliability have been widely examined and reported. However, most studies have been conducted in high-income contexts, and there are few studies on low-income contexts.

Of the few studies that use the SRQ in poverty contexts, most use scales adapted from English. Van Egmond and colleagues adapted the academic SRQ (Ryan & Connell, 1989) to assess the academic motivation of schoolgirls in Malawi (Van Egmond et al., 2017) and Mozambique (van Egmond et al., 2020); De Man and colleagues have utilized the treatment SRQ (TSRQ: Williams et al., 1996) in two studies, one that adapted the TSRQ to measure the motivation towards maintaining a healthy diet of diabetics and pre-diabetics in rural South Africa (De Man, Wouters, Delobelle, et al., 2020b), and another that was adapted to assess motivation towards exercising among diabetics in rural Uganda (De Man, Wouters, Absetz, et al., 2020a); Czaicki et al. (2018) also adapted the TSRQ to measure motivation towards adhering to medication to treat HIV/AIDS; and Kaplan and Madjar (2015) used an SRQ scale to assess Bedouin adolescents' motivation regarding participation in pro-environmental activities. The associations of the SRQs used in these studies generally were as would be predicted by SDT, as autonomous motivation positively correlated with adaptive behaviors, so there seems to be some degree of convergent validity. All of these studies report satisfactory internal consistency for the SRQ scales. However, not all studies report the descriptive statistics for the measures, but for those that do, the distributions for the scale in Czaicki et al. (2018) and van Egmond et al. (2017) are skewed and would be considered unfit to use in parametric statistical analyses, and to a lesser and tolerable degree, Kaplan and Madjar (2015) also reported a somewhat skewed distribution. Thus, while there is some evidence of validity and reliability in adapted SRQ scales, but many aspects remain unexamined. The skewedness of the responses is also of concern as it limits the ability of scales to detect individual differences.

Sayanagi et al. (2021) report on the development of an SRQ-styled scale to measure rural farmers' motivation towards an agricultural training program in Madagascar. Rather than translating and adapting existing SRQ measures, to assure content validity, they developed items based on farmer responses from Sayanagi and Aikawa (2016) and Sayanagi et al. (2016). However, the responses to the first version of the scale yielded a variance of almost zero. Despite several modifications, the distributions remained very skewed. Ultimately, the fifth prototype of the scale attained marginally acceptable distributions and internal consistency. Unlike most scales used in high-income countries, the items asked in second person instead of stating in first person. Additionally, respondents were asked the frequency that they acted or thought as in the items instead of how much they agreed with statements. For example, whereas a traditional SRQ item on would ask how much the respondent agreed with the statement, "I participate because I enjoy the project," the corresponding item that was developed stated, "How often do you participate because you enjoy the activities of the project?" Sayanagi et al. (2021) speculate that the lack of opportunities for education, and also the state of extreme poverty, may have constrained the farmers' ability to think in degrees as required by Likert scales, or limited their familiarity with this kind of high-order cognitive task.

As Sayanagi et al. (2021) point out, asking in second person is a method that is sometimes used with young children. However, whether the method validly measures constructs is still an open question that warrants investigation. Such investigation will be challenging, because as aforementioned, there are no qualitative measures that have had their validity assessed and convergent and divergent validity cannot be tested statistically.

2.3 *Future Directions for the Measurement of Autonomous Motivation in Poverty Contexts*

That traditional Likert scales may not always validly measure psychological constructs makes the already challenging task of measuring agency/autonomous motivation in poverty contexts even more difficult. Since the qualitative why questions approach has been demonstrated to be useful, for the time being, using mixed-method research, with qualitative data used to corroborate the validity of quantitative measures, would be the prudent way to go. It will be time- and labor-intensive, not to mention expensive, to conduct such research, but it is a necessary step to lay the foundations for solid empirical research.

3 Concluding Remarks

This chapter has discussed the underlying assumptions of psychometrics and illustrated the difficulties of measuring autonomous motivation, or agency, in poverty contexts. Because psychometric methods for poverty contexts are still in their infancy, there is still much work to do to test and refine the hypothesis proposed in Chap. 6 for the facilitation of agency in populations that seemingly are low in agency.

There are still very few psychology researchers that work in poverty contexts, but since the field of psychology is competitive and the "publish or perish" ethos is prevalent, the fact that research will be ineffective in terms of producing publications will cause most psychologists to hesitate from entering the field. However, interest is growing, and prominent psychologists have called out for more participation in the fight against poverty (Davis & Williams, 2020). The study of agency, on how to enhance the ability and capacity of disempowered populations to take initiatives that would enable them to work out of their difficulties, would be a promising research topic through which psychologists could make a meaningful contribution.

Psychological research in poverty contexts would probably have to be conducted with researchers and non-researcher specialists from different disciplines, as is the case for this author and the endeavor of this volume. For interdisciplinary work to function, one must reflect upon and communicate the implicit assumptions of their own discipline. The author hopes that he has done a satisfactory job in conveying the nuances of psychological research to non-psychologists, and that more psychology researchers will become interested in conducting research for the reduction of poverty.

References

Bandura, A. (1997). *Self-efficacy: The Exercise of Control*. W. H. Freeman and Company.

Chandler, C. L., & Connell, J. P. (1987). Children's Intrinsic, Extrinsic and Internalized Motivation: A Developmental Study of Children's Reasons for Liked and Disliked Behaviors. *British Journal of Developmental Psychology, 5*, 357–365.

Czaicki, N. L., Dow, W. H., Njau, P. F., & McCoy, S. I. (2018). Do Incentives Undermine Intrinsic Motivation? Increases in Intrinsic Motivation within an Incentive-based Intervention for People Living with HIV in Tanzania. *PLoS ONE, 13*, e0196616.

Davis, R. P., & Williams, W. R. (2020). Bringing Psychologists to the Fight Against Deep Poverty. *American Psychologist, 75*, 655–667.

De Man, J., Wouters, E., Absetz, P., Daivadanam, M., Naggayi, G., Kasujja, F. X., Remmen, R., Guwatudde, D., & Van Olmen, J. (2020a). What Motivates People with (pre)diabetes to Move? Testing Self-determination Theory in Rural Uganda. *Frontiers in Psychology, 11*, 404.

De Man, J., Wouters, E., Delobelle, P., Puoane, T., Daivadanam, M., Absetz, P., Remmen, R., & Van Olmen, J. (2020b). Testing a Self-determination Theory Model of Healthy Eating in a South African Township. *Frontiers in Psychology, 11*, 2181.

Deci, E. L. (1971). Effects of Externally Mediated Rewards on Intrinsic Motivation. *Journal of Personality and Social Psychology, 18*, 105–115.

References

Deci, E. L., & Ryan, R. M. (1995). Human Autonomy: The Basis for True Self-esteem. In M. H. Kernis (Ed.), *Efficacy, Agency, and Self-esteem* (pp. 31–46). Plenum.

Dinar, A., Albiac, J., & Sánchez-Soriano, J. (Eds.). (2008). *Game Theory and Policymaking in Natural Resources and the Environment*. Routledge.

Fischbacher, U., Gächter, S., & Quercia, S. (2012). The Behavioral Validity of the Strategy Method in Public Good Experiments. *Journal of Economic Psychology, 33*, 897–913.

Franzen, A., & Pointner, S. (2013). The External Validity of Giving in the Dictator Game: A Field Experiment Using the Misdirected Letter Technique. *Experimental Economics, 16*, 155–169.

Henrich, J., Heine, S. J., & Norenzayan, A. (2010). Most People Are Not WEIRD. *Nature, 466*, 29–29.

Kaplan, H., & Madjar, N. (2015). Autonomous Motivation and Pro-environmental Behaviours Among Bedouin Students in Israel: A Self-determination Theory Perspective. *Australian Journal of Environmental Education, 31*, 223–347.

Laajaj, R., Macours, K., Hernandez, D. A. P., Arias, O., Gosling, S. D., Potter, J., Rubio-Cortina, M., & Vakis, R. (2019). Challenges to Capture the Big Five Personality Traits in Non-WEIRD Populations. *Science Advances, 5*, eaaw5226.

Lepper, M. R., Greene, D., & Nisbett, R. E. (1973). Undermining Children's Intrinsic Interest with Extrinsic Reward: A Test of the "overjustification" Hypothesis. *Journal of Personality and Social Psychology, 28*, 129–137.

Levitt, S. D., & List, J. A. (2007). What Do Laboratory Experiments Measuring Social Preferences Reveal About the Real World? *Journal of Economic Perspectives, 21*, 153–174.

Messick, S. (1995). Validation of Psychological Assessment: Validation of Inferences for Persons' Responses and Performances as Scientific Inquiry into Score Meaning. *American Psychologist, 50*, 741–749.

Pick, S., Sirkin, J., Ortega, I., Osorio, P., Martínez, R., Xocolotzin, U., & Givaudan, M. (2007). Escala para medir agencia personal y empoderamiento (ESAGE) [Scale for the measurement of personal agency and empowerment (ESAGE)]. *Revista Interamericana de Psicología [Interamerican Journal of Psychology], 41*, 295–304.

Rosenberg, M. (1979). *Conceiving the Self*. Basic Books.

Ryan, R. M., & Deci, E. L. (2017). *Self-determination Theory: Basic Psychological Needs in Motivation, Development, and Wellness*. The Guilford Press.

Sayanagi, N. R. & Aikawa, J. (2016). The Motivation of Participants in Successful Development Aid Projects: A Self-determination Theory Analysis of Reasons for Participating. *JICA Research Institute Working Paper No. 121*. Retrieved from https://www.jica.go.jp/jica-ri/publication/workingpaper/wp_121.html

Sayanagi, N. R., & van Egmond, M. C. (in press). SDT and International Development. In R. M. Ryan (Ed.), *The Oxford handbook of Self-determination Theory*. Oxford University Press.

Sayanagi, N. R., Aikawa, J., & Asaoka, M. (2016). The Relationship Between Motivation and Outcomes in Development Aid Projects: Implications from an SDT-based Approach in Kenya. Paper presented at The 6th International Conference on Self-Determination Theory. Victoria, BC.

Sayanagi, N. R., Randriamanana, T., Razafimbelonaina, H. S. A., Rabemanantsoa, N., Abel-Ratovo, H. L., & Yokoyama, S. (2021). The Challenges of Psychometrics in Impoverished Populations of Developing Countries: Development of a Motivation Scale in Rural Madagascar. *Japanese Journal of Personality, 30*, 56–69.

Toshima, T., & Seiwa, H. (1993). *Shinrigaku no tame no jikken manuaru: Nyumon kara kiso/hatten e [Experiment manual for psychology: Introduction, basics, and advanced]*. Kitaoji Shobo.

Van Egmond, M. C., Navarrete Berges, A., Omarshah, T., & Benton, J. (2017). The Role of Intrinsic Motivation and the Satisfaction of Basic Psychological Needs Under Conditions of Severe Resource Scarcity. *Psychological Science, 28*, 822–828.

Van Egmond, M. C., Hanke, K., Omarshah, T. T., Navarrete Berges, A., Zango, V., & Sieu, C. (2020). Self-esteem, Motivation and School Attendance Among Sub-Saharan African Girls: A Self-Determination Theory Perspective. *International Journal of Psychology, 55*, 842–850.

Wechsler, D. (1950). Cognitive, Conative, and Non-intellective Intelligence. *American Psychologist, 5*, 78–83.
Wechsler, D. (2008). *Wechsler Adult Intelligence Scale: Fourth Edition (WAIS-IV)*. Pearson.
Williams, G. C., Grow, V. M., Freedman, Z. R., Ryan, R. M., & Deci, E. L. (1996). Motivational Predictors of Weight Loss and Weight-loss Maintenance. *Journal of Personality and Social Psychology, 70*, 115–126.

Chapter 10
Visualization of the Stages of Agency Development

The Design and Performance of the *Chile Soridario* Program for the Poorest in Chile

1 Introduction

This chapter represents an in-depth case study of the *Chile Solidario* Program (CHS), designed and implemented by the national government of Chile to assist the poorest segment of the population to move out of poverty trap. The special feature of CHS was its emphasis of "agency development" as key condition for overcoming the difficulties of daily life and setting the goals for better life at present and in the future. Following the description of the key features of CHS, its results in the realm of agency development are presented based on official documents and, with a view to visualizing the process of agency development, a conceptual scheme of stage transition is formulated and illustrated by views and sentiments expressed by program participants. The key role of social workers in providing psychosocial support along the process of stage transition is emphasized and conditions for their effective performance are identified.

The situation of the poorest is characterized by multifaceted "difficulties" of life that accompany economic "deprivations," which lead to various vicious circles that hinder the formation and development of agency required to improve the situation. The *Chile Solidario* Program (CHS) is designed to support the poorest people to move out of this situation by means of accompaniment (psychosocial support) and the provision of social services. The central focus of CHS is to make the available social services effectively accessible for eligible people through the assistance of social workers and subsequently to keep them connected to administrative systems so that they use services to their own advantage, improving their current situations and also preparing themselves for the task of charting a better future. In this chapter, we will review the design, implementation, and achievements of the program, stylize the stages of formation and strengthening of the agentic capacity among program participants, and explore the conditions that enable stage transition.

© The Author(s), under exclusive license to Springer Nature Singapore Pte Ltd. 2022
M. Sato et al., *Empowerment Through Agency Enhancement*,
https://doi.org/10.1007/978-981-19-1227-6_10

2 *Chile Solidario* Program (CHS): Background, Design and Expected Results[1]

In1990, the first government of the *Concertación* took office in Chile after nearly two decades of dictatorship under the military regime (1973–90). Social policy of the first democratic government was framed by two principles, one particular for that particular period, the other longer-term and associated with development strategy. The first principle was to respond to the 'social debt' accumulated during the years of military dictatorship, the most notable expression of which was the poverty incidence as high as 40% in the country. The second principle postulated a "growth and equity" strategy. This was maintained, with varying emphasis and terminology, throughout the four governments of the *Concertación* (the four governments are: Aylwin, 1990–94; Frei Ruiz-Tagle, 1994–2000; Lagos Escobar, 2000–2006; Bachelet, 2006–2010). Each government designed and implemented its flagship initiatives, and the *Chile Solidario* Program (CHS) was the emblematic initiative of the government of Lagos Escobar, 2000–2006.

Chile Solidario Program (CHS), designed to assist the poorest segment of the population to move out of poverty trap, was first introduced in 2002 and gradually phased in over time. The immediate background to the formulation of CHS was that the proportion of the poorest in the total population remained constant while that of the poor followed a declining trend over the 1990s. Two factors were recognized as reasons for this: first, the mechanism that led to the overall economic growth did not reach the poorest strata of the population; and second, support measures for poor people were not utilized by the poorest of the poor. Based on this recognition, the design of CHS took into account the situation of the poorest people and the need for proactive engagement by support providers so that the marginalized families would be connected to available support measures and also to economic activities. Both the supply side and the demand side of public services were addressed: on the supply side, conscious attention was paid in order to make public services easier to use for the poorest people, and on the demand side, psychosocial support consisting of "accompaniment, counseling and consulting" was provided by trained workers. What is important in the design of CHS was that the basic approach of social policy had been changed from a vertically divided policy targeting individuals to a comprehensive policy targeting families. Based on such a new approach, CHS was designed as a comprehensive program directed to both the demand and supply sides of social services.

---

[1] This and the next two sections draw heavily on Raczynski (2008).

2.1 Design of Chile Solidario *Program (CHS)*

In the second half of the 1990s, the reduction of poverty and indigence in the country that began in 1987 and accelerated between 1990–96 as a result of a more active social policy and an improvement in the employment situation and wages, reduced its rate of descent and, in the case of indigence, showed stagnation around 6% of population (about 225 thousand families).

The diagnoses of the time indicated that the stagnation in the reduction of indigence was a consequence of the fact that social policy and its main instruments, social programs, did not reach or only partially reached this segment of the population. It was either because they did not handle information on the benefits and programs to which they could access and/or because they faced personal barriers (communication difficulties, low self-esteem, shame and fear, learned hopelessness). The diagnosis defined indigence as the combination of insufficient monetary income and human resources (poor health, education, training and labor productivity conditions) and the absence of effective social networks in the face of negative events such as illness, accidents, unemployment, disability, old age, as well as recessive economic cycles. In other words, the situation of indigence was conceived as a multidimensional problem that required comprehensive support, and *Chile Solidario* Program (CHS) was designed to improve existing living conditions and to shape future prospects.

In this framework, CHS aimed to improve the living conditions of families in extreme poverty, generating opportunities and providing resources that allow for the recovery or creation of effective functional capacities in the personal, family, community and institutional environments. CHS sought to realize in families in extreme poverty minimum conditions for quality of life and also real opportunities and possibilities to improve their standard of living. As indicators were established 53 minimum conditions grouped under seven dimensions of life.

CHS adopted an action strategy that touched both sides of service and program transactions: the beneficiary side (families) and the provider / administrator side (public institutions). On the one hand, it carried out work with families to generate in them basic conditions of functionality and self-commitment for their departure from the socioeconomic conditions in which they found themselves; on the other hand, it deployed actions aimed at sensitizing those responsible for public programs and services so that they would make their services and benefits more flexible in order to ensure timely and pertinent delivery of support to families in extreme poverty.

The design of CHS did not start from scratch. It was supported by the *Programa Puente*[2] (PP) of the Solidarity and Social Investment Fund (FOSIS), which in turn had as a precedent some work experiences with sectors in poverty at the local level carried out by municipalities and NGOs. CHS proposed the extension of PP to the population in extreme poverty throughout the country, the incorporation into it of

---

[2] *"Puente"* signifies "bridge."

other important components of social policy and the delivery of a guaranteed payment to the family for a period of 24 months.

2.2 The Four Components of CHS

CHS consists of four main components: psychosocial support to the family (component 1), guaranteed cash income transfers (components 2 and 3), and preferential access to public entitlements and services (component 4).

(1) Psychosocial support (*Puente Program*: PP)

Accompaniment to the family in extreme poverty is provided by professionals or workers trained for the task, for a period of 24 months, through a system of periodic home visits following a methodology developed for this task. The professional / worker, called 'Family Support' (*Apoyo Familiar*: AF), supports the family in the process of realizing a certain standard of quality of life expressed in the list of seven dimensions and 53 minimum conditions. The AF invites the family to join the program and signs a "Family Contract" of reciprocal commitment with it. This component is the bridge to CHS.

(2) Solidarity Bond

The family begins to receive monetary benefit ("*Bono Solidaridad*", Solidarity Bond) when it has signed the Family Contract and shows signs that it is making efforts toward the fulfilment of the terms of the contract. This voucher is given to the mother or, failing that, to the oldest woman in the household. Only exceptionally is it given to the man head of the family. Each family incorporated into PP that collaborates in the tasks associated with it receives monthly payment for 24 months. The amount of the payment decreases with the passing of time. This modality was chosen to encourage the family to stay in the program but not depend on it as a permanent source of income.

(3) Guaranteed monetary subsidies

The 225,000 families integrated into CHS will have the guarantee of allocation of the existing monetary benefits to which they are entitled according to their family conditions. These are:

Single Family Subsidy (SUF), for all those under 18 years of age and pregnant women. Children under 6 years of age must attend health centers and those of school age (6–18 years) must attend schools.
Old Age Assistance Pension (PASIS), for all those over 65 who do not have social security.
Disability Assistance Pension (PASIS) to all the cause of each family.

Subsidy for Drinking Water and Sewerage Service (SAP), which covers 100% of the monthly bill up to 15 cubic meters of consumption to all families with a drinking water connection and meter.

Subsidy for school retention that is paid at the end of the school year to establishments that maintain as regular students the children of CHS families who attend between 7th grade and 4th grade.

Exit bonus: granted monthly for the period of three consecutive years to the family that has completed the 24 months of PP. It has an amount equivalent to the SUF and the last month of Solidarity Bond.

(4) Preferential access to public benefits / services

Different institutions and public organizations in the areas of health, work, housing, justice, among others, agree with MIDEPLAN to attend to the CHS beneficiaries in the defined programs. The programs included are:

Job training, leveling studies, drug rehabilitation, prevention of domestic violence, technical aid for people with disabilities, JUNAEB benefits and others.

Preferential subsidy for hiring for unemployed heads of families integrated into CHS.

Pension contribution for unemployed heads of families who at the time of losing their job have been contributing to the pension system.

In this way, the CHS is an articulated system of benefits that "streamline" the social protection network for families in situations of extreme poverty. It is more appropriate to see it as not a program but rather a system, understood as a network of programs that are coordinated according to and responding to the specific needs of each family. The psychosocial support component is novel insofar as, until then, it was generally not present in programs targeting poverty in the country. Another distinctive feature of the CHS is the explicit definition of "social minimums of quality of life." The hypothesis underlying it is that a family needs to have these minimums resolved in order to be able to activate and deploy its individual and group capacities and potentialities. Furthermore, in the Chilean context, the decision to work with the family and not with individual people of certain characteristics is novel. The family in extreme poverty is the focus of the intervention and they access specific support according to their particular situation.

After the 24-month stage of psychosocial support and activation of collaboration networks, comes the post-psychosocial support follow-up stage that lasts for 36 months. In this stage, it is sought that the family completes and maintains compliance with the minimum conditions, providing psychosocial support only in cases where it is essential, either because in the initial 24 months the minimum conditions were only partially achieved or because the family has experienced vital events or social dynamics that require additional support. The priority issue at this stage is to ensure that the family remains on the path to improving their situation and to identify and respond to new demands for the public offer that families may have.

2.3 Minimum Conditions of Quality of Life

Here is the List of 53 Minimum Conditions of Quality of Life to be met by families. (Source: Carneiro et al. (2015) Table A.1)

Identification
I1 All family members registered in the Civil Registry.
I2 All members of family have an ID card
I3 The family has CAS updated at the municipality of residence.
I4 All men over 18 have military situation sorted.
I5 All adult members of the family have regularized their bureaucracy, as appropriate.
I6 Individuals with a disability should have the disability certified by COMPIN (Medical, Prevention and Impairment Commission) and registered in the National Disability Center.

Health
H1 Family service registered in the Primary Health Care.
H2 Pregnant women have their health checks updated.
H3 Children under 6 have their vaccinations updated.
H4 Children under age 6 have their health checks updated.
H5 Women 35 years and older have the Pap test updated.
H6 Women who use birth control are under medical supervision.
H7 Elderly are under medical supervision.
H8 All members of the family who have a chronic illness are under medical supervision.
H9 Family members with disabilities that can be rehabilitated participating in a rehabilitation program.
H10 Family members are informed on health and self-care.

Education
E1 Preschoolers attend a nursery school program.
E2 If mother works and there are no adults to take care of children, these should be in some form of child care.
E3 Children up to 15 years are attending an educational establishment.
E4 Children who attend preschool, primary or secondary, benefit from assistance programs appropriate school.
E5 Children over age 12 are literate.
E6 Children with disabilities able to study are incorporated into the educational system, regular/special.
E7 That there is an adult responsible for the child's education and that is in regular contact with the school.
E8 Adults have a responsible attitude towards education, recognizing the value of formal education.
E9 That adults are literate.

Family Dynamics
F1 Daily conversation about topics such as habits, times and places for recreation.
F2 The family has adequate mechanisms to deal with conflicts.
F3 That there are clear rules of coexistence within the family.
F4 Equitable distribution of household tasks (regardless of the sex and according to the age).
F5 Family knows about community resources and development programs.
F6 People involved in domestic violence are incorporated into a program of support.
F7 Families who have children in the protection system somewhere visit them regularly.
F8 Families with young members in the correctional system should support him/her.

Housing
C1 Family has its housing situation clarified regarding tenure of house and site in which they live.
C2 If the family wants to apply for housing, it should be doing it.
C3 Access to clean water.
C4 An adequate power system.
C5 They have a system of proper sewage disposal.
C6 That house is not raining, not flooded and is well sealed.
C7 That housing has at least two habitable rooms.
C8 That each family member has his bed with basic equipment (sheets, blankets, pillows).
C9 Basic equipment to feed the members (pots, pans, cutlery for all family members).
C10 They must have a proper system of garbage disposal.
C11 That the home environment is free from pollution.
C12 That the family has access to the subsidy payment of potable water consumption, if applicable.

Labor Market
L1 At least one adult family member works on a regular basis and have a stable salary.
L2 No child under 15 years drop out of school to work.
L3 That people who are unemployed are registered in the Municipal Information Office (OMIL).

Income
G1 That the members of families entitled to SUF have it (at least are applying to it).
G2 That family members entitled to Family Allowance have it.
G3 That family members entitled to PASIS (welfare pension) have it (at least are applying to it).
G4 The family has income above the poverty line.
G5 The family has a budget organized according to their resources and priority needs.

From the perspective of this chapter, the 53 conditions may be classified into four different categories: i.e., (1) Administrative Procedures (AP), (2) Utilization of Public Services (PS), (3) Conditions of Life (CL) and (4) Management of Family Life (FL). This classification is tentative, since there are items that may belong to more than one category as we see later.

(1) Administrative Procedures (AP): I1,2,3,4,5,6, H1, C1,2, L3, G1,2,3
(2) Utilization of Public Service (PS): H2,3,4,5,6,7,8,9,10, E1, 3,4,6, F6, C12
(3) Conditions of Life (CL): E2,5,7,8,9, C3,4,5, 6,7,8,9, 10,11, L1,2, G4
(4) Management of Family Life (FL): F1,2,3,4,5,7,8, G5

Broadly speaking, Quality of Life (QoL) is most directly related to conditions of life, or beings and doings that constitute life as is. Utilization of public services are important indirect determinants of QoL insofar as that has strong impacts on the conditions of life. Administrative procedures are one step further removed from QoL in that what they affect directly is the access to public services, which in turn are expected to bring about improvements in conditions of life. However, it is possible that establishing proper relations with government offices and having access to public services have not only an instrumental value in improving objective conditions of life but also an intrinsic value as constituents of self-identity and self-esteem, as they help to diminish the sense of marginalization and alienation.

Let us examine the items in the QoL list in some detail.

(1) Administrative Procedures (AP): I1,2,3,4,5,6, H1, C1,2, L3, G1,2,3

The items in this category may be divided into two subgroups, i.e., I1,2,3,4,5,6 as one and the rest as the other. The items in the first subgroup are preconditions for the access to any public service, including those mentioned in the second subgroup. They do not bring any immediate, direct benefit in improving objective conditions of life. In contrast, those in the second subgroup refer to the steps needed to secure access to public services in particular areas and entitle the applicants to some specific benefits. This is most clear in the case of G1,2,3 where entitlements to welfare payments are actually converted into their receipt by taking proper administrative procedures. (In fact, G1,2,3 may also be classified as items belonging to Utilization of Public Service (PS).)

(2) Utilization of Public Service (PS): H2,3,4,5,6,7,8,9,10, E1,3,4,6, F5,6, C3,4,5,10,12

No explicit mention of 'public' service is made in the description of the items listed here but it is presumed that they involve public services with most, if not all, families. In particular, C12, with its reference to the 'subsidy payment,' will be considered most certainly related to public service. There are a number of items that merit particular mention. H10 is interesting in that it refers to the condition of 'information on health and self-care.' As such it may not relate to public service in this domain. It is also of interest from the viewpoint of self-management with regard to the family's own health conditions. F5 is concerned with access to resources and opportunities that exist in the community and the public domain. F6 is of particular interest in that it relates to intra-family relationship and that there is a 'program of support' on domestic violence as public service. C3,4,5,10 relate directly to conditions of life in the physical infrastructure domain of water, power and sanitation. (In fact, C3,4,5,10 may also be classified as items belonging to Conditions of Life (CL).)

(3) Conditions of Life (CL): E2,5,7,8,9, C3,4,5, 6,7,8,9,10,11, L1,2, G4

E2,7,8 relate to care of children, with E7 and E8 referring to the responsibility of adult members of the family toward schooling of children. L2 also relates to the same theme. These items presumably could be pustulated as conditions for children's QoL at present as well as in the future. E5 and E9 relate to 'literacy', i.e., capacity to read and write, which may be viewed as a factor with both an instrumental and intrinsic value in life. C3,4,5, 6,7,8,9,10,11 are concerned with the physical conditions of life of a family in and around its residence, which are expected to have direct bearing on QoL of the family. L1 and G4 relate to the monetary condition of the family that sets the budget constraint to QoL of the family.

(4) Management of Family Life (FL): F1,2,3,4,7,8, G5

The items in this subgroup are connected to the management of family life. F7 and F8 are concerned with the attention and care to be given to children in public custody. This is presumably a factor affecting QoL of children under such conditions and possibly also broader intra-family relations. F1,2,3,4 and G5 are concerned with various aspects of 'management' of intra-family relations. They are related to both material and psychological aspects of QoL. It is important to note that they are closely interwoven with the question of agency on the part of family members. This question will be further explored later in this chapter.

The definition of the minimum quality of life is valuable and significant because it represents an important operational advance that (1) shifts the view of the public offer from each program (and the institution that is in charge of it) to the specific needs of the family in extreme poverty; (2) it facilitates the evaluation of the CHS system as a whole in terms of its contribution to compliance with the minimums and their sustainability over time; (3) consolidates in the participating families a sense of right to comply with these minimums, at the same time that it establishes commitments and a responsibility of the family in achieving them.[3]

2.4 Goals and Expected Results

1. Quantitative goal regarding the number of families in extreme poverty included in the program:

    225 thousand families until 2005 (Lagos Presidential term), to which 50 thousand more were added for 2006.

---

[3] The definition of minimum conditions of quality of life has been criticized from various viewpoints (Raczynski, 2008, p. 19).

2. Expected results in the incorporated families, in three moments
   (a) 70% of relevant families are expected to graduate from the *Program Puente* (PP):
   - Integrate with the local environment where the family resides;
   - Participate in mutual support practices;
   - Join the public network of social support in the locality;
   - Effectively access the social benefits aimed at them; and
   - Have a per capita income above the indigence line.

The indicator fulfillment of these goals is that 70% of families have a "successful exit" from PP, that is, have met the 53 minimum conditions.

   (b) During the post-graduation monitoring period of PP, it is expected that:
   - Families with "successful exit" maintain compliance with the 53 minimums over time and continue to be inserted in their environment with practices of mutual support, access to the public network in case of need and have an income that is not below the indigence line; and
   - "Insufficient exit" families complete the minimum quality of life that was pending in their case and do not reverse those achieved.

   (c) After 5 years in the system, the CHS expects the families to:
   - Maintain the achievement of the 53 minimum conditions and access the subsidies, benefits and social programs of the State to which they are entitled;
   - Have and can maintain an income above the indigence line;
   - Participate in mutual support practices and be integrated into the local environment where you reside; and
   - Have the autonomous capacity to cope when faced with new life events and socioeconomic risks.

3 Psychosocial Support: *Programa Puente*

Programa Puente (PP) is the gateway to the CHS and is the responsibility of FOSIS, the institution that designed it and developed its methodology, management modality and the associated registration system. The execution of the work is based in the municipality, within which a family intervention unit (UIF) is created, composed of a Head (JUIF) and a body of family support workers (AFs). The head of the UIF organizes the work of the AFs, assigns a group of families to each AF (according to the contracted schedule), encourages collaboration and the contribution to the CHS of the associated institutions established in the national collaboration agreements, and seeks and motivates the collaboration of others in public, private, and community domains, so that they contribute with their actions and benefits to the work with the CHS families in each locality.

To respond to the situation of these low-income families, excluded from the existing social and assistance networks and lacking the minimum requirements to have an adequate quality of life, PP carried out personalized work with each participating family in their home conducted by AFs, prepared and trained to accompany and support the family in strengthening their capacities for self-commitment and self-management in pursuit of a better quality of life.

The function of the AF is defined as follows:

- Directly and personally supports families in gradually obtaining the 53 minimum quality of life conditions contemplated by the system according to the specific requirements and priorities defined by each family, work that is carried out with an intervention methodology specially designed for these ends, which is materialized in work sessions at home and incorporated in periodic contracts of mutual commitments between the family and the AF for the achievement of the minimum conditions for the family.
- The foregoing is complemented with the processing of the respective bonuses and subsidies to which the family is entitled and the facilitation of the family's access to a varied set of locally executed social programs, available to the system. [Strictly speaking, it is about the household, the set of people who live in a private home and share the household budget.]

The AF seeks to promote the development of the family's potential, transforming it into the agent of its improvement process and generating actions aimed at bringing the family closer to the social services and benefits available in the territorial network. "Through a personalized intervention carried out by a promoter, it connects the family with networks and opportunities that can contribute to the progressive satisfaction of basic needs" (MIDEPLAN, 2002).

The AF works individually with each of the families that have been assigned to it with a methodology whose goal is to mobilize the family's self-management capacities to comply with and maintain the minimum quality-of-life conditions over time. This is done through work sessions at the family's home, establishing a personalized and trusting relationship with it. For these sessions, the following sequence, contents and intensity are defined:

- In the first two months, through easy-to-understand methods and pedagogical materials especially designed for these purposes, the AF carries out 8 work sessions with the family, one per week, based on the "family platform," a methodological instrument to facilitate the realization of a diagnosis and a participatory work plan between the AF and the family. Among the issues identified in the platform are the composition, characteristics and relationships within the family, the human, social and material capital that it has, and the priorities that the household establishes for the achievement the 53 minimum quality-of-life conditions across the seven dimensions of well-being. Based on this diagnosis and

prioritization, a work plan is defined in agreement with the family, in which the family and the AF assume responsibilities, which must be fulfilled by each party.
- In months 3–4, home visits become biweekly and in months 5 and 6, monthly. In these visits, the diagnosis is deepened, progress in the work plan is monitored and new commitments are defined between the family and the AF.
- From the 7th month the sessions are bimonthly and after the first year quarterly. The contents of the sessions are about monitoring and reinforcing weak points in the family, and the identification and access to the benefits it requires.
- At month 24, the family graduates from PP (psychosocial support), which is classified as "successful" when the family has managed to meet the 53 established minimums and as "insufficient" if they need to meet one or more of the 53 minimum conditions.

Parallel to this work, the AFs support the JUIF in activating the collaboration and offer of the associated institutions. In this field, the CHS does not define a specific methodology. It only indicates that it is responsible for publicizing at the local level the agreements signed at the national level and that inter-institutional collaboration practices will be more successful if the managers and officials of the services are involved in working with the family and they together design activities and benefits that respond to the needs of families in extreme poverty in the locality, particularly those which do not have regular contacts with available services.

4 Results of *Chile Solidario* Program (CHS)

4.1 Incorporation of Beneficiary Families

Every year about 50 thousand new families were invited to participate in the system. Of these, on average, 4.9% did not participate in the system either because they did not want to or because it was not possible to locate the family. The rest, 95.1% started work with a PA. 5.5% of the families contacted interrupted the process, either due to the decision of family support, the family or both. The rest, 89%, have participated regularly in the System.

The initially projected coverage was to incorporate 225 thousand families between 2002 and 2005. Between 2002 and 2005, 207,277 families were contacted, 8% less than initially projected. In 2006, the projected figure exceeds this goal by 15%. If the calculation is made in relation to the families effectively incorporated (participants), the corresponding percentages are –29 19% in 2005 and + 3% in 2006. In other words, with a one-year lag, the CHS exceeds the initial coverage goal of 225 thousand families proposed.

4.2 Reduction of Indigence

The CASEN 2006 survey allows a first estimate of the contribution of the CHS to the reduction of indigence. The components of the CHS that have a direct impact on the level of household income are the protection and graduation bonus, and the monetary subsidies. The comparative information for the years 2000 and 2003 and 2006 that is reproduced in table 18 indicates that with the CHS the weight of these subsidies increased in the total income of households in the lowest quintile; from 8.6%, to 11.5 and 16.7%, respectively. For the year 2006, the information published is disaggregated by tenth and it can be seen that in the lowest tenth just over a quarter of the family's monetary income corresponds to monetary subsidies and these subsidies increase the income of these families by 35.6%. In short, CHS families have access to more monetary subsidies and these improve the immediate consumption capacity of the families. The receipt of the bonuses and subsidies is highly valued by the beneficiaries. The money they obtain for this concept is used to solve needs such as the payment of outstanding accounts, rent or dividend debts, food, purchase of school supplies and medicines, and if it is enough, small savings for the home.

4.3 Changes in the Minimum Quality-of-Life Conditions of the Participating Families

Table 10.1 records the percentage of families that met all the minimums of each dimension at the time of admission to the CHS and at the time of exit from the psychosocial support phase. There it is observed that the percentages increase considerably, between 24 and 50 percentage points, between the two moments. In other words, this indicator reveals a notable advance in the situation of families in

Table 10.1 Fulfillment of the minimum quality-of-life conditions on Entry / Exit of the *Programa Puente* (PP)

Dimension	On Entry (%)	On Exit (%)	Advance during PP (%)
Identification	36.2	80.9	44.7 / 63.8
Health	42.3	91.9	49.6 / 57.7
Education	63.6	87.2	23.6 / 36.4
Habitability	14.5	60.7	46.2 / 85.5
Employment	39.6	84.1	44.5 / 60.4
Income	28.3	72.4	44.1 / 71.7
Family Relations	52.6	91.2	38.6 / 47.4

Source: Raczynski (2008), Table 15, p. 30. [Original source: Asesoría para el Desarrollo (2005b) Tabla 4.]
Note: It is considered that a dimension is fulfilled if all the conditions in it are satisfied

meeting minimum conditions. The goal of 70% of families with all the minimum conditions fulfilled is achieved in all dimensions except one, which is habitability.

Table 10.2 details the goals met for each minimum condition. It is detected that the minimum conditions that are fulfilled to a lesser extent are income above the indigence line (fulfillment of 77.2%), sealed house (83.2%), drinking water subsidy (84.2%), application to housing program (84.3%), domestic violence care (84.7%), registration in the national disability registry and disability rehabilitation (89.8%). Income, employment, habitability and disability are the conditions where it is most difficult to overcome the gaps with respect to the defined minimums. They are also the conditions that when entering PP showed a larger gap. All of these antecedents verify that the CHS achieves the goals that it has set for the time of graduation from PP. More than 70% of the families meet the minimum conditions that have been defined and the families are better connected with the local network of services and benefits.

4.4 Effects of the Programa Puente (PP) on the Behaviors, Projects and Future Orientations of Participating Families

In this regard, the empirical evidence available is scarce. The quantitative study already cited by Galasso (2006) verifies that CHS families are more optimistic about their future socioeconomic status than the control group, by 7–8% in rural areas and 10–11% in urban areas. However, another study, of a qualitative nature, suggests that recently graduated families show a greater willingness to advance, but that there would be few cases that manage to persevere when facing severe adverse conditions such as prolonged episodes of unemployment, serious illnesses, situations of domestic violence. These circumstances compromise their self-image and weaken their projection capacity (Asesorias para el Desarrollo, 2005b).

The study also observes that families have two different attitudes towards the CHS. The first corresponds to families who value only the material help of the CHS and not the psychosocial support, demand more help in this area and are dissatisfied or critical of what they have obtained. The second corresponds to families who value psychosocial support and material benefits and demand training and work tools, since with this they increase skills to overcome the situation in which they find themselves. These latter families are more satisfied with what the CHS has provided them, as they take advantage of the opportunities it offers them and work on the realization of family and work projects.

Families in the first group tend to be dependent on subsidies and other direct support provided by the CHS. They are often plagued with family problems whose treatment exceeds the possibilities of the CHS response: mental health, domestic violence, alcoholism and drug trafficking and consumption, and other delinquencies. These situations make psychosocial support work difficult and nullify its potential effects on the psychology and mentality of the family. What to do with

Table 10.2 Minimum quality-of-life conditions met at the entry into and the exit from *Programa Puente* (PP)

Dimension	On entry (%)	On exit (%)
Identification	**80.2**	**93.8**
I1 Registered in the Civil Registry	98.9	99.9
I2 Have an ID card	46.8	90.2
I3 CAS updated	89.5	95.4
I4 Military situation sorted	87.8	96.5
I5 Regularized bureaucratic requirements	89.8	95.6
I6 Disability certified and registered	68.8	85.2
Health	**81.7**	**97.3**
H1 Registered in the Primary Health Care	90.1	99.4
H2 Pregnancy health checks updated	94.5	98.9
H3 Children < 6 vaccinations updated	97.4	99.5
H4 Children < 6 health checks updated	96.2	99.4
H5 Women > 35 Pap test updated	62.3	95.8
H6 Birth control under medical supervision	77.6	97.8
H7 Elderly under medical supervision	79.3	97.5
H8 Chronic illness under medical supervision	79.6	96.4
H9 Participation in a rehabilitation program	70.9	89.8
H10 Informed on health and self-care	69.7	98.9
Education	**88.6**	**96.6**
E1 Preschoolers attend a nursery school	74.2	92.6
E2 Some form of child care	89.4	98.1
E3 Children <15 attending an educational establishment	94.2	97.9
E4 Appropriate school assistance programs	86.4	97.8
E5 Children > 12 are literate	96.9	99.1
E6 Disabled children in regular/special education	85.9	94.0
E7 An adult responsible for the child's education	95.8	98.9
E8 A responsible attitude towards formal education	94.2	98.6
E9 Adults are literate	80.5	92.5
Family Dynamics	**81.6**	**95.4**
F1 Daily conversation	83.5	97.0
F2 Adequate mechanisms to deal with conflicts	78.8	95.3
F3 Clear rules of coexistence within the family	84.8	96.3
F4 Equitable distribution of household tasks	82.1	97.7
F5 Knowledge on resources and programs	74.7	98.9
F6 Support program for domestic violence	71.2	84.7
F7 Regular visits to children in the protection system	89.9	96.6
F8 Family support to minors in the correctional system	88.3	96.8
Housing	**73.8**	**92.5**
C1 Tenure of house and site clarified	78.9	98.2
C2 Apply for housing	44.4	84.3

(continued)

Table 10.2 (continued)

Dimension	On entry (%)	On exit (%)
C3 Access to clean water	90.1	97.7
C4 An adequate power system	85.0	95.8
C5 Proper sewage disposal	73.1	93.1
C6 House well sealed from water damage	44.2	83.2
C7 At least two habitable rooms	77.6	94.1
C8 Bed with basic equipment for each member	64.4	87.9
C9 Basic kitchen equipment	87.6	97.1
C10 Proper garbage disposal	90.2	98.6
C11 Home free from pollution	81.3	96.7
C12 Access to subsidy for potable water	69.9	84.2
Labor Market	**64.3**	**93.6**
L1 Regular work and stable salary	52.6	85.8
L2 No child <15 drop out of school to work	93.8	99.0
L3 Registered for unemployment	46.5	96.1
Income	**71.2**	**91.4**
G1 Entitled members receiving SUF	82.6	94.1
G2 Entitled members receiving Family Allowance	88.0	96.6
G3 Entitled members receiving PASIS (welfare pension)	86.0	92.4
G4 Income above the indigence line	34.5	77.2
G5 Effective budget management	65.0	96.6

Source: Raczynski (2008, Table 16, pp. 31–32). Original source: Asesoría para el Desarrollo, 2005b, Tabla 5
Note: See Section 2.3 for details of each entry

these families is an open question. It is worth wondering if different care paths should be opened for families according to the specific problems that are behind their situation of indigence.

The families that have managed to consolidate a level of autonomy and agency that allows them to move ahead in pursuit of improved living conditions and persevere in their efforts are in the minority. Even so, the achievement is significant. "Family empowerment" crystallizes in the mother, the main recipient of psychosocial support and recipient of the social protection voucher. For her, the fact of receiving the bonus and being able to administer it based on family needs is a sign of dignity and recognition of her role in the family, and, if the relationship that is built between her and the AF is one of trust, she finds a space to talk about herself and her difficulties, a conversation in which she obtains more and better information, learns to set small goals for herself, and when she achieves them, she forges a forward look, strengthening her self-confidence and self-esteem.

There are two important observations in the aforementioned study. First, empowerment is realized only among women who have prior capacities to visualize problems, deficiencies and alternative solutions, such capacities being further strengthened with psychosocial support work. In other words, the work of the AF has positive results in the presence of pre-existing capacities, activating and developing them. Second, the empowered woman head or spouse of the family requires the support of her family after the psychosocial support stage; if she does not have it, the possibility for her and her family to advance autonomously is reduced. It is observed that in families where family dynamics are positive and there is communication between the partners and with their children, the probability of projecting forward and persevering is evidently higher than in homes marked by maltreatment, isolation and absence of communication.

Another goal of CHS is for families to be aware of and manage information about the social services available at the local level. The study by Galasso (2006) verifies that CHS families are indeed more informed about local social services than families in the control group (differences of 10 percentage points in rural areas and 16 in urban areas). The aforementioned qualitative study reaffirms this finding.

4.5 Functioning of UIFs and AFs

There are important differences between the localities in relation to the organization and quality of work of the UIFs and the AFs. There are several reasons for these differences:

- Characteristics of the localities and municipal management: the support and priority that the municipality (mayor and his team) gives to the CHS; the commitment and leadership capacity of the Chief of UIF for the task; the shortage of suitable professional personnel in rural and more isolated localities to take on the work of AF; the local environment, in particular the incidence of poverty in the locality and the complexity of the factors behind it; and the geographical extension, dispersion of the local population and transport difficulties between localities.
- Employment situation of AFs: a situation common to many localities is a high workload of AFs. The studies show figures that vary between 40 and up to 160 families in charge of an AF in 2005, with the average of 74 families per AF. In addition to the high workload, labor contracts do not provide social security or per diem. There are two different contracting modalities—municipality and FOSIS—with different working conditions and hours, which has had a deleterious impact on the work environment in the UIFs and between the AFs.
- Instability and rotation of AFs: a situation which affected the continuity of work and has had a negative impact on psychosocial support work with the family.

4.6 AF's Work with the Family: Tension Between Welfare and Social Promotion

The AF, with the support of the FIU to which it belongs, is a key agent that, through its attitudes and behaviors and the relationship it establishes with the family, determines the effects and impact that the CHS achieves. Studies on the way in which AF s approach their work reveal that at the discourse level they share the principles of the CHS: social promotion, involving the family in solving the problems that afflict it, fostering acceptance and fulfillment of commitments, promoting projects, in short, strengthen the autonomy and agency of the family. However, in their daily work they find it difficult to get out of "welfare" given the urgencies that families experience. Faced with the urgency of help, there is a tendency for AFs to carry out a task themselves because the solution will be faster, instead of supporting the family to do so by making a commitment and fulfilling it. There is therefore the risk of installing a relationship of "perverse accompaniment" that creates dependence on the part of the family.[4]

The observations above point to a risk and underline the importance of looking for appropriate ways to support and properly channel the work of the AFs. The conditions in which the AFs carry out their work—high burden of families, transportation difficulties, insufficient infrastructure conditions (office, workplace), lack of instances and time for teamwork and exchange of experiences between them, insufficient training and support in technical aspects, as well as the absence of supervisory and self-care workshops—accentuate this risk. Interviews with AFs reveal a strong demand for supervisory and support actions that allow distancing oneself from lived situations and sharing experiences, providing feedback on daily work with families, and carrying out case analyses. The initial training and induction to the PP for the UIF and AF does not seem to be enough. Many AFs express need for regular support on the job (Raczynski, 2008, p. 38).

---

[4] There is an interesting exploratory study that characterizes mutual sentiments between the family and AF based on a survey of 68 family representatives and 23 AFs in six localities. The study concludes that in 37% of the cases the link is adequate, another 37% not so good, and 25% inappropriate. The dimensions of the qualifications are: level of commitment, stability, closeness, horizontality, flexibility and promotion (Raczynski, 2008, p. 37. [Original source: FOCUS-FOSIS, "Characterization and Evaluation of the Link between AFs and people and families participating in the PP", Final Report, July 2004.]) .

4.7 Difficulties Or Insufficiencies in the Offer of Complementary Programs

Insufficiencies in complementary programs and/or delay in reaching household members who urgently need support, reduces the potential of the CHS. The evidence available in studies on this point coincides in areas that show weaknesses in this regard. They are:

- Employment and income generation in the local environment. If employment or the possibility of a micro-enterprise does not exist, the family's probability of moving out of indigence is remote. Specifically, the weaknesses detected are associated with limitations of the Municipal Office of Labor Intermediation (OMIL), insufficient training and qualification courses available to CHS beneficiaries, and difficulties in marketing the product or service and/or the absence of market for the service at the local level, and, in the case of micro-entrepreneurship initiatives, the lack of access to credit to acquire the necessary inputs, design problems and product quality, among others.
- Housing. This is the dimension in which the CHS families showed a lower proportion of minimums fulfilled at the time of entry and remain in this situation at the end of the 24 months of psychosocial support. It is not that there is no improvement in housing, but that there is less than what is required as obtaining access to a better and proper home is not easy.
- Family dynamics. Another area in which the programmatic offer is insufficient is the issue of isolation and domestic violence, in the couple and with children. When a family faces problems, it seems almost impossible for the family to persevere in its efforts to move ahead. AFs face complex and deep-rooted relational problems for which they often do not have the required skills. There are cases involving drug use, alcoholism and situations involving illegal activities. Specialized services that could provide support in those matters are few and practically inaccessible.

5 Evaluation of *Chile Solidario* Program (CHS)

5.1 Evaluation by Participating Families

Here we show the results compiled from responses to a survey by questionnaire to the families participating in CHS in a series of tables (Tables 10.3, 10.4, and 10.5).

The following observations can be obtained from the examination and comparison of the three tables above:

Table 10.3 Evaluation of the CHS as a whole by participating families

	Number of families	Percentage (%)
Very satisfied	538	13.1
Satisfied	1658	40.4
A little satisfied	1143	27.9
Unsatisfied	406	9.9
Very unsatisfied	234	5.7
Unknown	123	3.0
Total	4102	100.0

Source: MIDEPLAN (2009a, Table No1, p. 23)

Table 10.4 Evaluation of AFs by participating families

	Number of families	Percentage (%)
Very satisfied	432	10.5
Satisfied	1421	34.6
A little satisfied	956	23.3
Unsatisfied	693	16.9
Very unsatisfied	490	12.0
Unknown	110	2.7
Total	4102	100.0

Source: MIDEPLAN (2009a, Table No2-A, p. 23)

Table 10.5 Evaluation of works on intrafamily relations by participating families

	Number of families	Percentage (%)
Very satisfied	345	8.5
Satisfied	1525	37.2
A little satisfied	1069	26.1
Unsatisfied	694	16.9
Very unsatisfied	349	8.5
Unknown	120	2.9
Total	4102	100.0

Source: MIDEPLAN (2009a, Table No2-E, p. 27)

- There is a great dispersion of responses in each table.
- Positive opinions outnumber the negative by a wide margin in assessing the CHS Program as a whole. The same is true when comparing "very satisfied" and "very dissatisfied".

5 Evaluation of *Chile Solidario* Program (CHS)

- Positive opinions outnumber negative ones in the evaluation of AFs. However, families who answer "very satisfied or" are outnumbered by those responding "very unsatisfied".
- The responses on work related to intra-family relationships are similar to those of the AF, but both "very dissatisfied" and "very satisfied" represent lower percentages and are almost at the same level.
- Positive views are most prominent for the CHS Program as a whole than for the relationship with AF or work related to domestic relations. An inverse pattern is observed in negative opinions.

Several conjectures suggest themselves based on these observations:

- A comparatively higher positive evaluation for the CHS Program as a whole can be explained by a high level of satisfaction with the components other than the PP (where AFs play a central role even in family relationships related work).
- The fact that there is a considerable percentage of negative opinions about AF seems to imply limitations of PP.
- That both extreme responses ("very satisfied" and "very dissatisfied") are more pronounced for the relationship with AF than for work on intra-family relationships is an intriguing mystery. Do emotions arise more strongly for people than for events?

5.2 Self-assessment of the Achievements Made by the Participating Families

Intervention by AFs in the CHS Program consists of "counseling" (psycho-social support through accompaniment and encouragement) and "consulting" (technical support through education and advice), both tailored to the conditions of the families. The counseling function addresses psychological matters related to perceptions, feelings and emotions such as self-esteem, self-control, self-efficacy and motivation for achievement. The central task is to promote and develop positive elements in perceptions, feelings and emotions and enhance expectations for positive change in life (MIDEPLAN, 2009a, p. 18).

As stated above, the central objective of *Programa Puente* (PP) is to initiate and promote a process of empowerment of target families with an adult education approach. The learning on the part of families is geared to the acquisition of capacity for self-management and autonomous resolution of problems, encompassing such competencies as recognition of opportunities, management and resolution of problems, determination of alternative courses of actions, establishment and utilization of relationships with providers of services. Such learning during the program is expected, as the program is completed in two years' time, to have enabled the formation of capacity to formulate projects and courses of action for their realization. In the Final Note (*Nota de Egreso*) at the time of the termination of PP, each

Table 10.6 Area of most significant learning

Family	52.5%
Institutions	31.8%
Community	4.4%
Others	11.4%

Source: MIDEPLAN (2009b, Grafico 2.1, p. 71)

Table 10.7 Subcategory of most significant learning under "Family"

Self-respect and positive attitude	50.4%
Intra-family relations	24.5%
Household management	12.0%
Development of abilities	8.0%
Development of values	8.0%

Source: MIDEPLAN (2009b, Tabla 2.1, p. 73)

participating family expresses their views and evaluations of their experiences with the program and also proposes a project for improvement of family life.

The central "empowerment" objective of the PP is closely related to the task of rehabilitating sound personal relations within the family and reestablishing it as source of mutual support and positive contributor to the resolution of problems. This is clearly indicated in the Final Note of many of the families as indicated in the "area of most significant learning" during the program (Table 10.6):

Of those who mentioned "Family" as the area of most significant learning, a half of them mentioned "self-respect and positive attitude" and a quarter "intra-family relations" as the most significant subcategory, far exceeding those mentioning learning of more technical nature such as "household management" and "development of abilities" (Table 10.7).

Inquiry was also made on the area of most significant functioning attributed to PP. Here "functioning" refers to behaviors in various aspects of family life, which impinge on the quality of life. They are supported by the knowledge, attitudes, skills and tools the family has. The following table registers the self-assessment by participating families regarding important functioning acquired or strengthened through their participation in PP (Table 10.8).

On exit from PP, the largest proportion (20.9%) of responses on most significant functioning referred to Family, understood as increased effectiveness on issues of coexistence, cohesion and self-respect.

14.9% of answers that indicate functioning in Housing; this is to say that PP helped the families to improve their living conditions in such forms as acquisition or improvement of their houses or their immediate surroundings. 14.1% of the responses indicate functioning in 'Income', which refers to the contribution of PP in the management of subsidies and savings, in addition to the increase of income from the newly granted "Social Protection Bond."

5 Evaluation of *Chile Solidario* Program (CHS)

Table 10.8 Area of most significant functioning attributed to *Program Puente* (at the time of exit)

Family	20.9%
Housing	14.9%
Income	14.1%
Positive attitude	10.5%
Public services	8.8%
Employment	6.5%
Health	4.1%
Education	3.4%
Registration	1.4%
Unknown	15.6%

Source: MIDEPLAN (2009b, Grafico 2.2, p. 80)
Note: In the table above "Income" refers to the receipt of cash transfer and subsidies, and newly acquired practice of saving

Table 10.9 Area of most significant functioning attributed to *Program Puente* (three years after exit)

a.	Acquisition of Social Protection Bond
b.	Access to micro-entrepreneurship development
c.	Management of family budget
d.	Improvement of housing conditions and equipment for the home
e.	Integration into and use of the Public Health System
f.	Access to benefits of assistance at school
g.	Subsidies for the processing of the National Identity Card

Source: MIDEPLAN (2009b, Grafico 2.2, p. 80)

The information gathered through in-depth interviews made to families three years after the exit from PP provides a view of functioning acquired in PP (as shown in the following table) that is very different from those mentioned at the time of exit from PP (Table 10.9).[5]

It appears that, three years after the completion of PP, families tend to remember and give credit to more concrete and tangible benefits than at the time of exit from PP. The mention of "micro-entrepreneurship" and "family budget" are of particular interest as manifestation of goal-setting and self-management capacities.

Conspicuous in absence in this list is the mention of "Family." It may be because the foundation of family relations had already been built during the two years of PP. Also, consciousness on intra-family relations may have weakened with the end of home visit by AFs.

---

[5] This and following paragraphs draw heavily on MIDEPLAN (2009b, pp. 77–81).

6 Visualization of the Stages of Agency Development

6.1 *Refleccions on the Effects of* **Programa Puente** *on the Development of Agency*

The available evidence on the effects of the CHS indicates that nothing ensures that meeting the 53 minimum conditions of quality of life is sufficient to achieve "autonomy"[6] of the family and produce a "springboard effect" that will lead them to successfully face future development challenges. The development of agency is neither easy nor automatic.

It seems that psychosocial support (counseling) is a necessary precondition for effectiveness of informational and technical advice (consulting) related to agency development. The feeling of intimacy and affection between the family and the social worker is necessary for the family to be able to overcome insecurity and low self-esteem and acquire a positive outlook on life. Some interviewees state that they recognize the importance of having developed better capacity to express and verbalize their emotions and that such capacity was enhanced during the conversations with AFs about events and difficulties. They say that such capacity not only contributes to the improvement of intra-family relations but also to increased sense of security, self-efficacy and positive attitude, contributing to the enhancement of agency. This being the case, care is needed so that emotional attachment will not create psychological dependence and instead that the family strengthen their independent planning and managing capacities (MIDEPLAN, 2009b, pp. 88–89).

In this context, the requirement of the declaration of a project at the conclusion of *Programa Puente* serves as an important instrument to gauge the degree of self-determination and self-management capacity in the family. A project is to consist of goals set by the family and courses of action to realize them. These "family projects" constitute the starting point for the trajectory of family life they make efforts to realize through a series of actions independent of the assistance of AFs (MIDEPLAN, 2009b, p. 90).

The following table gives the breakdown of areas of life focused in the family projects expressed in the Final Note at the time of exit from *Programa Puente* (Table 10.10).

Of these items, "Education" can be regarded as clearly indicating a future orientation. "Positive attitude / Happiness" seems to indicate future orientation but is in fact often no more than a vague expression of hope, with a low degree of project specificity and execution (MIDEPLAN, 2009b, p. 96).

The degree of success in achieving self-determination and self-management capacity varies across families. There seems to have emerged contrasting patterns of virtuous and vicious circles. Virtuous and vicious circles involve three elements: the

---

[6] The term "autonomy" has not been clearly defined or operationalized by *Programa Puente* or CHS. The texts only indicate that the family must be informed and connected and know how to access the public offer that responds to the problems and risks it faces.

Table 10.10 Areas of attention expressed in 'family projects' (on exit from *Programa Puente*)

Housing	40.9%
Employment	21.4%
Education	14.7%
Positive attitude / Happiness	12.0%
Family relations	4.9%
Income	3.2%
Health	2.1%
Other	0.9%

Source: MIDEPLAN (2009b, Grafico 2.1, p. 95)

condition of family life, attitude toward government offices, and the relationship with AFs (MIDEPLAN, 2009b, p. 94).

We need to understand the variability in the degree of success across three phases—i.e., pre-program, in-program and post-program. Families with relatively favorable initial psycho-social conditions benefited more from the program and prepared themselves for the realization of their life goals, while less favorably situated families benefited less from the program and failed to change outlook on their life prospects. In some cases of high attainment during the program, with increased sense of self-efficacy, self-confidence and optimism, goals set for the project reflect future-oriented aspirations in pursuit of higher standing in society—stable work, higher income, home ownership, and higher education for children. (MIDEPLAN, 2009b, p. 111) By contrast, there are cases of virtually no attainment during the program among the families with unfavorable initial conditions, typically characterized by alcoholism, drug use, and domestic violence.

It has been found that there are variations in the performance of *Apoyos Familiares* (AFs): some of them made more frequent and longer visits than others. Those families visited by less attentive AFs tended to have poor results in learning, low utilization of the program offerings, and low evaluation of the program. Similar negative sentiments were generated when there were frequent changes in AFs, as families felt abandoned and insecure about their relationship with the program. They need to establish expectations of sustained benefits on the basis of correct understanding of the program if their connection with government offices should continue beyond the period of accompaniment and psychosocial support conducted by AFs. For that to happen intimate and trustful relationship with an AF is indispensable, as family members need to feel safe in discussing most private family matters openly (MIDEPLAN, 2009b, pp. 86–87).

6.2 A Stage Model of the Process of Development of Agency

It seems to be possible to formulate a conceptual model of agency development consisting of four stages, based on the comments of participating families regarding their experiences and thoughts generated through their participation in CHS, PP in particular. It will be useful to illustrate the stages of agency development with the comments and characteristic behaviors of the participating families.

It seems that intra-family relations and intensity of accompaniment by AFs are the most important factors that affect the transition from one stage to next. This may be particularly relevant for the transition from stage 1 to stage 2, which is often not achieved when there are significant negative factors within the family or when the accompaniment by Afs is not sufficiently intense. Further investigation is required on these matters.

In what follows, we present a conceptual model of the process of development of agency. This model is informed by the insights and findings of the Behavioral Economics of Poverty (Chap. 4) and an implicit stage theory of user agency (Chap. 7). It is formulated as consisting of four stages. The model will be illustrated with comments from participating families.

Stage 1: Feeling of not being able to exercise control in one's own daily life due to conditions of uncertainty and permanent vulnerability.
There is no formation of an agentic subject.

"… *The only problems I have is my partner's job, which is not stable, and the house we are in, because now in the winter it rains, because of the rain that happened, we had to patch with nylon.*" *(Woman, 18 years old, Interrupted, Quillota).*

"*With the job that my partner has, we have not been able to put up a roof, because we still have to buy the milk that the child drinks, the diapers, we have to have all the things for the house, the electricity, the water, so it is not enough, because he earns the minimum no more*"*(Woman, Interrupted, Quillota)*

Source: MIDEPLAN (2005), pp. 16–17.

Stage 2: Sense of achievement in managing some aspect of daily life, accompanied by a social worker, generates a glimpse of a feeling of self-efficacy and internal strength to be able to withstand the harsh conditions of life.
This is a necessary preparatory stage for the formation of an agentic subject.

"*The Bridge helped us with the wood. To be able to cover up, they gave us that mass. A gentleman came to the house here, to look at the house, to do a survey of the house. And there he saw that the houses were not lined up, so there he gave us that [...] they came to check first if it was missing. Of course, and as I say, the windows, out in front they gave us the cans so that ... because the internits were broken. So, there they helped us a lot with that. Yes, the house looks prettier." (Lota Family, Bío-Bío Region)*

Source: MIDEPLAN (2009b), p. 76.

"... I have always agreed, because the Bridge Program ... before I didn't even have to take it, the little goats didn't have

not to grab, not a piece of bread; At least I sell now, a little bit, I am getting my profit, I already have to buy bread, a little sugar, something to make food ... we had, because before we did not even have to hold on ... (El Monte rsam)

"... for me it has meant a lot because as I say I was like in a hole, that is, I had no expectation of anything po', of coming out of nothing, that is, I thought that for me, my husband was my livelihood, it was everything and now I can't. The Puente program has helped me because I have had financial help, I have had psychological help that I never thought I would have, I have had a lot of advances, I have fixed my house with the Puente program, little by little." (Curacaví rijb)

Source: MIDEPLAN (2004), p. 27.

"The Health Program was also very important for us, because I was very reluctant to go to the post and he [the Support]

He told us "no po 'if you feel pain you have to go to the post", for example the subject of mammograms which is super important, then in those issues he guided us and helped us more to have more responsibility in the health issue. This is how I had amography, I have been seeing myself all year round by a doctor, for example they found me a fibroid ..."(Family of San Clemente, Maule Region)

Source: MIDEPLAN (2009b), p. 83.

"Well, now ... I graduated from the Chile Solidario Program. They sent me to do that job training course, and there they taught me a lot of things, what is work aspect, because I ... suddenly you go out to look for work and you arrive and leave. So they helped us prepare to look for work, how we have to speak, how to introduce ourselves ..."(Tomé's Family, Bío-Bío Region)

"My mother has always known everything about being involved in the Municipality, I can't'. I did not know how to do a procedure, there

[in the Puente Program] I learned what it is to do paperwork, to harass in the Muni"(Lo Espejo Family, Metropolitan Region)

Source: MIDEPLAN (2009b), p. 76.

"[We learned] how to listen, I think. Learn to listen more to my children. They also taught me to say, I don't know, to him "let's sit down and talk" if we have a problem, not to go yelling and shouting and things like that. So I don't know about sitting down and talking about it, not about shouting for the neighbors to find out, and all that. In that I liked it because I learned that.

Now, when we have something to talk about, we talk about it, we don't yell at each other". (Coronel's Family, Bío Region—Bío)
"We learned how to distribute the little and nothing of the money, to be able to spend it so that it would spread more. It is a new apprenticeship, because sometimes one would come and say, oh now, I have so much money and I go and buy this and I did not notice if it was cheaper elsewhere or if I was going to give up more". (Family of San Clemente, Maule Region)
Source: MIDEPLAN (2009b), p. 74.

Stage 3: Experience of achievements in multiple aspects of daily life, accompanied by a social worker, generates self-confidence and sufficient internal strength to be able to face problems and challenges.
The formation and gradual strengthening of agentic capacity begins.

"When we went to the meetings they held for us, the same supporters told us: we are going to do a business and administration course so that you... learn to manage it, not only give the money, but also that you learn to manage that money that you they are going to give, then they gave us the explanation, they taught us to manage a capital". (Family of San Bernardo, Metropolitan Region)

"I learned to be more active with people, all that ... With the same authorities when one goes to speak, talk to an office, one has more personality ... Because where I go, I will do all my paperwork alone, I do not go with anyone. I found it good
[the Program], because you are going to talk to people, you have more confidence ... you give yourself more confidence ...
before it was shameful..."(Coronel's Family, Bío-Bío Region)

"She came often. Every time I touched him. Sometimes he came, as I say, three or four times a month. But it helped me a lot. It helped me a lot that she was, because now when I need a role I go to her, and she immediately has it for me. (...). About health, I wondered about the children, how they were. In other words, she talked about several things: about my situation, as a couple ... it helped me a lot, as I said, to talk, a lot". (Coronel's Family, Bío-Bío Region)

"I think there were many good learning experiences, in each meeting that there was it was different and something new was learned, one learned something different."(Family of San Clemente, Maule Region)

"And the visits they have made to us, I think they have done us very well, the visits of Miss Assistant when she goes to my house, which I like when she goes because we talk" (GF Coihueco rim)

"It also changed me, when the visitor came to my house, to see me in the situation that I found myself with the poverty that I had, and there it was like

a light I couldn't trust anyone, I became independent but it went badly, but when the visitor arrived, my life changed"(GF Macul—Peñalolén uij)

"They encouraged me a lot because with that game that they came ... that is, I say 'game' because it was as an incentive, because they encouraged me as a therapy, as they gave me therapy from my personal life in terms of the help that They were giving me, I don't know if you understand me, it was therapy because they helped me morally"(Lo Espejo Family, Metropolitan Region)

Source: MIDEPLAN (2009b), pp. 77, 83, 84, 89, 90.

"... to talk to her to ask her for help, the only thing I ask for help is to pull myself up for the meantime, to handle myself better." (Penco uimm)

"For me the best outside of the material, the help as a person that they have given me, they threw me up that has immense value." (GF María Pinto-Curacaví rem) ".

"... they are pending of us. Problems we have, and they help us to solve them." (GF Quillón-Bulnes rea) ..a "We miss her, because when she goes you sit down to talk with her, and as if you knew her all your life, she listens, and it also kind of gives you hope. , one tells one about one's personal things" (GF María Pinto-Curacaví rem)

Source: MIDEPLAN (2004), pp. 28–30.

Stage 4: Hope, vision, goals and plans for the future and action towards their realization.
The process of agency development continues, eventually to reach full agency.

"Before, my husband never participated in the children's meetings at school, now he does. When we have to go to a meeting for Isaías, we both go together, we find out... uh... we talk with Isaías more than with the other children. It's like with him. We had, what is it like?, more contact, more closeness with him, and with Alanis, who is our granddaughter who lives with us." (Lota Family, Bío-Bío Region)

"Since I graduated from the Puente Program, the change I had with my son is that he began to look and feel superior, my son wanted to get to fourth grade and when we left the Puente Program he told me: "Now I want to buy you things, study, depend of a career, mom". He wants to be a kinesiologist. He tells me, "When I have studies I will go to work to pay for my university ..." (Lo Espejo Family, Metropolitan Region)

Source: MIDEPLAN (2009b), pp. 73, 74

7 Concluding Remarks

In this chapter we have reviewed the experience of *Chile Solidario* Program (CHS), a government initiative to help the poorest segment of the population move out of poverty. The most notable feature of CHS is its unique component called *Programa Puente* (PP) which provides psychosocial support in the form of accompaniment and counseling to participating families with a view to fomenting agentic capacity among them. Its positive effects in terms of agency development were qualitatively significant when and where they were realized. At the same time, however, it should be noted that the scope of such achievement is quantitatively limited.

The transition through stages as presented above seems to be the only possible path of agency development for the marginalized indigent families could follow. First, negative elements in objective life conditions and in psychological and mental states need to be dealt with, intra-family relations often being the most significant underlying factor. Positive experience of achievement is of critical importance in the generation of a sense of self-efficacy and self-confidence, which in turn providing a psychological base for the development of "agency," i.e., "disposition and capacity for self-determination and self-management." Agency would be first exercised in dealing with matters of immediate concern and then, with sufficient experience of self-determination and self-management, would be further extended to address future issues.

The *Chile Solidario* Program (CHS) is novel and unique in addressing the extreme poverty from the perspective of "agency development" through "psychosocial empowerment." The experiences of CHS merit further attention and analysis. There are positive messages on new prospects for agency development and escape from the poverty trap, it is true. At the same time, however, it is to be remembered that the paths of stage transition in agency development are fraught with difficulties since they (i) take time, (ii) need adequate counselling and consulting supports, and (iii) are vulnerable to adverse influences. Both of these hopeful and cautionary lessons offer important inputs for the design and execution of anti-poverty and human development programs.

References

Galasso, E. (2006). *With Their Effort and One Opportunity. Alleviating Extreme Poverty in Chile*. Document, Development Research Group, World Bank.
MIDEPLAN. (2004). *Study Effects of Psychosocial Intervention in Women Directly Participating in the Chile Solidario System*.
MIDEPLAN. (2005). *Study of Families in a Situation of Extreme Poverty That Have Not Accepted to Join Or Have Interrupted Their Participation in the Chile Solidario System*.
MIDEPLAN. (2009a). *Chile Solidario Social Protection System: User Satisfaction and Psychosocial Factors*.
MIDEPLAN. (2009b). *Family Paths to Exit from the Puente Program*.
Raczynski, D. (2008). *System Chile Solidario and Policy of Proteccion Social in Chile: Lessons from the Past and Agenda for the Future*. CIEPLAN.

Chapter 11
Conclusion

This book represents a collaborative research endeavor to address the question: "What moves people to take initiatives?" The three authors of this book approached this question from the vantage points of respective disciplines of Anthropology, Psychology, and Economics. The central concept in the articulation and elaboration of the question is "agency and its development." Our research project has focused on the understanding of factors and mechanisms involved in the development of agency mainly in three related contexts—participatory development, extension work, and service transactions. The main objectives of the project are to (1) identify critical roles of agency in human behaviors, (2) examine related concepts and relevant propositions, (3) put forth our understanding and working hypotheses on factors and mechanisms impinging on the exercise and development of agency, and (4) present results of our attempts at measuring agency and/or visualizing its development.

This publication is woven with three disciplinary warps and three thematic wefts, the former moving through the latter more or less independently. The three common themes expressed as titles of the three parts are: "Part1: Understanding Agency and its Development," "Part2: Enhancing Agency: its Plausible Mechanisms and Influential Factors," and "Part3: Visualizing and Measuring Agency." Let us summarize the achievements in each of the three parts of this publication.

1 Part1: Understanding Agency and Its Development

Part 1 provides conceptual and theoretical examination of "agency," starting with the definition and articulation of the concept and the determination of its place and role in relation to some key concepts in each discipline. It is to be remembered that it is as a way to address the central, practice-oriented question of this book "What moves people to take initiatives" that the authors focus on the concept of "agency" in our academic discussions. We did not intend to engage in academic research for research's sake, but tried to distill whatever each discipline offers to illuminate the issue and help inform and guide the practice. We wholeheartedly concur with Jo Rowlands when she says (Rowlands, 1997, p. vi):

> I wanted to undertake a theoretically and intellectually grounded exploration of the concept that would enable an analysis of the practical and organisational implications of its use....
> My intention is to encourage more precise usage and to explore how a more disciplined use of the concept of empowerment might provide a useful tool for activism, gender planning, project planning, and evaluation.

Let us first present the definitions and related arguments from the three disciplines represented in this volume (Anthropology, Psychology, and Economics), followed by an attempted synthesis.

1.1 Agency: Definition and Significance

1.1.1 Definition of "Agency"

Part 1 "Understanding Agency and its Development" presents relevant reviews of literature in the three disciplines represented in this volume (i.e., Anthropology, Psychology, and Economics) on the theme of "agency and its development." It is notable that, unlike in sociology or philosophy, the term "agency" is not necessarily explicitly defined or employed as a central concept in any of the three disciplines.

For our collaborative research, we adopted as our common starting point the definition of "agency" given by the American Psychological Association (APA):

> "the state of being active, usually in the service of a goal, or of having the power and capability to produce an effect or exert influence"

From an anthropological perspective, Mine Sato combines this definition with other two (by Amartya Sen and Nail Kabeer) from development studies to form a synthetic one:

> [Def. A] "an individual's or shared power/ability to produce an effect or exert influence on some issues in pursuit of specific goals and values, which is context-bound as influenced by culture. (However, agency, on some occasions, can be also power/ability to transform culture.)"

This definition is uniquely "anthropological" in that it explicitly refers to "cultural context" in which "agency" is exercised.

Based on the psychological methodology and clarifying the character and role of "constructs," Nobuo Sayanagi relates "agency" to more familiar and better operationalized concept of "autonomous motivation" in the Self-Determination Theory. He defines "agency" as:

> [Def. P] "the ability and capacity to self-determinedly act towards goal(s) of improving the environment and/or circumstances"

1 Part1: Understanding Agency and Its Development

It is to be noted that "self-determinedly" in this definition refers to the subjective experience of volition (regardless of whether there are any external influences) rather than the objective state of decision-taking independent of external influences.

From an economic viewpoint on the characterization of an individual as "agent," Toru Yanagihara sees "agency" as an internal factor that enables a person to decide on and manage one's actions and defines it as:

> [Def. E] "disposition and capacity for self-determination and self-management of one's own actions and activities"

This definition neatly fits the traditional economics conception of "endowments" of an individual at a point in time and opens the way to place "agency" as an additional component or layer of "human capital."

It is noteworthy that all the definitions identify "agency" as "power/capacity/ability," unlike the APA definition ("the state of having power and capability") that the three authors used as common reference and the starting point. This reflects our common orientation toward practice-relevant investigation to find effective levers of influence on the process of "development of agency."

To compare and contrast the three definitions presented above, it will be useful to recall the conception and characterization of "agency" by Amartya Sen consisting of the following four elements: (i) self-determination, (ii) reason orientation and deliberation, (iii) action, and (iv) impact on the world (Chap. 3, 3.2). The following Table 11.1 compares and contrasts the three definitions.

It may be worthy of mention that the degree of specificity of goals of action is highest in Def. A, followed by Def. P, and lowest in Def. E. This difference is related to their respective natures in relation to (iii) action and (iv) impact on the world presented in the table above. Def. A makes much of actions and impacts in specific contexts; Def. P centers on action and motivation behind it (rather than its outcomes) in relation to more general goals; and Def. E is focused on the underlying driving force and enabling factor for self-directed action in general and not concerned with any specific actions or activities.

Table 11.1 Comparison of the three definitions

	(i) self-determination	(ii) reason/deliberation	(iii) action	(iv) impact
Def. A	No	Maybe (implicit)	Yes	Yes
Def. P	Yes	Maybe (implicit)	Yes	No
Def. E	Yes	Maybe (implicit)	No	No

Note: The characterization in the table above is based on the explicit expressions in the definitions alone and that it does not reflect any discussion of the determinants or outcomes of "agency" in the respective disciplines.
Source: Compiled by the author.

1.1.2 Significance of "Agency"

As stated at the outset, this volume revolves around the central question: "What moves people to take initiatives?" In what ways is "taking initiatives" significant? In other words, in what ways is "agency" significant?

In answering this question, we follow Amartya Sen's conceptual formulation (Sen, 1999):

- Intrinsic value Exercising agency is in and of itself is a desirable achievement ("Development as freedom").
- Instrumental value Agency in goal-setting and self-management contributes to improved life-conditions.
- Constructive value Agency in reasoning enables examination and evaluation of attitudes and preferences

We have endeavored to identify these roles of agency in our thematic arguments and case studies.

1.2 The Place and Role of "agency" in the Three Disciplines

1.2.1 Anthropology

Review of two branches in Anthropology, Academic Anthropology and Development Anthropology, has been conducted. In Academic Anthropology, "agency" is best understood in relation to "culture" insofar as the former presupposes certain values that are embedded in the latter. It is alright to describe an "exercise of agency" but not so with "development of agency" as the latter goes against cultural relativism, the fundamental grain of the academic discipline. In contrast, Development Anthropology is practice-oriented adopting the value premises of the development community. The key concept in this school is "empowerment." There are many documents of experiences of empowerment work but there has not been conscious effort toward theorization based on those experiences. To fill the gap, the present author proposes "Anthropology of development practices" with a view to providing a theoretical perspective on the process and mechanism of "empowerment," or "agency development."

1.2.2 Psychology

The most influential psychologist on the theme of "agency" has been Albert Bandura. While Bandura has written extensively on agency, he does not provide an explicit definition. However, we can surmise his definition of the term from the statement: "To be an agent is to influence intentionally one's functioning and life circumstances." Bandura asserts that "self-efficacy," or "beliefs in one's capabilities to organize and execute the courses of action required to produce given attainments," is the central mechanism of agency. Another motivational theory that deals with agency is SDT. SDT does not provide an explicit definition of agency, but it is safe to interpret that it is used synonymously with "autonomy," or "acting volitionally with a sense of choice." SDT emphasizes the subjective sense of self-determination, which contrasts with Bandura's position which puts emphasis on the intentional influence upon one's circumstances. Theoretically and operationally, the best psychological approach to "agency" is to relate it to "autonomous motivation," the central construct of SDT. The formulation of SDT provides a rich discussion of factors and mechanisms of self-regulated behavior and also well-proven measures of degrees of autonomy in the motivation toward behavior.

1.2.3 Economics

"Agency" can be related to three key concepts in economics, i.e., (1) rationality, (2) human capital, and (3) human capability.

(1) Agency and rationality.
   In standard microeconomics, "agents" are postulated to be fully rational, i.e., fully informed of relevant facts and fully capable of making the optimal decisions that maximize their objective functions. This conception of agents has been long criticized by the "bounded rationality" school on the ground of limited cognitive capacity: agents may intend to be rational but they are incapable of attaining "full rationality." Behavioral Economics (BE) carries this thinking several steps further and fundamentally rejects the general applicability of standard economics. Agents choose and decide under the influences of various psychological and social factors not traditionally considered in economics. They are "bounded" not only in "rationality" but in "self-control" and "self-interest." In the BE paradigm, agency relates not only to cognitive capacity but also to socio-emotional capacity.
(2) Agency and human capital theory.
   The concept of human capital as originally proposed by Theodore Schultz and Gary Becker was only concerned with the "cognitive capacity" as determinant of earnings. Recently James Heckman and his collaborators, consisting of economists and psychologists, have added the "noncognitive capacity" (later relabeled as "socio-emotional skills") as another aspect of human capital, arguing and demonstrating that it is also important as determinant of earnings and other socioeconomic outcomes. With our definition of agency (Def. E in 1.1.1) as endowment, it is straightforward to add agentic disposition and capacity as another aspect of human capital. In fact, agency may be seen as the core element, or the deepest layer, of human capital in that it is the fundamental driving force and enabling factor of all human actions and activities. Human capital

theory is usefully employed in the theoretical and empirical studies on formation of capacities and development of agency.
(3) Agency and the capability approach.
Agency is importantly featured in the capability approach (CA). Discussions of agency in this school are heavily influenced by its founder, Amartya Sen. Sen emphasizes both internal and external conditions of an individual as determinant of the person's agency. One weakness in the argument on agency in the capability approach is the lack of dynamics needed to address development of agency. On this, there is obvious complementarity between the CA and human capital theory.

The main features of (1) and (2) represent recent scholastic innovations in economics motivated by the desire to make economic research theoretically more comprehensive and empirically more relevant by incorporating viewpoints and findings from psychology and neuroscience. By contrast, (3) reflects attempts spearheaded by Amartya Sen to bridge economics and philosophy (ethics, in particular). There are a number of interconnections among these three areas of research, as illustrated above.

1.3 Understanding Agency and Its Development

1.3.1 Anthropology[1]

As anthropologist, the author relates discourses on "agency and its development" to and compares them with more practically-oriented discussions on "empowerment," and finds the former "individualized" and "de-contextualized. Conscious about these deficiencies of the former, she provides her own understanding of the process of "agency development" based on in-depth case studies of a rural empowerment training course in Nicaragua and the Life Record Movement groups in Japan. From the first study, the process is identified as a sequence of "affirmations": (i) "power from within" of self, (ii) "power with" others, and (iii) "power to" and "power over" surrounding structures, emphasize the importance of social communication (involving individual particularities of people involved) and (locally-contextualized) practical knowledge. From the examination of the second case focused on the power of "story-telling" as means of "emancipation, self-formation, and democratized communication," "power with" emerges as the core of the processes of a series of subtle transformations, accompanied by manifestations of "power to" and "power over." "Power from within" was not consciously pursued in group activities but seems to have been realized in the process.

---

[1] Includes relevant findings from Parts 2 and 3 as well.

1.3.2 Psychology

The author presents an understanding of the term "agency" as essentially synonymous with that of "autonomy" or "acting volitionally with a sense of choice" based on SDT in psychology. As stated in defining "agency", what matters is the subjective experience, or "autonomous motivation." There is strong empirical evidence associating agency with autonomous motivation. Agency based on autonomous motivation is likely to promote *eudaimonia*.

1.3.3 Economics

"Agency" is understood to be a latent, underlying factor behind any purposeful human action. It is conceived to be an element of human capital for each individual and is treated as a stock variable (as if it is an entity). An important conceptual distinction is made between "activation" of a given stock of agency in the short run and "development" (i.e., increase in the level of the stock) of agency in the long run. Agency is conceived to be a generic disposition and capacity to be activated and utilized in specific actions and activities when and as so motivated. Development of agency is understood as a process of capital formation and discussed in relation to facilitating and limiting factors impinging on that process. For example, life/work experiences could exert positive or negative influences depending on the nature of the experiences and the condition of the person concerned.

2 Part 2: Enhancing Agency: Its Plausible Mechanisms and Influential Factors

Concepts and propositions are only useful to the extent they inform and support practices in the real-world. In this part the authors have discussed "agency and its development" in various real-world contexts and conditions from the perspective of the respective disciplines.

2.1 Anthropology

The author first reviews the main literature on empowerment and agency to develop a theoretical framework for the agency development process, identifies black boxes of the theories, and clarifies the three critical factors for analyzing case studies. An in-depth case study of a development project in rural Nicaragua designed for the specific purpose of agency development is provided with particular attention to (1) context specific factors, (2) design feature of the project, and (3) mechanisms of agency development in the three types of power (power from within, power with, power to, and power over). The findings and understandings are related to theoretical frameworks adapted from academic research on human resource development.

2.2 Psychology

Three factors, corresponding to the three "basic psychological needs" as postulated in SDT, constitute facilitators of agency. They are: "autonomy support (AS)," "competence support (CS)," and "relatedness support (RS)." Based on available empirical evidence, it is hypothesized that, in addition to their direct effects on agency enhancement, there are interactions between them. While the existing literature on agency enhancement emphasizes AS, the author argues that AS is not effective in low perceived competence settings such as poverty contexts and requires additional CS in the context of RS.

2.3 Economics

The "User-Centered Approach (UCA)" is proposed widely as a remedy for supply-side domination in service provision. The author examines user-centered approaches to service transactions and the empowerment of service users, one context in which "agency" as human capital on the part of service users is importantly featured, from the perspective of institutional economics. First, conceptual and analytical approaches to service transaction and utilization are presented, followed by articulation and classification of the nature of services and conjectures on two types of failures. Second, in discussing the effectiveness of the UCA models (co-production and self-management), typologies of user-provider relations and of user agency in service transaction and utilization is presented. Third, conceptual distinction between and empirical illustrations of the activation and development of user agency are provided and related to different types of empowerment interventions. Based on these arguments, an implicit stage theory of user agency is schematically presented: pre-outreach → outreach → counselling → consulting → independence (full autonomy)

3 Part3: Visualizing and Measuring Agency

3.1 *Anthropology*

The author examines the experiences of the Life Record Movement (LRM) in post-WWII Japan from the perspective of agency development focusing on the following three questions: (1) facilitating factors and inhibitors for the initiation, development and sustainability of LRM activities; (2) documentation of texts and narratives by participants and supporters; and (3) plausible mechanisms of agency development hypothesized based on the case study. On the last question, previous academic discussion of LRM is reviewed and useful insights are drawn through the examination of the key concepts employed.

3.2 *Psychology*

The author reviews traditional methods in which autonomous motivation (agency) has been measured, and critiques the adaptation of such methods in research on poverty contexts. Specifically, the validity of measurement of traditional Likert scales adapted to poverty contexts is unclear, and in some cases, the obtained measurements violate the basic assumptions of parametric statistical testing. The author proposes that mixed-method research, which corroborates quantitative measurements with qualitative data, is necessary to solidify the foundations for psychological research, which is still in its infancy in poverty contexts.

3.3 *Economics*

The author presents an in-depth case study of *Chile Solidario* Program (CHS), designed and implemented by the government to assist the poorest segment of the population to move out of poverty trap. The special feature of CHS was its emphasis of agency development as key condition for overcoming the difficulties of daily life and setting the goals for better life at present and in future. Following the description of the key features of CHS, its results in the realm of agency development are presented based on official documents and, with a view to visualizing the process of agency formation/development, a conceptual scheme of stage transition is formulated and illustrated by views and sentiments expressed by program participants. The key role of social workers in providing psychosocial support throughout the process of stage transition is emphasized and conditions for their effective performance are identified.

4 Achievements and Tasks Ahead

4.1 Achievements

4.1.1 Advances in Each Discipline

Anthropology

In the field of Anthropology, as explained, there have been a very limited number of discussions on "agency development" as well as defining the term itself, mainly due to Cultural Relativism. The author [Mine Sato] thus believe that the most significant achievements through this book project were opening up a forum of discussion on agency development from anthropological views, through making structured and focused discussions regarding agency, agency development and culture to clarify their hidden and unexplored relations (Chap. 2), Proposing an alternative approach in applied anthropology "Anthropology of development practices" (Chap. 5) as well as Extracting working models of agency development from two case studies in contextualized manners (Chap. 8). This project should be also a pioneering contribution to Anthropology through exploring how anthropological texts actually deal with "agency development"

Psychology

The most important contribution of the three Psychology chapters as a whole is a clear definition and articulate discussion of "agency" from the perspective of SDT. SDT is a widely accepted theory in psychology and other scholars from adjacent disciplines based on its theoretical coherence and sound empirical support. By relating "agency" to "autonomous motivation," one of the key concepts of SDT, these chapters—combining theory, comparison with other relevant approaches, and attempted measurement of "agency" in an agricultural development program---offer a useful new way of understanding the psychological construct of "agency" and the promotive factors for "agency enhancement." It is worthy of mention that this new understanding has immediate relevance to the design and execution of projects and activities in development at the grassroots.

Economics

The most important achievement is our formulation of "agency" as a core component of human capital and resulting possibilities of discussing "empowerment" as activation or development of agency (Chap. 4). This question was first addressed and illustrated in the context of the "user-centered approach" to service transactions, where the role and character of empowerment in the co-production and self-management models were analyzed and strengths and limitations of empowerment programs were examined (Chap. 7). The empowerment issue was further pursued in relation to a poverty program and a stage theory of "agency development" was proposed with a view to visualizing the process and mechanism of agency development, theoretically informed by the Behavioral Economics of Poverty (Chap. 4) and an implicit stage theory of user agency (Chap. 7) and empirically based on the statements by program participants (Chap. 10). We believe that Chaps. 7 and 10 constitute important contributions from the vantage point of economics to our collaborative endeavor to seek answers to the overriding question "What moves people to take initiatives?"

4.1.2 Synthesis

"Empowerment" is a term widely used in the practice of development professionals and social workers. Logically, the notion of empowerment needs to be based on the conception of "power." The situation to be worked on is viewed as "the lack or scarcity of power" and the goal is envisaged as "increased power." Surprisingly, however, explicit discussion of power is rather uncommon in the discourse and practice of empowerment. We have cited and relied on Rowlands (1997) for her unique contribution in this regard. In particular, we found two particularly appealing concepts she proposed: "power from within" and "power to". We believe that this book, as a whole, has made important contributions as our research was conducted to answer the overriding question: "What moves people to take initiatives?" In our view, this is, and should be the core issue of "empowerment" addressing both "power from within" (source of power) and "power to" (effect of power).

In this book, the three strands—Anthropology, Psychology, and Economics—of "understanding agency and agency development" have been presented (Part1), followed by the tripartite discussions on "the mechanisms and factors involved in agency enhancement" (Part2) and on "the visualization and measurement of agency" (Part3). The authors believe that all three strands have made unique contributions in the respective disciplines as summarized above. Here, we try to draw insights, suggestions, and implications for the practice of agency development aimed at "empowerment," or "enabling and facilitating people to take initiatives," identifying areas of complementarity across the disciplines.

The Anthropology chapters provide thick descriptions of the process of empowerment through profound understanding about oneself supported by leaders and encouraged by peers. There are many elements that are context-specific and even person-specific. Those details, which tend to be disregarded in the formulation of programs and projects, may prove to be crucial factors in their success. …

The Psychology chapters shed a sharply focused light on the nature of motivation that is conducive to "people taking initiatives." Based on the well-verified theoretical formulations of SDT, they offer an important insight into human motivation, provide practical guidance for the design of programs and projects, and enable ongoing monitoring of their outcomes.

The Economics chapters present coherent conceptual frameworks and theoretical models useful for clarifying the conception of "agency" and for visualizing the process of "agency development." Of particular practical significance is the findings, informed by the insights of the Behavioral Economics of Poverty and varied experiences of User-Centered Approach, on the diversity of preparedness conditions for productive engagement both on the program participant side and the service provider side. Attempts at fine-tuning to cope with this difficulty are likely to prove costly in terms of time, attention, effort, and money and thus tend to be ignored or shunned. Sensitivity with this issue on the part of designers and workers could make a difference in practice, however.

As summarized above, the Psychology chapters offer directly useful guidance and tools for the design and implementation of the practice of "agency development." Of particular importance is the scale designed to measure the degree of autonomy in the motivation toward a determinate action. By comparison, contributions of the Anthropology and Economics chapters are of indirect characters. The Anthropology chapters offer insights into the nature of profound change involved in the process of realizing "power from within" paying attention to context- and person-specific factors. The Economics chapters provide useful conceptual frameworks for visualizing the dynamic process of "agency development" and the distinctive modes of engagement by workers for different stages of the process.

It is noteworthy that all the three basic psychological needs postulated in SDT—autonomy, competence, and relatedness—are importantly featured in the Anthropology and Economics chapters as well, serving as the common threads throughout the volume and enabling coherent treatment of overlapping issues across the three strands.

4.2 Tasks Ahead

4.2.1 For Research in Each Discipline

Anthropology

This book project is just a starting point. Further case studies should be conducted to extract lessons and working theories/models of agency development in context-specific manners to be shared widely. The authors hope that we can situate this attempt into mainstream applied/development anthropology to make a platform to bridge practice and theory.

Psychology

First and foremost, there are still very few psychologists that work in poverty contexts, where the facilitation of agency is very much needed. The authors strongly hope that this volume will interest more psychologists to enter the field. Additionally, the authors hope that the detailed assumptions behind psychological theory and research will inform workers from other disciplines to better understand and utilize psychological concepts and methods in their research and practice.

Economics

There are a number of fronts where further theoretical and empirical studies are desired. First, the Behavioral Economics of Poverty needs to be related more closely and systematically with the understandings and orientations in the practice of development and social work, as the former tends to deal with general tendencies disregarding diversities in the life and psychology of the poor. Second, various experiences of the User-Centered Approach need to be further explored with a view to an updated systematization and possible theorization on the conditions for successful program performances. Third, the case of the Chile *Solidario* Program (CHS) could be further explored through documentary and statistical studies with a particular focus on the system surrounding the recruitment, training and staffing of social workers.

4.2.2 For Interdisciplinary Research

As continuation of this book, a logical next step will be conducting truly joint research working on the same case. Such research will be highly useful to organize findings in cross-disciplinary manners and, in the process, to understand similarities/differences across the three disciplines as well. One candidate will be the Chile *Solidario* Program (CHS). Another will be the Life Improvement Program conducted in rural Japan after World War II.

It might be also helpful to form a network with other interdisciplinary research teams in the related fields with a view to exchanging experiences and lessons in search of effective approaches and practices.

References

Rowlands, J. (1997). *Questioning Empowerment: Working with Women in Honduras*. Oxfam.
Sen, A. (1999). *Development as Freedom*. Anchor Books.

Index

A
Accessibility, 81
Accompaniment, 187, 188
Actor-Network Theory (ANT), 18
Actor-oriented approaches, 20
Adult life education, 167
Affirmation, 83
Agency, 11, 29–35, 37, 89–92, 97, 98, 113, 114, 123, 179, 181
Agency achievements, 56
Agency activated (AA), 54
Agency activation, 124
Agency augmentation, 124
Agency development, 11, 38, 187
Agency freedoms, 56
Agency in existence (AE), 54
Agentic capacity, 44, 187
Aid, 83
Aid ethnography, 24
Alianza Comunitaria, 76
Alkire, S., 66
Altruism, 50
Antagonistic observer, 20
Anthology, 161
Anthropologists, 12, 13
Anthropology, 11
Anthropology of Development, 20
Anthropology of development practices, 24
Anti-poverty approaches, 95
Applied anthropology, 19–23
Appreciative Inquiries, 172
Aspirations, 42, 68
Attitudes, 113
Autonomous motivation, 34–35, 80, 89, 96, 98, 109, 111, 115, 116, 175, 181

Autonomy, 33, 97, 111–113, 115
Autonomy support, 98, 100, 105, 106, 111, 115
Autonomy-supporting, 94
Autonomy supportive, 98, 110, 115

B
Basic psychological needs, 97, 116
Behavioral economics, 37
Behavioral Economics of Poverty, 41–43
Behavior changes, 94, 95, 99, 101, 102, 104, 108, 109, 111, 115, 116
Behaviorism, 30, 94, 100, 101
Behaviorist, 27, 30, 96, 109
Behaviorist theory, 109
Behavior modification, 94, 100–104, 107
Benedict, Ruth, 17
"Big Five" personality inventory, 49
Boas, Franz, 16
Bottom-up, 72
Bounded rationality, 37, 40
Bounded self-interest, 40
Bounded willpower, 40
Brazil, 74
Bricolage, 16

C
Capability, 54–55
Capability approach (CA), 37, 38, 91, 93
Capacity development, 95, 100
Capital stock, 44
Cernea, Michael, 21
Chambers, Robert, 21

© The Author(s), under exclusive license to Springer Nature Singapore Pte Ltd. 2022
M. Sato et al., *Empowerment Through Agency Enhancement*,
https://doi.org/10.1007/978-981-19-1227-6

231

Chile Soridario, 187–216
Chronic Disease Self-Management Program (CDSMP), 144
Circle activities, 166
Clifford, J., 18
Cognitive abilities, 170
Cognitive capacity, 39
Cognitive psychology, 30
Collaboration, 77
Commitment, 84
Communion and agency, 31
Community development, 77
Compassion, 168
Competence, 80, 99–101, 104, 112, 115
Competence support, 105, 106, 108, 110, 111, 114, 115
Compositions, 166
Conditional cash transfers, 104, 107–110
Connectedness, 171
Consientizacion, 73
Constraints, 39
Construct, 27, 30, 175, 181
Construct validity, 178
Consulting, 131, 188
Content validity, 177, 183
Context, 12
Context specific factors, 67
Controlling, 102, 110
Convergent and divergent validity, 183
Convergent validity, 177, 180, 182
Co-production, 123
Core competencies, 52
Cornwall, A., 23
Counseling, 127, 131, 188
Criterion-related validity, 177
Cultural evolutionism, 14–15
Cultural relativism, 13, 16–17
Culture, 12
Culture and agency, 11
Culture of poverty, 90

D
Decision-making, 92
De-contextualization, 66
Default rules, 41
Definition of agency, 34, 175
Democratization of communication, 157
Deprivations, 187
Developing countries, 14
Development agencies, 21
Development aid, 89, 91–93, 95
Development anthropology, 11

Development practitioners, 24
Development project, 71
Dewey, John, 157
Diaries, 168
Digital storytelling (DST), 154
Discretion, 123
Disposition, 38
Divergent validity, 177
Divine agency, 29
Dormitory, 158

E
Economic agents, 37
Emancipated, 157
Empathy, 168
Empowerment, 22, 124
Engaged activists, 20
Escobar, A., 20
Ethnographies, 12, 13
Eudaimonia, 33
Executive function, 47
Exercise of agency, 39
Exercising agency, 85
Extreme poverty, 89
Extrinsic motivation, 96

F
Facilitation of agency, 178–179
Facilitators, 80
Factor validity, 177
Family Dynamics, 193
Family Life (FL), 194
Female factory workers, 157
Ferguson, J., 20
Foucault, 20
Framework for Enabling Empowerment (FrEE), 93, 95, 113–114
Framing, 41
Freire, Paulo, 73
Front-line service providers, 127
Full rationality, 37
Functioning, 54–55
Fundamental attribution error, 90

G
Game theory experiments, 178
Geertz, Clifford, 12, 18
Gender equalities, 67
Gender norms, 170
General Headquarters (GHQ), 158

Index

Generalized self-efficacy, 32
Giddens, Anthony, 66
Governmentality, 20

H
Haiku, 154
Heckman, James, 45
Hedonic concept of happiness, 34
Heuristics, 39
Hope, 42
Human capital theory, 37, 38
Human development, 79, 123

I
Ibrahim, S., 66
Identification, 192
Impact evaluations, 123
Implementation failures, 130
Individual differences, 27, 29, 175
Individualization, 66
Informational, 102
Information processing, 39
Informative, 109
Initiatives, 65
Insiders, 24
Intentions, 113
Inter-coder agreement, 180
Internal consistency, 179, 180
Internalization, 97–99, 102, 108, 112
Internalize, 104, 107, 108
Internalized, 100, 108, 110
International Development, 19
Intra-family relations, 208
Intrinsically motivated, 96
Intrinsic motivation, 96, 97, 112
Items, 176

K
Kabeer, N., 12
Kinoshita, Junji, 168

L
Labor union, 158
Leadership, 167
Levi-Strauss, Cloud, 15, 16
Lewis, Oscar, 17
Life Composition Movement (LCM), 167

Life improvement approach (LIA), 95, 110–111
Life record movement, 153–172
Likert scales, 176, 183
Locus of control, 113
Long, N., 20
Loss aversion, 41
Low perceived competence, 106

M
Malinowski, Bronislaw, 15
Marcus, 18
Marginalized population, 172
Mauss, Marcel, 15
Mead, Margaret, 17
Measurement of agency, 175
Mental mode, 41
Microeconomics, 39–44
Millennium Development Goals (MDGs), 23, 89
Minimum Conditions of Quality of Life, 192
Minimum quality-of-life conditions, 199–200
MMO, 71
Modernist anthropology, 15–16
Modernization theory, 15
Moral agency, 29
Morgan, Luis, 14
Mosse, David, 23
Most Significant Changes, 172
Mother's History, 159
Motivation, 38, 123, 168
Motivational Interviewing (MI), 146
Muchaku, Seikyo, 162
My Home, 158
My Mother, 159

N
Narrative approaches, 154
Need for autonomy, 97, 102, 107, 109
Need for competence, 97, 102, 104
Need for relatedness, 97, 103
Needs for autonomy, competence, and relatedness, 97
Need support, 110
New Institutional Economics, 127
Nicaragua, 72
Nohara, Tetsuo, 71
Noncognitive skills, 45
NPOs, 76
Nurse-Family Partnership (NFP), 148

O

Operant conditioning, 101
Operational definitions, 176
Optimization, 39
Outreach, 134
Ownership, 65

P

Participatory observations, 12, 24
Participatory rural appraisal (PRA), 21, 71
Peacock, J., 12
People-centered primary care, 136
People's Learning and Action (PLA), 21
People's participation, 24, 67
Perry Preschool Program, 47
Personal agency, 181
Personal empowerment, 127
Personality, 38
Personality psychology, 45
Personality skills, 45
Personality traits, 45
Physiological drives, 98
Plausible mechanisms, 78–85
Poor, 169
Positive attitude, 208
Postmodern anthropology, 18–19
Postwar democracy, 167
Poverty, 89
Poverty alleviation, 65
Poverty reduction, 93
Poverty trap, 90, 187
Power from within, 66, 68
Power over, 66, 68
Power to, 66, 68
Power with, 66, 68
Practical knowledge, 24, 86
"Practice"-type services, 127
Pre-counseling, 131
Predictive validity, 177
Preference for leisure, 50
Preference parameters, 49–50
Preferences, 38, 39
Proactive engagement, 188
Project ethnography, 23
Protagonist, 84
Psychic costs, 149
Psychological constructs, 27–28
Psychological needs, 115
Psychological well-being, 98
Psychometrics, 28, 175
Psychometric tests, 176
Psychosocial support, 126, 187
Punishments, 101

Q

Qualitative research, 178, 180
Quality of life, 65, 192–195
Quality of motivation, 181

R

Radcliffe-Brown, A. R., 15
Rapport, 166
Realities, 169
Reinforcements, 100, 101
Relatedness, 104, 115
Relatedness support, 105, 106, 110–112, 114, 115
Relatedness supporting, 108, 115
Relational empowerment, 127
Reliability, 179, 183
Reluctant participant, 20
Replicability, 82
Resources, 85
Rewards, 96, 100, 101
Risk aversion, 50
Risk preference, 50
Risk tolerance, 50
Routines, 39
Rowlands, J., 65
Rural villages, 166

S

Said, Edward, 18
Satisficing, 39
Sawai, Yoshiro, 158
Self-acceptance, 171
Self-agency, 31
Self-confidence, 84
Self-determination, 38
Self-determination theory (SDT), 27, 80, 89
Self-efficacy, 32–34, 84, 113, 177, 181
Self-esteem, 153
Self-exclusion, 133
Self-formation, 154
Self-management, 38, 123
Self-regulation questionnaire (SRQ), 182
Self-reliance, 171
Self-respect, 68, 79, 153, 171, 208
Semi-structured interviews, 12
Sen, A., 12, 37
Sense of agency, 30, 31, 68
Service provision, 123
Service transaction, 123
Service users, 123
Shimizu, Ikutaro, 162

Index 235

Smallholder horticulture empowerment project (SHEP), 95, 111–112
Social communication, 86
Social constructionism, 22
Social Emotional Learning, 52
Social-Emotional Skills, 52
Social networking services (SNS), 171
Social policy, 188
Social preferences, 50
Social services, 187
Social workers, 187
Sociocultural Anthropology, 11
Sociodrama, 153
Socioemotional skills, 45
Solidarity, 170
Spencer, Herbert, 15
Spillover effects, 171
Stages of agency development, 187–216
Stage transition, 187
Standard microeconomics, 39
Step-by-step, 170
Step-by-step approaches, 168
Story-based methods, 153–172
Storytelling, 82
Stress, 42
Structural validity, 177
Structured, 112
Structures, 66
Subjective changes, 172
Subjective norms, 113
Support for competence and relatedness, 109
Sustainable Development Goals (SDGs), 23, 89

T
Test-retest reliability, 179
Theoretical definitions, 176
Theory of planned behavior (TPB), 93, 113
Third World, 20
Time discounting, 49

Time preference, 42
Token economy, 101–104
Top-down, 65
Totemism, 16
Training, 73
Training program, 77
Transaction-intensity, 123
Transformations, 172
Trust, 82
Tsurumi, Kazuko, 154
Tylor, E., 12, 14

U
Uncertainty, 51
Unconditional cash transfers (UCCTs), 109
Undermining effect, 96, 108
Uptake, 123, 126
User-Centered Approach (UCA), 123
User-Provider Relations, 131–134

V
Validity, 176, 181, 183
Visualizing, 171
Voices of the Poor, 159
Volition, 38

W
Well-being, 55–56, 68, 123
Well-being achievements, 55
Well-being freedoms, 55
Why questions approach, 181–183
Will, 29, 30, 65
Women's empowerment, 23
World Bank, 21
Writing circles, 156

Y
Yamabiko Gakko, 158